Ciao Italia

TRADITIONAL ITALIAN RECIPES
FROM FAMILY KITCHENS

Mary Ann Esposito

HEARST BOOKS
New York

It is the policy of William Morrow and Company, Inc., and its imprints and affiliates, recognizing the importance of preserving what has been written, to print the books we publish on acid-free paper, and we exert our best efforts to that end.

Library of Congress Cataloging-in-Publication Data

Esposito, Mary Ann.
    Ciao Italia: traditional Italian recipes from family kitchens /
Mary Ann Esposito.
        p.   cm.
    Includes index.
    ISBN 0-688-10317-0
    1. Cookery, Italian. 1. Title.
TX723.E67 1991
641.5945—dc20   91-10308
                                                                                     CIP

Printed in the United States of America

10

BOOK DESIGN BY BINNS & LUBIN/BETTY BINNS

ILLUSTRATIONS BY JENNIFER HARPER

DEDICATION

*For Nonna Galasso and Nonna Saporito, who
kept my families' Italian heritage and traditions alive
and taught us to respect them, and for my mother, Louise
Galasso Saporito, who never once took a shortcut
to anything, and whose ingenuity and generosity
go far beyond her contributions to the pages of this book.*

Contents

ACKNOWLEDGMENTS

Writing this book has been a journey back to my roots and years of growing up in an Italian home. As I wrote, experiences that I had long ago tucked into my library of memories surfaced from their far recesses, and I found myself caught up in the emotions of remembering. More than once, tears fell to stain the pages.

I could not have written this work without the understanding of my family, the encouragement of my husband, Guy, and the patience of my children, Beth and Chris, who, more often than not, found themselves the taste testers of yet another heirloom recipe, and who longed for "an American meal once in a while."

Special thanks to my mother, Louise Florence Saporito; to Aunt Phoebe Zampini and Aunt Santina Galasso, who parted with some of their treasured family recipes; and to author Rose Tavino Manes, my cheerleader in all things Italian, for her advice and encouragement.

Invaluable help in proofreading was given by Christine Hoppe and Tomasina Gabriele of the Italian Department at the University of New Hampshire. Kudos to Mary Norris, who helped me type the manuscript, and to Constance Kane, culinary adviser to my television series, for her artistic talents in helping with the display and preparation of food for the cover of the book.

A debt of gratitude and thanks to my editor, Harriet Bell, who would accept nothing less than perfect and who taught me that perseverance would produce "the light at the end of the tunnel."

Also to my copyeditor, Judith Sutton; photographer Bill Truslow; Donna Petti Soares; Cynthia Fenneman, Director of Public Broadcasting for Channel 11; Tracy Kane; John Wackman; Karen Webster; and my agent, Bill Adler—*mille grazie.*

Introduction

I WISH MY grandmothers were alive today. They were unique women, born and raised in an ancient land. When they left Italy for America by steamer in the 1890s, the only world they had ever known disappeared from the horizon forever, but not from their hearts and minds. They struggled, like so many others in their adopted land, to forge a new life, but were determined to keep alive many of the traditions of Italian life, passing them on to their children and grandchildren. I am grateful to them for making me realize the unique heritage I have, and need to preserve. I woke up to that realization late in life, when I made my first trip to Italy, completing the cycle my grandmothers began.

My love of things Italian, especially food, took time to develop. Food was always the connector in our lives: It brought people together in times of joy and sadness. Italians believe that food holds the family together. In an Italian family, love is expressed through kisses, kudos, and the kitchen. There is never an occasion when food is not the great comforter, the big go-between, the means of celebrating, or the show of friendship and neighborliness.

When someone is born, wed, or buried, there food will be, giving sustenance, making one feel secure. Food is the vehicle of love that is passed on in an Italian family, generation after generation. It is tradition. The Saporito and Galasso families kept that tradition alive, as I do today, and hope that my children will tomorrow.

I didn't appreciate those traditions when I was young, but as I grow older, they mean more to me. In those early years, I was content to let my Neapolitan and Sicilian grandmothers and my mother carry on with tradition, while I tried to escape it. Nowhere was this more evident than in all the cooking that was done for our large family, which consisted of seven children, me being the oldest.

I still see the twenty or so loaves of bread that were baked each week, even on the hottest of summer days. I also remember the mountains of vegetables and fruits we canned each season and the crates of live chickens that were freshly dressed and found their way to the large Ben Hur freezer that took up half the kitchen. All these chores, and they were bone-tiring ones, left me with a definite distaste for cooking. I didn't want to have anything to do with food, but it seemed I could never get away from it. I was always roped into skinning tomatoes or helping to roll out pasta or pizza dough.

I hated the thought of holidays because it meant the cooking load would get only heavier. Just about everyone we knew would wind up with our homemade cookies, breads, and pizza. When I wondered why all those people we delivered food to at holiday time couldn't make their own, my mother would give me a firm lecture about sharing.

I still believe that my mother and grandmothers went overboard with food preparation, but that was what they knew how to do best, and it gave them great satisfaction, I suppose, not only to be known as good cooks, but also to be able to give the results of that talent away to others. After all, when Anna, Maria Assunta, and Louisa cooked a meal for you, you knew it was going to be something very special. And when they gave someone a loaf of bread, some homemade pasta, or a cake, it was the reaction of the receiver that was their reward: a smile, a stumbling thank-you, or the display of complete surprise. They were keeping alive the Italian trait of openness, caring, and respect.

When I became engaged, my mother had a dinner party for me. She invited the entire Esposito family to come for a splendid meal. Naturally, I helped with the preparations. There were *cappelletti in brodo* to start, then homemade Italian sausages and *braciole*, followed by chicken in wine and peas and mushrooms, homemade breads, and salads. These were followed by heavy desserts: whiskey cake in a cloud of meringue, crisp tubes of cannoli stuffed with ricotta cheese and chocolate, honey balls profusely sprinkled with candy confetti, and fresh fruit salad. The "other side" of the family, as the guests were called, were oohing and ahhing through the entire meal. There were many compliments to my mother, who spent this special evening in the basement kitchen, dishing up a never-to-be-forgotten banquet. My father did sit down with the dinner guests, but only long enough to inhale each course and then disappear to the basement to get the next offering.

Finally, after the last crumb of dessert had settled, my mother, obviously tired and relieved, made her way up to the dining room to ask how everything was. Her eyes sparkled as everyone pronounced her the best cook ever. This was her satisfaction, but it seemed more important to me at the time that she had missed being present at the table. After all, how many times was I going to get engaged? I didn't realize that food was her world and her feelings were expressed by what she had prepared. I vowed that life would be different for me. I had better things to do than cook all day!

That was many years ago, and if anyone had gazed into a crystal ball then and told me that I would spend ten years making trips back and forth to Italy to learn more about the traditional methods of preparing Italian food, I would have choked on a meatball!

But that was exactly what I did in fact do. I left the teaching profession to devote time to raising a family of two children and to renovating a pre–Revolutionary War house. The first thing that desperately needed fixing was the 1920s-style kitchen. I designed a spiffy kitchen with a work island that was seven feet long and could be used for rolling out pastry and pasta. Once my kitchen was complete, my mother came to visit and gave me a pasta machine—and suddenly old feelings surfaced about those early days at home when I stood in the kitchen for hours on end, hanging thin strands of straw-colored pasta over broom handles positioned between two chairs. It was as if a spell had come over me. Not long after that visit, I took out my pasta machine and went to work. I was thrilled that I still remembered the old technique of making pasta. I made my well of flour on my wood island and in the middle, I cracked my eggs. I started beating the eggs ever so gently, incorporating the inside wall of flour as I went. Soon I had a ball of dough that was just like what I remembered from home. I rolled and cut my pieces of dough and put them through my brand-new machine; in no time at all, I was hanging pasta over broom handles.

That gift of a pasta machine was also my magic carpet to Italy. I began to read all I could about Italian foods, not only recipes, but the history of food as well. I tried new recipes and old traditional ones, but I still wanted more. I enrolled in a cooking course in Italy near Sorrento in the southern Campania region.

There I was among gourmands, food writers, and stylists, all eager to get the latest information on the right way to cook Italian. Before long I realized something: All the things that Lorenzo, the chef, was teaching were, for the most part, already familiar to me. When he made pasta, I mused on how many times I had seen this done at home . . . and how many times I had rolled and cut that dough myself. I looked around. Everybody else was so impressed with hanging noodles they had made themselves. I realized that these traditions had been kept alive by the three women who were closest to me. Time to move on, I thought. I knew there was more to Italian cooking—much more when you consider that Italy is made up of twenty-three diverse regions, each with its own distinct way of cooking. My grandmothers brought with them the old cooking secrets of Avellino and Caltinasetta, but that was just a small part of what was Italian cooking. To me this was fascinating; I wanted to know more, and experience in Italian kitchens was the answer. I spent the subsequent ten years in and out of kitchens in northern, central, and southern Italy, each time fascinated by the localization and versatility of Italian food, as well as its simplicity of preparation and tasty rewards. I learned a lot, so much in fact that one year I was invited to teach others how to cook Italian food in Torgiano, a little town in the Umbrian countryside. At a cooking school called Tre Vaselle, I shared the cooking spotlight with the in-residence chef. We taught classes to Americans of diverse backgrounds. It was one of the most rewarding experiences of my life.

If someone had gazed into that same crystal ball and told me that I would be teaching Italian cooking on television, all over the country, I would have choked on two meatballs! But that's where my interest in food has taken me now . . . and I love every minute of it. *Mille grazie*, Nonna Galasso, Nonna Saporito, e Mamma! Because of them I can pass on the tradition to you, and I feel a certain comfort and pride in knowing that the rich heritage my grandmothers brought with them in their journey from Italy to America, so long ago, will be preserved.

This book contains my most cherished recipes: Some are family heirlooms, others are from cooking experiences in Italy, and still others are my own devisings, which may not be traditional in the strictest sense, but still adhere to the principles of good Italian cooking instilled at home.

From Nonna's Pantry

W<small>HEN I WAS</small> a child, Sunday was the day to visit Nonna Saporito, in Fairport, New York. The trip from Buffalo to the little canal town near Rochester seemed interminable. Grandma's old green-shingled house was near the railroad tracks and the train station where Grandpa worked. Trains whizzed by the kitchen door all day long and the whole house shook with a steady, but soothing, tremor. As soon as my family arrived, I kissed Grandma and headed for the walk-in pantry at the back of the kitchen. There were always special treats in there, like *torrone*, a nougat confection made from egg whites, sugar, and almonds. *Biscotti* sat in a large glass cookie jar next to Grandma's eggplant relish; braids of garlic and onions hung from the ceiling and dried oregano dangled from an old hook. On the floor was a basket full of embroidery threads that Grandma used to crochet decorative edges on plain hankies she bought at the five-and-dime store. Every visit produced a new hankie for me to add to the stack I already had.

The pantry smelled like a cross between olive oil, dried herbs, wine, cheese, and garlic. These staples were the reason for Grandma's genius in the kitchen, and I wish now that I had paid more attention to what was in that pantry when I was young. All the things I came to learn about Italian food, and the customs surrounding them, could have been learned from my grandmother, if only I had taken the time to ask.

The house where Grandma Saporito lived still stands, but on a recent visit, many years overdue, to film an introduction to one of my cooking shows, disappointment set in. After hugging Aunt Phoebe, I made my way to the pantry. It had become a laundry room! The window was still in the same place, from where I could once reach out and easily grab a handful of cherries from Grandma's tree, and the smell of the room was unmistakably the same, but there were no longer shelves holding Italian ingredients. Grandma's old maple rolling pin and her chitarra for making pasta stood against the wall, antique reminders of her hard work. As I left the room that had once harbored so many treats for me, my attention was drawn to the wall where I remembered the herbs hanging. Still taped in their original place were two faded yellow prayer cards with the pictures of St. Lucy and St. Joseph.

What my grandmother had in her pantry long ago is not so very different from what I have in mine today. Bottles of various grades of olive oil, as well as red wine and balsamic vinegars, and colorful boxes of imported macaroni in various shapes and sizes line the shelves. Homemade pasta rests in pieces of aluminum foil. Anchovies, capers, dried porcini mushrooms, dried beans, corn meal for making polenta, and Arborio rice are some of my treasured staples. Cans of imported plum tomatoes are lined up like tall tin soldiers, as are glass jars of marinated eggplant that I put up the previous summer, and an enormous crock of sun-dried tomatoes I labored over is wedged into one corner.

Large tins of semolina flour, unbleached flour, and whole wheat flour are available to choose from when I bake. Cravings for Italian sweets can be satisfied by using the dried figs, candied citron, pine nuts, almonds, and chocolate that sit in clear glass jars.

In my refrigerator, Italian cheeses for eating and grating are neatly labeled; fresh herbs packed in salt stand at the ready; and simple yeast granules wait for their chance to bubble and brew and work magic.

If Nonna Saporito could walk into my pantry, she would no doubt feel right at home. She would put on her flowered apron, gather up the ingredients she needed, and, within minutes, my kitchen would be permeated with the familiar smell of her cooking.

Anchovies These little Mediterranean fish are preserved either in salt or in olive oil. I use them like Nonna did, to flavor pasta sauces, and as a flavor enhancer for fish soups. Buy them in any grocery store. I save the oil from the anchovies to use in cooking or on salads.

Butcher's pepper and coarse salt Coarse black pepper and coarse salt were always stored in big jars near Grandma's stove. She never measured anything and that is the one trait I know I've inherited from her. To me, to be without coarse black pepper is to be without an arm. Both coarse pepper and coarse salt can be found in your grocery store. I prefer coarse sea salt, which has more minerals than regular salt, to the somewhat finer kosher salt. If you can't find coarse pepper, buy whole black peppercorns and grind your own.

Capers These little seed pods of the caper bush can really add zing to a dish. You can buy them packed in salt or in brine. I use them in sauces and salads. Nonna liked them with fish.

Cheese Pecorino Romano, a sheep's milk cheese, was Nonna's all-purpose cheese. It was grated over most pasta dishes. Parmigiano-Reggiano was used sparingly. Mozzarella was smoked and sometimes grilled. Provolone was eaten with olives and ricotta was always in the refrigerator, ready to be fried in a little olive oil and eaten with a sprinkling of black pepper or used in manicotti and lasagna. I always have these cheeses on hand.

Citron This fruit, a member of the citrus family, is boiled and candied and used in breads, cakes, and pastries. It is essential to many Christmas breads, like *panettone*. Many specialty food shops have it, or it can be ordered from mail-order catalogues. If you can't find it, candied lemon and orange peel can be substituted.

Dried beans Lentils, chickpeas, and cannellini, or white kidney beans, as well as fava beans were kept in glass jars for soup. Grandpa loved dried, salted *fave* and ate them like nuts, one after one. I keep a variety of dried beans on hand for making soups, salads, and antipasti. These are available in grocery or ethnic food stores.

Eggplant I remember big crocks sitting on the floor of the pantry, holding *melanzane sott'olio*, raw eggplant preserved in vinegar and oil. A wooden cover with a weight on top kept the eggplant pressed down and under the oil. When it was needed for Grandpa's lunch or for an antipasto, Nonna scooped some out onto a dish and served it with good crusty Italian bread to mop up the tasty oil. See page 214 for a recipe for this delicious appetizer.

Extracts Almond and vanilla flavorings were always on the shelf, but there was a heavy supply of anise too, a licorice-tasting flavoring that

Nonna put in her *brigidini*, waffle cookies, and *biscotti*. I buy my anise extract in Italian specialty shops.

Farina Grandma's flour was kept in a big tin on the floor. I keep unbleached flour in large tins, as well as finely milled semolina flour for pastries and coarse-ground semolina to mix with unbleached flour for pasta.

Fruits There were lots of home-canned fruits in the pantry. Queen Anne cherries from Nonna's tree were preserved in a sugar syrup, as were plums, peaches, and pears. Rich purple grape juice that I can still taste left my lips and teeth stained for hours. The applesauce she pressed by hand was one of my favorites and I especially liked it when she made her applesauce cookies, her only concession to *cucina Americana*. I don't can fruits but I do make applesauce.

Herbs These were hung everywhere to dry. They included mint, oregano, bay leaf, thyme, basil, and rosemary; I think rosemary was Nonna's favorite. I like to use fresh herbs whenever I can. Oregano and thyme are fine dried but the others lose their oils rapidly and are almost useless. Instead of drying herbs, I freeze them or pack them in salt for future use.

Nuts Nonna kept pine nuts, hazelnuts, walnuts, and almonds on hand and used them in cakes, cookies, and breads and to make fancy desserts for holidays and the feast days of her two favorite saints, St. Lucy and St. Joseph. For them, she pulled out all the stops. I keep an assortment of nuts on hand in glass jars in my pantry; for longer storage, I refrigerate or freeze them.

Olive oil Nonna used extra-virgin olive oil on salads, lesser grades to cook with. It was bought in 5-gallon drums and decanted into old wine bottles. She always kept it in the pantry, where it was cool and dark. I buy mine in 5-liter cans because it is more economical than the smaller bottles. I decant the oil into clean wine bottles and store them as Nonna did.

Olives in oil Jars of black, shriveled, very bitter tasting tiny olives were staples in my grandmother's pantry. Those preserved in brine have more flavor than those in oil. You can find these in the grocery store.

Onions White onions are milder than the more common yellow ones, and I always keep some on hand for certain recipes.

Pasta Nonna made her own pasta on a *chitarra*, a handmade wooden affair that had taut strings pulled across a wooden frame. She laid her dough on it and rolled a long thin pin across it to cut *spaghetti alla chitarra*. When the pasta dried, she stored it in clean dishcloths for future use. You can buy good imported Italian pasta in most grocery stores. I prefer to make my own, but when I am in a hurry, I use the Del Verde or De Cecco brands.

Peperoncini Nonna relied on dried hot red peppers to add flavor to many of her dishes; sometimes their impact was as if someone was lighting a fire on your tongue. She always sneaked some into her sauce. You can find these in the spice section of your grocery store or in gourmet food stores. Sometimes I bring them back from Italy.

Plum tomatoes No Italian pantry would be without these. Nonna had jars she put up herself as well as good imported varieties. Every summer she cooked bushels of plum tomatoes to preserve for winter use. I buy canned imported plum tomatoes in the grocery store; the San Marzano variety is exceptionally meaty and sweet.

Polenta Coarse yellow or white cornmeal was used to make a rustic *polentina*, or a soupier version of polenta, covered with tomato sauce. It was also used to make a polenta cake. You can buy the imported Italian varieties or domestic cornmeal. Do not buy instant polenta—it does not have the same texture as the long-cooked version.

Rice Grandma complained a lot about how hard it was to come by Arborio and *riso ordinario*, two types of Italian rice, in America. Lucky for us, today we can buy Italian rices in the grocery store. Use Arborio for risotto, *riso ordinario* for soups and desserts.

Tomato paste Nonna used this a lot in soups and sometimes in sauce. She told me how tomatoes were dried on old boards in the sun in Italy to make this thick pulp. I buy the handy tubes you can keep in the refrigerator: Squeeze out what you need and refrigerate the rest.

Tuna in olive oil A little can of tuna in olive oil can be the inspiration for a cool tuna and rice salad, or combine it with pasta or just eat it with bread. Nonna mixed it with cannellini beans for a Lenten meal. You can find tuna in olive oil next to the regular cans of tuna in any grocery store.

Wine   Grandma never bought wine: She used what Grandpa made. Only red wine was drunk and used for cooking. The only store-bought wines that showed up on the table were the bottles brought as gifts when a child was born, someone got married, or there was a funeral. Don't buy cooking wines, they are expensive and not worth it; there are many good inexpensive Italian table wines that are perfectly fine for cooking.

Wine vinegar   Grandpa made this "by accident" from old red wine when his home brew did not exactly turn out right, and Grandma kept it in big gallon jugs. She used it exclusively for salads. I buy red wine vinegar in gallon containers, but you can also buy it in smaller sizes. Use it on salads and in cooking.

Equipping the
Kitchen

*E*VERY COOK has a way of making life in the kitchen manageable
and efficient. Most Italian cooking does not require a lot of fancy pots
or gadgets, and I am a big fan of doing things *a mano*, by hand.

There are some things, however, that are indispensable to every
cook. The list that follows includes the things that I use most frequently.

Baker's peel   A long-handled wooden paddle for transferring pizza and
bread to a hot baking stone.

Baking stone   An unglazed stone placed in the bottom of the oven is
essential for baking some of the Italian breads in this book, like Pane
Toscano (page 106). It helps the bread rise while baking and gives it
uniform color and texture and a crispy crust.

Bowls   I use an assortment of sizes. Have several deep ones for making
bread dough and ovenproof high-sided bowls for baking fruits and making molded vegetable and pasta dishes.

Cannoli forms   I use old wooden forms, but you can buy stainless steel
ones in the grocery store.

Cheese grater The old-fashioned four- or six-sided stand-up model is the best. A food processor breaks down the oils in the cheese too much. A Mouli grater is fine too, but I like the control and texture that a hand grater allows me.

Colanders I have several sizes for straining sauces and draining vegetables and pasta.

Cookie sheets Nonstick cookie sheets save time and aggravation.

Deep fryer For frying pastries like *cenci, struffoli,* and *pizza fritta.*

Dehydrator I find a dehydrator indispensable for making my own dried tomatoes to preserve in olive oil. An inexpensive one costs about sixty dollars, but have you priced a 4-ounce jar of sun-dried tomatoes in olive oil? A dehydrator will pay for itself in one garden season.

Dowel rods Buy ¼-inch-thick ones at the hardware store to prop between two chairs for hanging pasta to dry.

Food processor Making pasta dough and preparing fillings are only two of the many uses for this absolute necessity.

Funnels Useful for decanting olive oil into smaller containers and making flavored vinegars.

Garlic press Handy for those recipes that call for garlic juice and mashed garlic.

Kitchen shears For cutting everything from poultry to pizza.

Lemon reamer This little gadget makes quick work out of squeezing lemons.

Marble pastry slab For rolling out *pasta frolla* or other pastry doughs that require a cold surface.

Meat hammer or pounder I like the weighted smooth-surfaced ones without teeth because they don't shred the meat.

Mezzaluna A single-blade half-moon knife with two wooden handles that is rocked back and forth when chopping vegetables and herbs.

Oil cans Decanting olive oil into a spouted stainless steel oil can keeps counters and stovetops neat and tidy.

Pasta cooker A 7- or 8-quart stainless steel three-piece set that includes one small and one large colander insert for draining pasta easily. These can be purchased in good cookware stores.

Pasta fork Wooden or plastic specially-shaped forks for lifting and stirring pasta.

Pasta machine There are many brands on the market; Atlas, Cross, and Mercato are all good. I do not recommend electric pasta machines as they are expensive and slow and do not always allow you the control to turn out a satisfactory product.

Pasta platters Sauced pasta dishes are best served in shallow platters rather than bowls so that the sauce does not settle to the bottom.

Pastry brushes Assorted natural-bristle brushes for glazing breads and fruit tarts and for greasing bowls and molds.

Pastry bags With assorted tips for decorating desserts and for filling pastries and stuffed pastas.

Pastry blender Wooden-handled types are best for blending pastry dough and mashing potatoes for gnocchi.

Peppermill An ABSOLUTE necessity for grinding peppercorns.

Pizza pans I cook pizza on a hot oven baking stone, but the round, perforated aluminum pans also help to give a crusty bottom crust.

Ravioli forms or attachment The forms are inexpensive and turn out twelve ravioli at a time. The attachment for a hand-crank pasta machine is more expensive but gets the job done quickly.

Rolling pins For pasta, I use a 27-inch-long thin wooden pin, for rolling pastry dough, a 16- to 18-inch pin.

Sausage funnels Long- or short-necked funnels for making sausages in casings.

Strainers Long-handled ones for scooping filled pasta such as ravioli and gnocchi from the cooking water.

Tart pans Removable-bottomed pans in various sizes for making pastry shells.

Wooden board For rolling out pasta and kneading bread.

Wooden spoons Assorted sizes for a multitude of kitchen tasks.

Antipasti

APPETIZERS

No MATTER where you travel in Italy, the array of what the Italians call *antipasti* can be endless. *Antipasto* means "before the meal," and antipasti prepare the palate for greater things to come. Most Italians would not recognize what passes for antipasti in many American restaurants. Limp beds of iceberg lettuce (found nowhere in Italy) strewn with canned black olives, slices of boiled ham, and salami cannot do justice to the real thing. Nor are cold antipasti the only ones you'll find on an Italian table.

Antipasti can be light and simple or more hearty and elaborate. The important thing to remember when deciding on what antipasto to serve is to make sure it fits the type of meal you are having. A formal five-course Italian dinner calls for a light, not too filling starter such as the classic prosciutto with melon or figs. At a formal dinner in Garda, in northern Italy in the Alto Adige region, our antipasto was fresh asparagus, cooked *al dente* and served at room temperature with a light dressing of olive oil. On the other hand, if a simple meal consisting of just meat and a vegetable is to be served, a more substantial antipasto like fried polenta and cheese would be perfect. Sometimes antipasti are substantial enough to be a meal in themselves. There are many ways the ingenious cooks of Italy use vegetables, breads, meats, fruits, cheeses, and grains to create antipasti.

At home, antipasti were reserved for special occasions, and the standard ones were prosciutto and melon for a more elegant meal, and marinated eggplant with crusty bread for the beginnings to a rustic *cena*, or supper.

My favorite antipasti recipes have been collected from my family and friends and from my travels in many different regions of Italy.

Bruschetta

GRILLED BREAD WITH GARLIC AND OIL

The region of Umbria is famous for *bruschetta*, or grilled bread, rubbed with fresh garlic and served with a generous drizzle of extra-virgin olive oil over the top. This is true garlic bread and the secret to its success is to use a dense, crusty loaf of Italian bread, such as earthy Pane Toscana (page 106). Using a spongy store-bought bread is courting disaster, because it will only shred and is not dense enough to hold the fruity olive oil. The recipe that follows is a favorite antipasto that has many variations.

SERVES 6

6 *slices Italian bread, about 1 inch thick*
2 *to 3 cloves garlic, peeled*

Extra-virgin olive oil
Freshly ground black pepper, optional

Grill the bread slices on an outdoor grill or toast them in the oven on a baking sheet until nicely browned on both sides, about 5 minutes. Rub each slice on one side only with a clove of garlic. As you do, tiny flecks of garlic will be caught in the crevices of the bread. Place each slice on an individual serving plate and drizzle with extra-virgin olive oil. Grind black pepper over the slices, if you wish.

Variation: Top each piece with fresh-made mozzarella and a few strips of dried tomatoes packed in olive oil (page 218). Garnish with fresh basil leaves.

Crostini di Spinaci

SPINACH CROSTINI

Crostini are small slices of bread that are fried in olive oil or butter and then topped with anything from black truffle paste, a favorite in Umbria, to this simple but delicious combination of spinach and melted Gorgonzola.

SERVES 6

½ cup extra-virgin olive oil

12 slices Italian bread (from a narrow baguette-type loaf)

½ cup crumbled Italian Gorgonzola cheese (about 2 ounces)

1 cup cooked spinach, squeezed dry and chopped

In a large frying pan, heat the olive oil. Add the bread slices and fry on both sides until golden brown. Drain on brown paper.

In a small pan, heat the Gorgonzola cheese over low heat, stirring, until it melts. Stir in the spinach. Mix well. Divide the cheese mixture evenly among the bread slices and serve immediately.

Crostini di Fegatini

LIVER CROSTINI

Edgardo Sandoli's chicken liver crostini are very popular in his restaurant, La Cucina di Edgardo. They are a specialty of his home in Venice.

SERVES 6

½ cup extra-virgin olive oil

12 slices Italian bread (from a narrow baguette-type loaf)

1 tablespoon butter

¼ red onion, finely minced

1 slice prosciutto, finely minced

½ pound chicken livers, trimmed and chopped

2 fresh sage leaves, minced, plus 12 whole leaves

Salt and freshly ground black pepper to taste

1 teaspoon flour

¼ cup Homemade Chicken Broth (page 30)

1 tablespoon capers

In a large frying pan, heat the oil. Add the bread and fry on both sides until golden brown. Drain on brown paper.

Wipe out the frying pan with paper towels and melt the butter over medium heat. Add the onion and sauté until soft. Add the prosciutto, chicken livers, minced sage, and salt and pepper and sauté over medium-high heat until the livers are browned. Sprinkle the flour over and stir in the broth. Add the capers and cook until the mixture thickens slightly.

Transfer the mixture to a blender or processor and puree. Divide the mixture evenly among the bread slices, top each one with a sage leaf, and serve.

Crostini di Pomodori

TOMATO CROSTINI

The secret to the success of these crostini is to use ripe plum tomatoes and fresh basil. Make these for a summer cookout and serve them while the rest of the meal is cooking on the grill.

MAKES 12

1½ cups seeded and chopped fresh plum tomatoes (about 3 medium tomatoes)

12 slices Italian bread (from a narrow baguette-type loaf)

1 to 2 large cloves garlic, peeled

2 tablespoons extra-virgin olive oil

1 tablespoon minced fresh basil

1 tablespoon minced fresh oregano

Salt and freshly ground black pepper to taste

Put the tomatoes in a strainer and set aside to drain. Grill or toast the bread slices. Rub each slice with the garlic and drizzle each one with ½ teaspoon of the oil. Set aside.

Transfer the drained tomatoes to a bowl and add the remaining ingredients. Mix well. Divide the mixture evenly among the bread slices and serve immediately.

P LINY once wrote, "There is no plant which bears a fruit of as great importance as the olive." The ancient Greeks and Romans revered the olive not only as a food but also for its medicinal and practical applications. Roman soldiers even rubbed olive oil on their skin. Olive oil was also used for fuel in lamps.

I especially love the stately olive trees that dot the countryside of Tuscany and Umbria, their graceful beauty immortalized by great artists like Giotto and Perugino. There are more than 40 species of silvery-leafed olive trees in the Mediterranean area. The regions of Tuscany, Umbria, Sicily, Calabria, Liguria, Puglia, and Campania produce some of the best olive oils in the world, and each one has its own particular flavor, color, and density, depending on the type of olive and the type of soil. Lower acidity in the soil produces a better olive oil.

Olives are harvested for oil production from mid-October to early November. Billowing nets are draped under the olive branches to protect the falling olives from bruising as they drop from the trees. Olives contain only 20 percent oil; the rest is 40 percent water and 40 percent pulp. Once the olives are picked, they are dumped into the top of a large crushing machine, where thousands of knifelike blades pierce the pulp and oil begins to drip into collection vats. The pulp is whirled at high speed with cold water to separate the oil from the pulp. This is where the term *cold pressed* comes from.

There are varying grades of olive oil and the standard for what is considered the best is set by Italian law. Extra-virgin olive oil comes from the first pressing of the olives and is the choicest grade, with the purest taste and color; it must contain less than 1 percent acidity (oleic acid). Other grades of olive oil include very fine virgin (1.5 percent),

Olive Oil

fine virgin (3 percent), and virgin (4 percent acidity). The color of olive oil can vary from golden yellow to yellow-green to very dark green, depending on the type of olive and the methods used to process it. Olive oil called *pomace* is rectified, or refined, oil that is made by a chemical process from the skins, seeds, and pulp of the olives remaining after all the oil has been extracted. It must be blended with virgin olive oil in order to make it saleable.

Use the different grades of olive oil in harmony with the dish being prepared. Like my grandmother I use extra-virgin olive oil on salads. For cooking, I usually use virgin olive oil, but for deep-frying some vegetables, like eggplant, I use peanut oil, because eggplant is notorious for absorbing oil and will absorb less peanut oil than olive oil. For desserts requiring deep-frying, I use vegetable oil.

Olive oil should be stored in a cool dark place. If you buy it in large gallon drums, decant it into manageably sized bottles. I still save wine bottles for this purpose. You can store olive oil for up to two years in a cool dark place.

Olive oil is the major cooking fat of Italy, but there are significant differences in its usage from region to region. Historically, the cuisine of northern Italy was based on butter and lard—one of the reasons why Bologna still retains the title "Bologna la Grassa" (Bologna the Fat), since its cuisine is rich in the use of butter and cream. In Tuscany, dark green olive oil and lard are used, and in Sorrento in the south, dark, thick olive oil is the cooking fat. You can buy different grades of imported olive oils in your grocery store. They may seem expensive, but there is nothing like the flavor and health benefits derived from this ancient fruit.

Peperoni Sott'Olio e Aceto

PEPPERS IN OIL AND VINEGAR

The last time I dined at Ristorante M.R. in Perugia, I ate nothing but antipasti. Mario Ragni, the "M.R." of the establishment's name, is a wonderful chef, combining fresh Italian ingredients in new ways. His antipasti bar is all one needs to feel really satisfied. I kept going back for the *peperoni sott'olio e aceto*, sweet peppers marinated in fruity olive oil and rich red wine vinegar. It reminded me of the pepper salad my grandmothers made at home.

SERVES 8 TO 10

8   bell peppers (an assortment of yellow, red, and green)

3   tablespoons chopped garlic

1/2 to 2/3 cup extra-virgin olive oil, depending on size of peppers

2   tablespoons balsamic vinegar

Salt and freshly ground black pepper to taste

Place the peppers on a lightly greased broiler pan and broil, turning them occasionally, until they are blackened all over. Put the peppers in a paper bag, close it tightly, and let the peppers cool for 20 minutes.

Meanwhile, in a large shallow nonmetal dish, mix the remaining ingredients well. Set aside.

Peel the peppers and remove the stems, cores, and seeds. Rinse and dry the peppers and cut them into thin strips. Add them to the dressing, mix well, and let sit, covered, at room temperature for 1 hour before serving.

Note: Try this as a topping for bruschetta.

Salvia Fritta

FRIED SAGE LEAVES

This simple antipasto of fresh sage leaves quickly fried in olive oil and sprinkled with coarse salt left me speechless when I had it at Club Lago di Tenno in the Trentino in northern Italy. Make this in the summer, when fresh sage is readily available.

½ cup olive oil   Coarse salt

Bunch of fresh sage, leaves only

In a large frying pan, heat the olive oil over medium-high heat. Add a small handful of sage leaves to the oil and fry just until they begin to shrivel. Drain on paper towels. Repeat with the remaining leaves. Put them on a plate, sprinkle with salt, and serve immediately. That's it!

Salame in Sfogliata

SALAME IN PUFF PASTRY

I developed this quick little nibble for a crowd of people. It uses pre-pared puff pastry, which is wrapped around some typical Italian ingredients. I use Genoa salame with black peppercorns in the filling, but prosciutto would be very nice too.

MAKES ABOUT 4 DOZEN

2   1-pound packages frozen puff   1½   pounds Genoa salame with
pastry (2 sheets each), thawed   peppercorns, thinly sliced

Dijon mustard   2   cups shredded sharp Provolone
                                             cheese (about ½ pound)

Preheat the oven to 425°F.

Work with 1 sheet of puff pastry at a time, keeping the rest wrapped and cold. Roll out the pastry on a lightly floured surface (I use a cold marble surface) to a 14-inch square. Brush the sheet with a thin layer of mustard. Cover with a layer of the Genoa salame, slightly overlapping the slices and leaving a ½-inch border all around. Sprinkle with ½ cup of the Provolone cheese.

Starting with a long side, roll up the puff pastry sheet tightly like a jelly roll. Pinch the seam closed and tuck under the ends of the roll. Cut the roll into 1 inch lengths and lay them on their sides, about 1 inch apart on an ungreased baking sheet. Repeat with the remaining pastry and filling. Bake the pastries until they are nicely browned, about 8 minutes.

Remove the rounds to a rack and let cool slightly. Serve warm.

Fiore di Pasta

PASTA FLOWER

I love cooking traditional pasta dishes, but I also like to give some of them a new twist. My inspirations seem to happen almost accidentally, like the day I decided to make a pasta antipasto. I marinated simple shell-shaped macaroni, threaded them on skewers, and stuck them into a melon half. By the time I had finished covering the melon with skewered shells, I had a very impressive looking "flower."

SERVES 15

MARINADE

¾ cup Basil Oil (page 214)

⅓ cup red wine vinegar or Basil Vinegar (page 213)

10 fresh basil leaves, chopped

4 cloves garlic, finely minced

1 teaspoon crushed red pepper flakes

Salt and freshly ground black pepper to taste

½ pound medium (#43) shell-shaped macaroni

½ cup grated Pecorino Romano cheese

1 cantaloupe, cut in half, seeds removed

In a large bowl, combine all the marinade ingredients and mix well. Set aside.

In a large pot of boiling water, cook the macaroni until *al dente*. Drain and immediately add to the marinade. Toss well to coat. Cover and refrigerate overnight.

Bring the macaroni to room temperature. Sprinkle with the cheese and toss to mix. Place the melon halves cut sides down on a large platter. Using 4-inch-long wooden skewers, thread each with 4 or 5 macaroni shells, and stick them into the melon halves, the bases of the "flowers." Cover the melon halves completely so no spaces remain; you should end up with very full flowers. Now your guests can just pick from them.

Conchiglie di Salmone

STUFFED SALMON SHELLS

Cold pasta salads smothered in mayonnaise or oil-and-vinegar-based dressings are not part of the Italian culinary tradition, but chilled macaroni salads are beginning to appear in many restaurants featuring *la tavola fredda*, the cold table. My interpretation of this new idea uses ordinary shell-shaped macaroni, the perfect containers for a smooth fresh salmon filling.

SERVES 25 TO 30

½ pound medium (#43) shell-shaped spinach macaroni	1 bay leaf
	2 teaspoons fresh lemon juice
FILLING	½ cup Basil Mayonnaise (page 217)
¾ pound skinless salmon fillet	
3 black peppercorns	Lettuce leaves
⅛ teaspoon salt	1 cup Basil Mayonnaise

In a large pot of boiling water, cook the macaroni until *al dente*. Drain and let cool. Spread the shells on a clean towel, separating them to prevent sticking.

To make the filling, place the salmon in a saucepan and add cold water to cover. Add the peppercorns, salt, bay leaf, and lemon juice. Cover the pan and bring to a boil. Lower the heat and simmer gently until the salmon turns a milky-pinkish color, about 5 minutes. Carefully lift the fish from the pan with a slotted spatula and let it cool on a dish a few minutes or drain on a rack. Discard the cooking liquid.

Transfer the salmon to a food processor or blender, add the Basil Mayonnaise, and puree to a smooth paste.

Fit a pastry bag with a medium star tip and fill with the filling. Pipe a small amount into each spinach seashell. Arrange the stuffed shells attractively on a bed of greens, cover, and refrigerate until serving time.

One hour before serving, remove the shells from the refrigerator and let come to room temperature, keeping them covered. Put the Basil Mayonnaise in a small bowl and serve as an accompaniment.

Note: If your salmon mixture appears to be too thin for piping, you can add 2 to 3 tablespoons of finely ground fresh bread crumbs to thicken it.

Crudità di Salmone

MARINATED SALMON

This is one of the most impressive antipasti I have ever eaten. Only fresh salmon will do. Buy boneless salmon fillet, rather than steaks. This dish is best made a day ahead. The salmon actually "cooks" in the refrigerator because of the lemon juice and cognac in the sauce. Serve with Pane Toscano (page 106).

SERVES 10 TO 12

SAUCE

1/2 cup fresh lemon juice

1/2 cup extra-virgin olive oil

1/4 cup cognac

1/8 teaspoon salt

1 teaspoon white pepper

2 large egg yolks

1 small clove garlic, finely chopped

1 tablespoon pink peppercorns in brine, drained

1/3 cup heavy cream

1 1/2 pounds salmon fillet

Lettuce leaves

1/4 cup Fresh Tomato Basil Sauce (page 87)

1/4 cup black caviar

Lemon wedges, optional

In a blender or food processor, combine all the sauce ingredients and blend until smooth and the consistency of a thin sauce. Set aside.

Working from the tail section toward the head, slice the salmon into very small, thin pieces with a sharp knife. As you cut them, flatten the slices with the side of your knife.

Spread a thin layer of the sauce over the bottom of a 12-×-15-×-2½-inch nonmetal dish. Arrange a layer of salmon slices over it, spoon some sauce over the salmon, and continue to layer the salmon and sauce until all the salmon is used. Spoon the remaining sauce over the top layer. Cover the dish with plastic wrap and refrigerate for at least 12 hours, or overnight.

To serve, arrange a bed of lettuce leaves on a large platter or on individual dishes. Place the salmon pieces, slightly overlapping, down the center of the platter or each dish. Spoon over the sauce remaining in the dish. Place a small dab of the tomato sauce on each slice of salmon. Sprinkle with the caviar and garnish with lemon wedges, if you wish.

Rigatoni Ripieni

STUFFED RIGATONI

This antipasto, developed from leftovers, would be just the thing for an Italian picnic or an informal party. The rigatoni become neat little tubes for holding the filling. Be sure to use thin tender green beans, they're easier to stuff into the rigatoni.

SERVES 10 TO 12

1¼ cups medium (#24) rigatoni	3 heaping teaspoons olive paste (see Note)
½ pound tender thin green beans	
1 tablespoon olive oil	Lettuce leaves
¼ pound prosciutto, thinly sliced	

In a large pot of boiling water, cook the rigatoni until *al dente*. Scoop the rigatoni out of the boiling water with a strainer and drain in a colander. Spread them on a clean towel in a single layer to cool.

Add the beans and olive oil to the boiling water and cook until the beans are *al dente*, about 5 to 6 minutes, depending on thickness. Drain and refresh them under cold running water. Pat dry with a towel, cut in half, and set aside.

Cut the prosciutto slices into 1-inch squares.

Spread each piece of prosciutto with about ½ teaspoon of the olive paste. Place 1 or 2 green beans at one edge of a square of prosciutto and roll the beans up in it. Stuff the prosciutto-wrapped bean(s) into one of the rigatoni; the beans should overhang the rigatoni evenly on either end. Repeat with the remaining ingredients.

Arrange the rigatoni attractively on a bed of lettuce. Serve immediately, or cover and refrigerate for several hours. Bring to room temperature before serving.

Note: Olive paste can be found in the gourmet section of your grocery store.

Torta di Pesto

PESTO TORTE

Pesto is the classic sauce from Genoa made from pungent basil leaves. The Genovese remove not only the stems but also the center vein of each leaf when making this sauce. Pesto is especially delicious in this *torta*, which can be prepared up to three days ahead.

SERVES 10 TO 12

1/2 cup pine nuts	3/4 cup Pesto (page 80)
1 pound butter, softened	24 1-inch-thick slices Italian bread (from a narrow baguette-type loaf)
3/4 pound cream cheese, softened	
1/4 pound mascarpone cheese, at room temperature	Extra-virgin olive oil
A few fresh basil leaves	

Preheat the oven to 350°F. Spread the pine nuts on a baking sheet and toast them until lightly golden, about 5 minutes; be careful not to burn them. Let cool.

In a food processor, or in a bowl, combine the butter, cream cheese, and mascarpone cheese. Process, or beat with a wooden spoon, until very smooth. Set aside.

Line a 9- × 5-inch loaf pan or a 6-cup round mold with a double thickness of damp cheesecloth large enough to hang over the sides of the mold. Scatter some of the pine nuts in the bottom of the mold and arrange the basil leaves, shiny side down, to make an attractive design.

Spoon one third of the cheese mixture into the mold and smooth it to make an even layer. Carefully spoon half of the pesto sauce on top of the cheese layer and sprinkle with the remaining pine nuts. Add another layer of the cheese mixture, spoon the remaining pesto sauce over it, and top with the remainder of the cheese mixture. Bring the cheesecloth edges up over the top of the mold. Press lightly on the top of the mold to settle the ingredients. Cover the mold with foil and refrigerate for several hours, or up to 3 days.

To serve, remove the foil and turn the mold upside down onto a serving dish. Remove the cheesecloth; let the *torta* come to room temperature.

In a large skillet, heat 1/4 cup extra-virgin olive oil and fry the bread slices a few at a time until golden brown on both sides, adding more olive oil as needed. Place the bread around the base of the *torta*, and spread it into slices or wedges to serve.

Melanzane in Carrozza

FRIED EGGPLANT AND FONTINA SANDWICHES

Lorenzo Fluss, my cooking teacher in Sorrento, taught me how to make many of his favorite foods, including antipasti. He always stressed that it is the quality of the ingredients and how they are prepared that makes all the difference. The success of this recipe depends on the initial salting of the eggplant to remove its bitter juices.

MAKES 12 TO 16

2 firm medium eggplants	2 cups toasted fresh bread crumbs
Salt	1 pound Italian Fontina cheese, cut
3/4 cup unbleached all-purpose flour	in 3- × 3- × 1/4-inch thick slices
2 large eggs	12 to 16 fresh sage leaves (see Note)
	Peanut oil for frying

Wash and dry the eggplant but do not peel. Cut the eggplant crosswise into 1/4-inch-thick slices. Layer the slices in a colander, sprinkling them liberally with salt. Set a large bowl filled with water on top of the slices to weigh them down and let stand for about 1 hour. This removes the excess water and the bitterness from the eggplant and helps prevent it from absorbing too much oil when fried.

Spread the flour on a plate. Break the eggs into a shallow bowl, add 1/8 teaspoon salt, and mix well with a fork. Spread the toasted bread crumbs on another plate.

Wipe the eggplant slices free of salt. Put 3 slices of Fontina on a round of eggplant, add a sage leaf, and cover with a second eggplant round. Continue making sandwiches until all the ingredients are used.

Dredge both sides of each sandwich in the flour, shaking off the excess. Dip the sandwiches in the eggs, then in the bread crumbs to coat on both sides. Put the sandwiches on a plate to dry slightly.

Pour enough peanut oil into a large frying pan to coat the bottom and heat over medium heat. When the oil is hot, carefully add just enough sandwiches to fit without crowding and fry them, turning once, until the eggplant is nicely browned and the cheese is just starting to melt. Drain the sandwiches on brown paper. Repeat with the remaining sandwiches, adding additional oil if necessary. Serve immediately.

Note: If you can't find fresh sage leaves, use flat-leaf parsley. Do not use dried sage—the flavor is medicinal tasting.

Zuppe

SOUPS

WHAT MAKES Italian *zuppe* special? Fresh vegetables and a good broth are essential, but so are a myriad of dried beans, bread, stuffed pasta, macaroni, rice, and even eggs that turn a humble dish of soup into a culinary wonder.

Italian soups can be meals in themselves. This is what supper, or *la cena*, often consisted of at home, and still does today in homes throughout Italy. When my grandmothers made soup, it was an all-day affair. First came the trip to "the chicken man" to find the toughest, but most flavorful old birds. Once chosen, they met their demise at home where the deft hands of my grandmother and mother then laboriously singed, plucked, and cleaned them. They were put into huge pots, feet and all, and simmered with herbs, chunks of fresh vegetables, and spices. While the soup simmered, dough was made for the pasta that would be added to the soup. Often I had the tedious task of cutting pasta strips into tiny squares called *quadrucci* that looked like confetti.

Most people have heard of the classic minestrone, or "big soup," so called because of the kaleidoscope of vegetables that go into it. We usually ate this boiling hot, but in regions of Italy like Campania, it is eaten at room temperature during the summer. In the Veneto, rice is a familiar staple in soup. The Tuscans make hearty soups like *ribollita*, twice-boiled soup thickened with beans and bread. The Romans prefer *stracciatella*, a mixture of eggs and Parmesan cheese dropped into a bowl

of hot beef broth, and the southern Italians love stylishly shaped macaroni, like little hollow ditalini, in their soups.

The base for soup can be meat, poultry, fish, or just vegetables. Meat
broth is the most common in Italy. As with the chicken broth, when
meat broth was made at home, it began with a tough piece of meat,
usually a brisket, or beef shin and neck bones. Then it was cook's fancy
as to what else went into it.

Today, people seem to have lost the art of making good soups and
this is a pity, because the ingredients to create them are probably in
your refrigerator right now. Soups are some of the quickest and easiest
dishes to prepare and no canned, heavily salted varieties can ever com-
pare. Although canned clear chicken broth or beef broth may be used
in some of my recipes, it is so easy to make these broths with beef or
chicken, water, a few herbs, and vegetables that you can do it ahead
and freeze the broth in small quantities for future use.

I make a lot of soup with just a few concessions to the modern age.
I order the chicken or beef that I need from my butcher, I use my food
processor for cutting up the vegetables, and I buy my ditalini. The rest
of the process is much the same as my grandmothers'.

Brodo di Pollo

HOMEMADE CHICKEN BROTH

Making chicken broth was a ritual with both my grandmothers. The process began in a noisy chicken store; then at home the hen would be simmered slowly with some cut-up vegetables and herbs and spices. When the soup was done, the vegetables and chicken were cut into small pieces and served in some of the broth for one meal. The rest was strained and used as a base for soups made with pasta, bread, or vegetables.

MAKES 3½ TO 4 QUARTS

4   pounds chicken parts, necks, and wings

1½ teaspoons coarse salt

1   clove garlic, peeled

1   large white onion, peeled and quartered

2   plum tomatoes, fresh or canned, quartered

1   bay leaf

2   sprigs each parsley and basil, tied together with string

Juice of 1 lemon

1   rib celery with leaves, cut in 4 pieces

2   carrots, peeled and cut in half

5   black peppercorns

Put the chicken pieces in a 7- or 8-quart stock pot and add the salt and cold water to cover. Cover the pot and bring to a boil. Skim off the foam that collects with a slotted spoon. Add all the remaining ingredients, reduce the heat, and simmer, covered, for 45 minutes to 1 hour. Skim off any additional foam that collects as the soup cooks.

Remove the chicken pieces with a slotted spoon and reserve the meat for another use. Pour the soup and vegetables through a large strainer lined with cheesecloth into another pot or a large bowl. With the back of a spoon, press on the vegetables to release all of the juices. Discard the solids left in the strainer. Cover the soup and refrigerate overnight.

With a spoon, remove the congealed fat from the top of the soup. The broth is ready to use or can be frozen for up to 3 months.

Cappelletti in Brodo

LITTLE HATS IN BROTH

I have many wonderful memories of making "little hat" soup with my mother and grandmothers. The cappelletti I usually choose for this soup are stuffed with a finely ground chicken filling, though on occasion I serve Grandma Galasso's version, stuffed with beef, pork, and veal. Sometimes I like to be untraditional and serve my cappelletti in brodo with a thin slice of lemon and fresh steamed spinach added with the broth to each bowl.

SERVES 8 TO 10

1 recipe Homemade Chicken Broth (page 30)

3 to 4 dozen Cappelletti di Pollo (page 52)

Grated Parmigiano-Reggiano cheese

In a large pot, bring the chicken broth to a boil. Add the cappelletti and cook until they bob to the surface. Ladle the broth and the cappelletti into individual serving dishes and sprinkle with grated Parmigiano-Reggiano.

Variation: If you prefer, substitute Cappelletti alla Nonna (page 51) for the chicken-filled cappelletti, and serve in either the chicken broth or Homemade Beef Broth (page 32). Sprinkle with grated cheese before serving.

Brodo di Manzo

HOMEMADE BEEF BROTH

When Italians make beef broth, they use tough cuts of meat like beef shin or beef brisket. My grandmothers and mother always added beef shoulder and neck bones to the simmering broth and even tossed in an old hen as well. This produced a rich-tasting broth that could be combined with pasta or rice or used as a juice over roasted meats. Many times the meats cooked in the broth were shredded into small pieces and put back into the broth for a hearty soup; sometimes the meats were used as fillings in stuffed pasta.

MAKES 3½ TO 4 QUARTS

1 pound beef shin	2 carrots, peeled and cut in half
1 pound beef brisket	1 rib celery with leaves, cut in half
2 or 3 beef neck bones	2 tomatoes, coarsely chopped
1½ pounds chicken parts	5 black peppercorns
1 tablespoon sea salt	4 or 5 sprigs parsley, tied together with string
1 large white onion, peeled and cut in half	

Put all the meats and chicken in a large stockpot and add the salt and cold water to cover, bring to a boil and boil for 5 minutes. Skim off the froth that accumulates with a slotted spoon. Lower the heat to medium and add all the remaining ingredients. Stir well with a wooden spoon and let the mixture simmer for 2½ to 3 hours. (The chicken will cook faster than the beef; remove it when tender, after about 1 hour. Let cool, remove the chicken from the bones, and reserve for another dish.) As the soup cooks, skim off the foam that collects on the top with a slotted spoon. When the meats are tender, remove them along with the bones; reserve the meat for another use. Pour the broth and vegetables through a colander lined with cheesecloth into another pot or a large bowl. Press on the solids with the back of a wooden spoon to release the juices; discard the solids in the colander. The broth is ready for use or can be frozen for up to 3 months.

Note: If you want to be a purist and have absolutely clear broth, mix 1 egg white with a cup of the cooled broth and return this mixture to the pot of strained broth. Bring the broth to a boil and, using a wire whisk, whisk the mixture vigorously until the residue begins to float to the surface. Let simmer gently, without stirring, to allow the residue to accumulate on the surface; then remove the residue with a slotted spoon and discard.

Zuppa di Pasta Grattata

GRATED PASTA SOUP

I remember my mother making a coarse type of pasta that was grated on a cheese grater and then cooked in boiling chicken or beef broth. The pasta had a distinct lemon flavor because of all the grated lemon zest that was mixed into the dough. This is a very old recipe with many variations.

SERVES 8 TO 10

¹/₂ cup plus 2 tablespoons unbleached all-purpose flour

³/₄ cup grated Parmigiano-Reggiano cheese

1 cup toasted fresh bread crumbs

Grated zest of 1 medium lemon

1¹/₂ teaspoons fresh lemon juice

2 large eggs, beaten

Salt and freshly ground black pepper to taste

4 quarts Homemade Chicken Broth (page 30) or Beef Broth (page 32)

To make the pasta, in a bowl, mix the flour, cheese, and bread crumbs together. In another bowl, mix the remaining ingredients together. Add to the flour mixture and mix well. Gather the dough into a ball; the dough will be quite rough. Wrap the dough in plastic wrap and refrigerate for at least 6 to 7 hours, or overnight, or until firm enough to grate.

Using the large holes of a cheese grater, grate the dough onto a clean towel.

In a large pot, bring the broth to a boil. Add the pasta and boil for about 5 minutes, or until the pasta floats to the surface. Serve immediately.

Note: This pasta freezes very well. If you like, double the pasta recipe and freeze half to have on hand for a quick soup. Spread the uncooked pasta out on a floured baking sheet and freeze until hard. Transfer to plastic bags and freeze. Do not defrost before cooking.

Zuppa di Pane di Nonna Saporito

GRANDMA SAPORITO'S BREAD SOUP

After I got my first job, I lived with my Grandmother Saporito. I'd often come home to her homemade bread soup. She'd ladle out a big bowlful, then sit and crochet while she took pleasure in watching me eat it. It was nothing more than good chicken broth and tiny "mosaic" cubes of bread that floated gracefully on top. Once I told her it was delicious but I wondered why the bread pieces were so small. The crochet needles dropped in her lap, her eyes looked up at me over the glasses perched on the end of her nose, and she began to recollect, with sadness in her voice, how poor her family had been in Sicily and how her mother always worried that there would not be enough bread to eat. Precious pieces of it were saved to put in soup and cut small so that it would go farther.

SERVES 8 TO 10

2 large eggs	1 recipe Homemade Chicken Broth (page 30)
½ cup milk	
¼ cup olive oil	Grated Pecorino Romano cheese, optional
6 slices stale Italian bread, diced	

In a large bowl, beat the eggs with the milk. In a large skillet, heat the olive oil over medium heat. Toss the bread cubes in the egg-milk mixture, coating well, and fry the bread in batches until browned on all sides. Remove the bread to a plate and set aside.

Meanwhile, bring the broth to a boil.

Ladle the broth into soup bowls, add some of the bread cubes to each serving, and sprinkle with grated Pecorino Romano cheese, if you wish.

Zuppa di Ceci

CHICKPEA SOUP

One of the old classic soups from home was made with *ceci,* or chickpeas. Jars of dried chickpeas were always in my grandmothers' pantries. I used to love watching these dried beans double in size after they had soaked in water. Canned chickpeas can be used in this recipe.

SERVES 6 TO 8

1   cup dried chickpeas

1   cup ditalini or elbow macaroni

½   cup olive oil

2   sprigs fresh rosemary or 1
     teaspoon dried

2   cloves garlic, finely minced

1   tablespoon anchovy paste

1   tablespoon tomato paste

¼   cup water

2   cups Homemade Chicken Broth
     (page 30)

3   cups crushed fresh (6 to 7 medium
     tomatoes) or canned plum
     tomatoes

     Salt and freshly ground black
     pepper to taste

     Extra-virgin olive oil

Put the dried chickpeas in a bowl, add cold water to cover, and let soak overnight.

Drain the chickpeas, place them in a large pan, and add cold water to cover. Bring to a boil and cook until the chickpeas are just tender, about 35 minutes. They should retain their shape and not be mushy. Drain and set aside.

In a saucepan of boiling water, cook the ditalini until *al dente*. Drain well, toss with 1 tablespoon of the olive oil, and set aside.

In a large pot, heat the remaining olive oil. Add the rosemary and garlic and sauté over medium heat, stirring until the garlic is soft and the rosemary is limp. Discard the rosemary sprigs. Lower the heat slightly and stir in the anchovy paste. Dissolve the tomato paste in the ¼ cup water and add with the chicken broth, tomatoes, and half the cooked chickpeas. Stir, bring to a boil, and let simmer for about 15 minutes.

Meanwhile, in a food processor, puree the remaining chickpeas until smooth.

Stir the chickpea puree into the soup and simmer for about 5 minutes. Add the cooked ditalini and simmer for 5 minutes more. Season with salt and pepper.

Ladle into soup bowls and pass extra-virgin olive oil to drizzle over the soup.

Note: This soup tastes even better the day after it is made. If it seems too thick, thin it slightly with a little chicken broth or water. Don't thin it too much—the beans and pasta make this a thick and satisfying soup.

Zuppa di Regina

QUEEN'S SOUP

When I told my mother-in-law that I was working on a collection of family recipes, she was generous enough to give me several of her most cherished recipes. I find this one intriguing . . . and, I might add, very good.

SERVES 6 TO 8

4 large egg yolks	6 cups Homemade Chicken Broth (page 30) or Beef Broth (page 32)
6 to 7 tablespoons unbleached all-purpose flour	Salt and freshly ground black pepper to taste
1/4 cup grated Parmigiano-Reggiano cheese	

In a bowl, beat the egg yolks until light colored. Add 6 tablespoons of the flour and the cheese and beat until the batter is smooth and thin but not too runny; the consistency should be like that of thick pancake batter. If the batter seems too thin, add a little flour; if too thick, add a little of the broth.

In a large pot, bring the broth to a boil. Hold a colander with holes about 1/8-inch in diameter over the top of the pot and pour the batter into the colander—it will stream out into the broth like strands of spaghetti. Boil for 5 minutes, or until the strands are set. Season with salt and pepper and serve.

Zuppa di Pesce alla Sarda

SARDINIAN FISH SOUP

Some people aren't aware that the island of Sardinia is part of Italy. Its cooking is rooted deep in history and the best way to describe its cuisine is just to call it simple—taking the offerings from the land and sea and using them in unadulterated ways. One example is the preparation of many fish dishes. Sardinian waters have a great variety of seafood, including bass, mullet, eel, tuna, spiny lobster, laguna fish, trout, and cuttlefish. While it is impossible to duplicate a Sardinian fish stew exactly, I substitute whatever is available here and it still sings to me of Sardegna. A mix of four different types of seafood is a good rule to follow for this dish.

SERVES 6

1	teaspoon saffron threads	1½	cups peeled and coarsely chopped fresh (about 3 medium tomatoes) or canned plum tomatoes
½	cup hot Homemade Chicken Broth (page 30)	½	cup dry white wine
5	tablespoons olive oil	2½	pounds mixed seafood (cleaned squid, lobster meat, tuna and swordfish steaks)
½	cup thinly sliced onion		Salt and freshly ground black pepper to taste
½	cup chopped fennel bulb, plus 1 tablespoon finely chopped fennel leaves	6	slices Italian bread, toasted
2	cloves garlic, chopped		Grated Pecorino Romano cheese
1	teaspoon crushed red pepper flakes		
1	tablespoon minced fresh parsley		

Soak the saffron threads in the hot chicken broth; set aside.

In a large Dutch oven or heavy pot, heat the oil. Add the onion and sauté for 2 minutes. Add the chopped fennel bulb and sauté for 3 minutes. Add the garlic and red pepper flakes and sauté for 1 minute. Add the fennel leaves, parsley, tomatoes, and wine and stir well. Strain the chicken broth, pressing on the saffron threads to extract all the liquid, and add to the pot; discard the saffron. Stir well and simmer for 5 minutes.

Meanwhile, cut the squid into ½-inch rings. Cut the lobster, tuna, and swordfish into 1-inch cubes.

Add the squid to the pot and season with salt and pepper. Cook over medium heat for 8 to 10 minutes, or until the squid is barely al dente, still firm but not rubbery. Add the remaining seafood and cook for 10 minutes longer.

Place a bread slice in each of 6 soup bowls and carefully ladle the soup over the bread. Pass grated Pecorino Romano cheese at the table.

Note: It is not customary in Italy to put grated cheese on fish dishes, but here the salty taste nicely complements the flavors of the seafood.

Zuppa di Verdure

VEGETABLE SOUP

The soup pot was always on the stove at our house—it was a good way for my mother and grandmother to feed seven hungry kids. But the soup itself was always a surprise. All sorts of leftovers went into the soup, including bits of meat, cheese, vegetables, and even eggs. When beans or pasta were added, it became what we called *zuppone*, or a big soup, since it was so filling and the beans and pasta made the soup swell to twice its regular size.

SERVES 6 TO 8

1½ cups dried cannellini beans

¼ pound pancetta, diced

2 tablespoons plus ½ cup olive oil

3 leeks, white part only, washed well and cut into ¼-inch slices

1 tablespoon tomato paste

2 tablespoons water

9 cups Homemade Chicken Broth (page 30) or Beef Broth (page 32)

1 small head cabbage, cored, quartered, and cut into thin strips

3 ribs celery, finely chopped

1 large carrot, thinly sliced

1 medium potato, peeled and diced

2 tablespoons chopped fresh parsley

Salt and freshly ground black pepper to taste

6 to 8 ½-inch-thick slices crusty bread

Grated Pecorino Romano cheese, optional

Extra-virgin olive oil, optional

Soak the beans overnight in cold water to cover.

Drain the beans, place them in a large pot, and add fresh water to cover. Bring to a boil and cook until the beans are just tender, about 45 minutes. They should not be mushy. Drain in a colander and set aside.

In a large pot, combine the pancetta and the olive oil and fry the pancetta over medium-high heat until it begins to render some of its fat. Add the leeks and cook until they are soft, about 5 minutes. Dissolve the tomato paste in the 2 tablespoons water and add to the leeks, along with the broth, vegetables, parsley, and salt and pepper. Cover, reduce the heat to medium low, and simmer for about 35 minutes, or until the vegetables are tender but not mushy.

To serve, heat the remaining ½ cup olive oil in a large frying pan. Add the bread and fry on both sides until lightly browned. Place a slice of bread in each soup bowl and ladle the soup over the bread. Pass grated Pecorino Romano cheese and olive oil for drizzling, if desired.

Zuppa di Riso ed Asparagi

RICE AND ASPARAGUS SOUP

When making this delicious soup from Reggio-Emilia, be sure to use very tender, thin asparagus. The best asparagus grows wild in Italy but it has just a short spring growing season.

SERVES 4

2 tablespoons butter	1 pound asparagus, trimmed and cut into 1-inch pieces
1 small white onion, finely chopped	
1 tablespoon tomato paste	4 cups Homemade Chicken Broth (page 30) or Beef Broth (page 32)
1 cup water	
1 teaspoon salt	¾ cup Arborio rice
½ teaspoon freshly ground black pepper	Grated Parmigiano-Reggiano cheese

In a large skillet, melt the butter and sauté the onion until soft. Dissolve the tomato paste in the water and add to the skillet with the salt and pepper. Add the asparagus, cover, and simmer until crisp-tender, about 3 to 4 minutes. Set aside.

In a large saucepan, bring the broth to a boil. Add the rice, reduce the heat, and simmer until the rice is *al dente*, about 15 minutes. Add the asparagus mixture to the rice and simmer for 2 to 3 minutes longer. Serve immediately, sprinkled with cheese.

Zuppa di Spinaci e Polpettine

SPINACH AND MEATBALL SOUP

Grandma Galasso had a knack for making delicious soups. My favorite, for which she had no set recipe, was a light spinach soup with *polpettine*, tiny meatballs, which she made from a combination of beef and veal. It was a tasty soup, even to me, who hated anything with spinach even more than the dreaded dose of cod liver oil she gave us each night to make us *più forte* (stronger).

SERVES 6 TO 8

½ pound ground veal

½ pound ground sirloin

1 large egg, lightly beaten

¼ cup fresh bread crumbs

1 tablespoon chopped fresh parsley

1 teaspoon grated lemon zest

1 teaspoon grated nutmeg

Salt and white pepper to taste

4 cups Homemade Chicken Broth (page 30) or Beef Broth (page 32)

2 cups spinach leaves, washed and torn into pieces

¼ cup grated Pecorino Romano cheese

Preheat the oven to 350°F.

In a bowl, combine the ground meat, egg, bread crumbs, parsley, lemon zest, nutmeg, and salt and pepper. Mix well but do not overwork the mixture. Using your hands, form small marble-size balls. You should have about 3 dozen meatballs. Place the meatballs on a rimmed baking sheet or in a shallow baking pan and bake for 30 minutes. Drain off the fat with a spoon.

Meanwhile, in a large pot, bring the broth to a boil. Add the spinach, cover, and boil for 5 minutes.

Add the meatballs to the hot broth and bring to a simmer. Stir in the cheese and serve immediately.

Minestra con Panno Sotto

SOUP WITH BREAD UNDER IT

Aunt Santina sent me the recipe for a peasant soup her mother, Mrs. Belurgi, used to carry to the workers in the fields near Veroli, Italy. The story goes that Mrs. B. would twist a large kitchen towel around her head and tie it securely. A large bowl of the soup would be propped atop her head, and off she went to the fields, arriving just before the bells of the church tolled the Angelus. When she arrived, the workers knelt and prayed and then had their soup.

SERVES 8 TO 10

1/4 cup olive oil

1 medium onion, chopped

2 cloves garlic, chopped

8 cups chopped fresh (about 5 pounds) or canned plum tomatoes

2 or 3 sprigs basil

Salt and freshly ground black pepper to taste

1 pound Swiss chard, leaves trimmed and cut crosswise into 3 or 4 pieces

1 loaf Italian bread, cut into 1-inch slices

About 1/4 cup grated Pecorino Romano cheese

In a large pot, heat the olive oil. Add the onion and sauté for 5 minutes. Add the garlic and sauté until the garlic is soft. Add the tomatoes, basil, and salt and pepper. Stir well and let simmer, covered, for 20 minutes.

Meanwhile, bring a large saucepan of water to a boil. Add the Swiss chard and boil for 5 to 6 minutes, or until crisp-tender. Drain well.

Add the Swiss chard to the tomato mixture, stir well, and simmer for 10 minutes.

Place a layer of bread slices in a deep platter. Spread just enough of the soup over the bread to cover it. Sprinkle with some of the Pecorino Romano cheese. Make a second layer of bread, tomato sauce, and cheese and continue until all the bread and soup is used. Serve immediately.

Zuppa di Zucca

PUMPKIN SOUP

Dottore Simonetti, one of the owners of Club Lago di Tenno in the Alto Adige region of Italy, near the Swiss border, knows how to impress his customers. Our nine-course luncheon, similar to what was served to the important ruling families of the Renaissance, began with a rich and creamy pumpkin soup. When making this soup, it is important to use pie pumpkins, which have a mild flavor and moist flesh; if pumpkins are unavailable, you can substitute butternut squash.

SERVES 4 TO 6

1 1½-pound pumpkin or butternut squash	1 tablespoon grated nutmeg
2 tablespoons butter	Salt and freshly ground black pepper to taste
1 medium onion, finely chopped	¼ cup toasted pine nuts
2 to 2¼ cups Homemade Chicken Broth (page 30)	1 tablespoon minced fresh thyme or 1 teaspoon dried
1 cup heavy cream or half-and-half	

Preheat the oven to 350°F.

Wash the pumpkin or squash, cut it in half, and scrape out the seeds and stringy pulp. Place the pumpkin or squash cut side down in a baking pan. Add ⅔ cup water to the pan. Cover with foil and bake for 45 to 50 minutes, or until soft. Let cool, then scoop out the flesh and puree it in a food processor or blender.

In a large saucepan, heat the butter and sauté the onion until very soft. Add the pumpkin or squash puree, 2 cups of the broth, the cream, nutmeg, and salt and pepper and stir well. Bring to a boil, reduce the heat to medium low, and simmer for 15 minutes. The soup should have the consistency of heavy cream; if it seems too thick, add a little more broth. Correct the seasonings. Scatter the pine nuts over the soup, sprinkle with the thyme, and serve.

Zuppa di Pomodori Freschi e Secchi

FRESH AND DRIED TOMATO SOUP

Rather than pay exorbitant prices for fancy, imported sun-dried tomatoes of varying quality, I dry my home-grown tomatoes and preserve them in olive oil (page 218) or freeze them. The flavor of dried tomatoes is very concentrated and delicious in this soup, which uses both fresh and dried plum tomatoes.

SERVES 6 TO 8

1 tablespoon butter	2 cups milk or 1 cup milk and 1 cup Homemade Chicken Broth (page 30)
1 tablespoon unbleached all-purpose flour	½ cup heavy cream, optional
4 cups pureed fresh plum tomatoes (about 2½ pounds)	1 cup Dried Tomatoes, not packed in oil, diced
1½ teaspoons salt	2 tablespoons chopped fresh basil
1 teaspoon baking soda	Grated Parmigiano-Reggiano cheese
1 tablespoon sugar	

In a large saucepan, melt the butter. Add the flour and cook over medium heat for 2 minutes, stirring constantly. Add the pureed tomatoes, salt, baking soda, and sugar. Stir to mix well and simmer for 10 minutes. Add the milk, cream, and dried tomatoes and simmer, covered, for 5 minutes.

To serve, ladle into soup bowls and sprinkle with the basil and Parmigiano-Reggiano cheese.

Pasta

W HO INVENTED pasta? Food historians have long debated this question, but most give the Chinese credit. However, if you study cooking manuscripts from different regions of the world, you will be amazed at how much similarity exists among various cuisines. In the case of stuffed pasta, for example, the Chinese have the wonton, a small piece of dough stuffed with a meat filling and served in soups or fried. The Poles have the pirogi. And the Italians have ravioli, cappelletti, and many other types of stuffed pasta that are added to soups or sauces. They even eat fried ravioli as sweets.

No cuisine is pure Italian, French, Chinese, etc. People have been trading food ideas and food crops through invasions, wars, and migrations for centuries and the ideas from one culture have been adopted and adapted by many others. What is important to remember in Italian cooking is what the Italians have done with pasta to make it their national dish. They layer it for lasagna, stuff it for tortellini, make narrow ribbons out of it for fettucine, flavor the dough with vegetables, and shape it into over three hundred versions of *maccheroni*.

I am intrigued by the idea that the Arabs introduced pasta in Sicily. If you recall Roman history, you will remember that as the empire grew, the need for more farmable land became acute, and Sicily was the fertile breadbasket Rome needed to provide durum wheat for flour. It seems only natural to conclude that Sicily thus had the right materials for pasta making.

Be that as it may, pasta was made from durum wheat then and still is today. Semolina is the very core of the durum wheat, and it produces a hard flour when it is milled. When you buy Italian *maccheroni* (macaroni), you are buying a product made from semolina.

In southern Italy, durum wheat flour and water are used to make *maccheroni* in hundreds of shapes that are extruded through brass dies. In northern Italy, notably in the areas around Bologna, eggs are added to flour to produce richer and lighter fresh pastas like tortellini, lasagna, and fettucine. Some places in Italy use only the whites of the eggs for making pasta.

However, it is made, pasta is loved the world over because of its versatility and ability to marry with just about any other food. It is filling, healthful, easy on the budget.

Of course, pasta made at home, *pasta fatta in casa*, is the best, but this is not to say that you can't buy good fresh or dried pasta. There are quite a few very good brands of dried imported pasta on the market.

If you want to make your own pasta, follow these few simple rules:

1. Do not make pasta at home with all semolina flour, as it does not absorb liquid well and the dough will be too hard to roll out. Semolina pasta is best made in large commercial machines. I use a combination of unbleached all-purpose flour with a high gluten content and semolina. This produces an elastic dough with a nice golden color that dries and stores beautifully.

2. Use large eggs. The size of the egg determines how much flour will be needed to make the dough. There is no exact proportion for this. You will know when you have added enough flour by "the feel" of the dough; it should be neither too wet nor too sticky. If your dough is too sticky, more flour is needed. If it is too dry, a little water should be added. At home, the rule was 1 large egg for every ¾ cup flour.

3. Always let the dough rest to relax the gluten in the flour after you have kneaded it. This step will make it easier to roll out.

4. Work on a well-floured surface when rolling out and cutting the dough.

5. Invest in a hand-crank pasta machine and some dowel rods over which to hang the pasta to dry. Use a long, thin rolling pin for rolling.

6. Let pasta dry completely before storing it, or it will mold. On humid days, drying will take longer than usual. Store pasta loosely wrapped in aluminum foil; it will keep for 3 months.

7. Never wash the pasta machine. Dust it off after use with a dry pastry brush.

8. Cook pasta in plenty of water, preferably in a large pasta pot with an insert drainer for lifting the pasta out of the water.

9. Do not add salt or oil to the cooking water. Salt does nothing for the taste and oil will make the pasta slippery so it will not hold the sauce as well. Some cooks add salt to the water to make it boil faster and more furiously.

10. Never overcook pasta. Italians like their pasta *al dente.* This means, literally, "to the tooth," or with a little bit of bite left. Many people tend to cook pasta until it is soggy.

11. Do not oversauce pasta. Italians like their pasta lightly coated—and they never top it with a snowstorm of grated cheese.

12. Fit the sauce to the pasta. Thin pasta should have a light sauce, chunky pasta a heartier sauce.

Pasta

BASIC EGG PASTA

When I was a kid, old broom handles propped between kitchen chairs, holding rows of golden yellow pasta in various shapes and sizes, were a familiar sight. Homemade spaghetti, fettucine, vermicelli, and lasagna noodles were staples in our house. Sometimes there were *farfalle,* or butterflies, resting on floured kitchen cloths, as well as plump ravioli filled with ricotta cheese. To make pasta, my mother and grandmothers would put a mound of flour on a large wooden board and make a "well" in the center. The eggs were broken into the well and beaten with a fork and a pinch of salt. The tricky part came next: moving the flour into the eggs, being careful not to break down the walls of the well—otherwise, the eggs would escape onto one's shoes and the floor. Admittedly, this technique takes a little practice, but once you've got it, it's really easy. Or you can make this classic recipe for pasta using modern technology—the food processor.

MAKES ABOUT 1½ POUNDS, ENOUGH FOR 4 TO 6 SERVINGS

4 *large eggs*	*½ cup semolina flour*
About 2½ cups unbleached all-purpose flour	*⅛ teaspoon salt*

To make the dough in a food processor, put the eggs in the bowl of the processor and process until smooth. In a bowl, mix 2½ cups all-purpose flour, the semolina flour, and salt together. Add the flour mixture to the eggs a cup at a time and process just until a ball of dough starts to form. Add a little water if the dough seems dry, a little more flour if it seems too wet. The dough should not be so sticky that it clings to your fingers. Turn the dough out onto a floured surface and knead it, adding additional flour as necessary, for about 5 minutes, or until smooth. Cover and let rest for 10 minutes before rolling out and cutting into the desired shape.

To make the dough the traditional way, combine 2½ cups all-purpose flour, the semolina flour, and salt and mound it on a work surface. Make a well in the center of the flour and break the eggs into the well. Beat the eggs with a fork. Then, using the fork, gradually incorporate the flour from the inside walls of the well. When the dough become too firm to mix with the fork, knead it with your hands, incorporating just enough of the flour to make a soft but sticky dough. You may not need all the flour. Brush the excess flour aside and knead the dough, adding additional flour as necessary, for about 10 minutes, or until smooth. Cover and let rest for 10 minutes before rolling out and cutting into the desired shape.

Cut the dough into 4 pieces. Work with 1 piece at a time, keeping the remaining dough covered. Roll the dough out on a floured surface as thin as possible, or use a pasta machine to roll the dough out to the thinnest setting. Drape the sheets of pasta over dowel rods suspended between 2 chairs to dry slightly, about 5 minutes.

If cutting the pasta by hand, roll up each sheet loosely like a jelly roll, then cut it into fettucine, vermicelli, or lasagna strips with a sharp knife. Or cut the pasta into the desired width with the attachment on the pasta machine. Hang the pasta strips over dowel rods as you cut them, or spread on floured towels; then cook immediately or dry for storage. (This dough can also be used for filled pasta, such as tortellini or ravioli.)

continued

Cook the pasta in a large pot of boiling water until *al dente*, 2 to 3 minutes, drain, sauce, and serve immediately. Or dry and store the pasta: Hang the strips over dowel rods suspended between 2 chairs until very dry. (I usually leave it on the rods for a day.) When the ends of the pasta begin to curl, it is dry enough to store. Wrap it loosely in aluminum foil and store for up to 3 months.

Pasta agli Spinaci

SPINACH PASTA

Adding spinach to pasta dough gives it a vibrant green color. The dough is a little harder to work with because of the added moisture from the spinach, and more flour is necessary per egg to achieve a dough that can be rolled.

MAKES ABOUT 1 POUND, ENOUGH FOR 3 TO 4 SERVINGS

3 *large eggs*	½ *cup semolina flour*
2 *tablespoons chopped cooked spinach, squeezed dry*	⅛ *teaspoon salt*
About 2¼ cups unbleached all-purpose flour	

Prepare the pasta dough following the directions on pages 46 to 47, but add the spinach to the food processor bowl with the eggs and process until smooth; mix 2 cups of the all-purpose flour with the semolina to start, adding additional flour if necessary. If making the traditional way, add the spinach to the well with the eggs and beat with a fork before proceeding as directed.

Roll out the dough, cut into the desired shape, and cook immediately or store as directed above.

Note: Either Salsa Fresca di Pomodori e Basilico (page 87) or the cream sauce used in Cappesante con Asiago (page 168) is very good with spinach fettucine.

Pasta al Pomodoro

TOMATO PASTA

One of the reasons pasta is a ubiquitous food is that it can be combined
with so many ingredients. When I make fettucine, I often add pureed
vegetables like carrots or beets to the dough. For tomato fettucine, I
add tomato paste, which turns it a wonderful bright orange color.

MAKES ABOUT 1½ POUNDS, ENOUGH FOR 4 TO 6 SERVINGS

4   *large eggs*
1½ *tablespoons tomato paste*
    *About 3 cups unbleached all-
    purpose flour*

½ *cup semolina flour*
⅛ *teaspoon salt*

Prepare the pasta dough following the directions on pages 46 to 47, but
add the tomato paste to the food processor bowl with the eggs and
process until smooth; mix 2½ cups of the all-purpose flour with the
semolina to start, adding additional flour if necessary. If making the
traditional way, add the tomato paste to the well with the eggs and
beat with a fork before proceeding as directed.

Roll out the dough, cut into the desired shape, and cook immediately
or store as directed on page 48.

Note: I like to serve this with Pesto (page 80). The vibrant green
color of the pesto contrasts nicely with the reddish-orange pasta. You
can use room-temperature pesto or, if desired, heat it slightly before
tossing it with the hot pasta.

Pasta al Pepe Nero

BLACK PEPPER PASTA

I sometimes like to add black pepper to my homemade pasta, particularly when I am making fettucine. Use coarsely ground pepper for a nice visual effect as well as a spicy taste.

MAKES ABOUT 1½ POUNDS, ENOUGH FOR 4 TO 6 SERVINGS

4 *large eggs*

1 *tablespoon coarsely ground black pepper*

About 2½ cups unbleached all-purpose flour

½ *cup semolina flour*

⅛ *teaspoon salt*

Prepare the pasta dough following the directions on pages 46 to 47, but add the tomato paste to the food processor bowl with the eggs and process until smooth; mix 2½ cups of the all-purpose flour with the semolina to start, adding more flour as necessary. If making the traditional way, add the black pepper to the well with the eggs and beat with a fork before proceeding as directed.

Roll out the dough, cut into the desired shape, and cook immediately or store as directed on page 48.

Note: Salsa Cinque Minuti (page 81) serves as an excellent complement to the spiciness of black pepper fettucine.

Cappelletti alla Nonna

GRANDMA'S MEAT CAPPELLETTI

Grandma Galasso liked to fill her cappelletti using a combination of beef, pork, and veal. I prefer mine with a chicken filling. Both are traditional and both are very good. Make these for Cappelletti in Brodo (page 31), or serve them with a light cream sauce or other sauce if you prefer. This recipe makes a lot, so you can use some immediately and freeze the remainder.

MAKES 150 TO 200

MEAT FILLING

2 tablespoons olive oil

1 center-cut pork chop, about ¼ pound, cubed

¼ pound boneless sirloin steak, cubed

¼ pound boneless veal roast, cubed

1 large egg

¼ cup grated Parmigiano-Reggiano cheese

2 tablespoons minced fresh parsley

2 teaspoons grated lemon zest

¼ teaspoon grated nutmeg

Salt and freshly ground black pepper to taste

1 recipe Cappelletti Dough (page 52)

To make the filling, in a large frying pan, heat the olive oil over medium-high heat. Add the meat cubes and brown them on all sides. Remove from the pan and let cool.

In a meat grinder or a food processor, grind the meats very fine. Put the ground meat in a large bowl.

Add all the remaining filling ingredients and mix well.

Roll out the dough and fill the cappelletti as directed on page 53. Then cook immediately or freeze as directed on page 53.

Cappelletti di Pollo

CHICKEN CAPPELLETTI

In Italy, *cappelletti*, "little hats," are traditionally served at Christmas time and other special occasions. They are time-consuming to make but we made hundreds of them in assembly-line fashion; Grandma made the dough, Mom rolled it out and cut the circles, and I put the dab of filling in the center of each circle. Some were cooked immediately in boiling homemade broth and the rest were frozen for future meals.

These cappelletti can be served in broth (page 31) or in a fresh cream sauce with a little fresh basil sprinkled on top, or other sauce of your choice.

The dough for cappelletti needs to be softer and wetter than basic pasta dough; if it is too dry, you will not be able to press the edges closed. You may have to experiment with the recipe below—the proportions are intended as a guideline. Egg size and the absorbency of the flour you use will determine the dryness of the dough.

MAKES 175 TO 200

CHICKEN FILLING

1   whole chicken breast, about 1¼ pounds

1   large egg, beaten

¼ cup grated Parmigiano-Reggiano cheese

2   tablespoons minced fresh parsley

2   teaspoons grated lemon zest

Dash of grated nutmeg

Salt and freshly ground black pepper to taste

CAPPELLETTI DOUGH

4   large eggs

⅛ teaspoon salt

⅓ cup semolina flour

2¾ to 3 cups unbleached all-purpose flour

To make the filling, put the chicken in a saucepan and add cold water to cover. Bring to a boil, reduce the heat, and simmer until the chicken is tender, 20 to 25 minutes. Remove the chicken and let cool. Remove the meat from the bones.

In a food processor, grind the chicken very fine. Transfer the chicken to a bowl and add all the remaining filling ingredients. Mix well, cover with plastic wrap, and refrigerate while you make the dough.

To make the dough, in a food processor, combine the eggs and salt and pulse to blend well. Mix the semolina flour and 2¾ cups of the unbleached flour together and add to the eggs about a cup at a time, pulsing until a ball is formed. If the dough is too sticky, add more flour; if too dry, add a little warm water. What you want is a stretchy, elastic dough that is slightly damp to the touch. On a well-floured surface, knead the dough until smooth, about 5 minutes. Cover the dough with a bowl or damp towel and let rest for 10 minutes.

Divide the dough into 4 pieces. Work with 1 piece at a time and keep the rest covered. Flatten the dough slightly with a rolling pin and then use a pasta machine to roll it out ⅛ inch thick. Don't make the dough too thin, or the filling will poke through when the cappelletti are formed. Or roll out each piece of dough on a lightly floured surface with a rolling pin.

Using a 1-inch round cookie cutter or a small glass, cut out rounds from each sheet of dough. (Form the scraps into a ball to reroll as directed.) Place about ½ teaspoon of the filling in the center of each round. Fold each round in half and pinch the edges together to make a half circle. Then take the two pointed ends and bring them together to meet; pinch to seal. Place the cappelletti on a floured towel or baking sheet as you form them.

To cook the cappelletti, bring a large pot of broth or water to a boil. Add the cappelletti about 3 dozen at a time and cook until they bob to the surface. Serve in the broth or in a sauce of your choosing.

To freeze the cappelletti, arrange them in a single layer, without touching, on baking sheets as you form them. Cover with foil and freeze on the sheets. When they are hard, transfer them to plastic bags. They can be frozen for up to 3 months. Add frozen cappelletti directly to boiling broth or water.

Cannelloni con Agnello

CANNELLONI STUFFED WITH LAMB

Cannelloni are tubes of pasta, or another type of dough, stuffed with a filling of either meat or cheese, or sometimes both. They are a wonderful first course or a meal in themselves. There are two different versions of cannelloni in Italy. One is made with a crepe-like batter (see Cannelloni con Verdure e Formaggio, page 55) and the other is made with a regular pasta dough, as in this recipe.

SERVES 8 TO 10

FILLING

2	tablespoons olive oil
1½	pounds ground lamb
2	teaspoons fennel seeds
2	teaspoons minced fresh mint
	Salt and freshly ground black pepper to taste

½	cup grated Pecorino Romano cheese
½	cup Fresh Tomato Basil Sauce (page 87)
1	recipe Tomato Pasta (page 49)
4	cups Fresh Tomato Basil Sauce
	About 1 cup grated Pecorino Romano cheese

To make the filling, in a large skillet, heat the olive oil over medium-high heat and sauté the lamb until it is browned. Add the fennel seeds, mint, and salt and pepper and cook for 5 minutes. Remove the lamb to a bowl and stir in the cheese and tomato sauce. Set aside.

Cut the pasta dough into 4 pieces. Work with 1 piece at a time, keeping the other pieces covered. Roll out the dough through a pasta machine to the finest setting. Cut each sheet into 5-inch squares, laying the squares on floured cloths as you make them.

In a large pot of boiling water, cook the cannelloni a few at a time for 2 to 3 minutes, until *al dente*. Remove from the water with a strainer, drain, and plunge them into a bowl of cold water to cool. Then lay them on a clean towel to dry slightly before filling them.

Preheat the oven to 350°F. Butter two 9- × -13-inch baking pans.

Spread 3 tablespoons of the lamb filling on each pasta square, roll them into cylinders, and place them in the prepared pans, seam sides down, in a single layer. Cover the cannelloni with the tomato sauce and sprinkle with the Pecorino Romano cheese.

Cover the pans with foil and bake for 30 minutes. Serve immediately.

Cannelloni con Verdure e Formaggio

CANNELLONI WITH VEGETABLES AND CHEESE

In this version of cannelloni, a *crespelle* batter is used, making a more delicate dish than the recipe that calls for a basic pasta dough. These make a wonderful first course or a light supper with a green salad.

SERVES 8 AS AN APPETIZER

1   recipe Crespelle Batter
    (page 56)

FILLING

1½ cups ricotta cheese, well drained

1   large egg, beaten

½ cup grated Parmigiano-Reggiano
    cheese

1   cup seeded and diced fresh
    tomatoes (about 2 medium),
    drained

⅔ cup chopped cooked broccoli

¼ cup minced fresh parsley

1   teaspoon grated lemon zest
    Salt and freshly ground black
    pepper to taste

8   tablespoons (1 stick) butter,
    melted

⅔ cup grated Parmigiano-Reggiano
    cheese

Cook the *crespelle* as directed on page 57. Set aside.

Preheat the oven to 350°F. Butter a 9-×-12-inch baking dish.

To make the filling, in a large bowl, combine the ricotta cheese, egg, and Parmigiano-Reggiano and mix well. Add all the remaining filling ingredients and mix well.

Spread about ¼ cup of the filling over each *crespella* and roll up into a cylinder. Place them in a single layer, seam side down, in the buttered dish. Drizzle the melted butter over them and sprinkle with the cheese.

Bake for 15 to 20 minutes, or until piping hot. If you wish, run under the broiler for a few minutes to brown the cheese. Serve immediately.

Crespelle con Formaggio

CHEESE FOLDS

Crespelle means "folds," folded pancakes that is. I first had them in Torgiano, where Chef Angelo of Tre Vaselle turns them out faster than lightning. The crespelle, made from a crepe-like batter, are cooked in a frying pan. The action is all in the wrist as you flip each crespella. I serve these as a first course.

SERVES 8 TO 10

FILLING

6   tablespoons butter

¾   cup unbleached all-purpose flour

6   cups milk

½   cup cubed Asiago cheese (about 2 ounces)

½   cup cubed Italian Fontina cheese (about 2 ounces)

½   cup cubed Provolone cheese (about 2 ounces)

⅓   cup grated Parmigiano-Reggiano cheese

Salt and freshly ground black pepper to taste

1   teaspoon grated nutmeg

CRESPELLE BATTER

About 1¾ cups unbleached all-purpose flour

⅛   teaspoon salt

1½ teaspoons grated nutmeg

2   large eggs, beaten

1   large egg yolk, beaten

1½ to 1¾ cups milk

1   tablespoon butter, melted

3   tablespoons grated Parmigiano-Reggiano cheese

To make the filling, in a large heavy saucepan, melt the butter over low heat. Add the flour and stir to blend well. Slowly add the milk, stirring constantly, and stir until smooth. Raise the heat to medium high and cook, stirring constantly, for about 10 minutes, or until the sauce just coats the back of the spoon. Turn off the heat and add the cubed cheeses, Parmigiano, salt and pepper, and nutmeg. Stir until smooth. Cover to keep warm and set aside.

To make the batter, sift 1¾ cups flour, the salt, and nutmeg together into a large bowl. Add the beaten eggs and egg yolk, 1½ cups of the milk, and the butter. Whisk the mixture until smooth and the consistency of pancake batter. If the batter seems too thin, add a little more flour; if too thick, add a little milk.

Lightly butter a 6- or 8-inch crêpe pan or a frying pan (I use a Teflon-coated one). Heat over medium heat. When the pan is hot, add ¼ cup of the batter and swirl the pan to make sure the bottom is evenly coated with a thin layer of batter. Cook for 1 to 2 minutes, or until lightly browned on the underside. Flip the *crespella* over and cook the other side until lightly browned. Remove the *crespella* to a sheet of wax paper. Repeat with the remaining batter, stacking the *crespelle* between wax paper as you make them. Lightly grease the pan every so often to prevent the batter from sticking.

Preheat the oven to 350°F. Butter a 9- × -12-inch baking dish.

Spread about 3 tablespoons of the filling over each *crespella*, making sure to cover the surface evenly. Fold each *crespella* in half, then in half again, and place them in the buttered dish, slightly overlapping them. Spoon the remaining filling over the *crespelle* and sprinkle with the Parmigiano-Reggiano cheese.

Bake for 20 minutes, or until piping hot. Run the *crespelle* under the broiler for 1 to 2 minutes to brown the top, and serve immediately.

Fettucine di Barbabietola con Mascarpone

BEET FETTUCINE WITH MASCARPONE SAUCE

This beet pasta is beautiful to look at, with a deep red color that fades to pink when it is boiled. I like to combine it with fettucine made from Pasta agli Spinaci (page 48) for an interesting color contrast. When I serve it on its own, I top it with a mascarpone cheese sauce that is very delicate.

SERVES 4 TO 6

PASTA

1   small beet

3   cups unbleached all-purpose flour

½   cup semolina flour

½   teaspoon salt

4   large eggs

SAUCE

6   tablespoons butter

1½   teaspoons finely minced garlic

2   cups heavy cream

1   cup (10 ounces) mascarpone cheese

6   tablespoons grated Parmigiano-Reggiano cheese

    Salt and freshly ground black pepper to taste

6   fresh basil leaves, minced

To make the pasta, cook the beet in boiling water until tender. Drain and let cool slightly. Peel the beet and mince fine. You will need 2 tablespoons minced beet for the dough; set aside.

Prepare the pasta dough following the directions on pages 46 to 47, but add the minced beet to the food processor bowl with the eggs and process until smooth; mix 2½ cups of the all-purpose flour with the semolina to start, adding additional flour if necessary. If making the traditional way, add the minced beet to the well after beating the eggs and beat with a fork before proceeding as directed.

Roll out the dough and cut into fettucine, following the directions on page 47.

To make the sauce, in a medium saucepan, melt the butter over medium heat and sauté the garlic until it is soft. Lower the heat and gradually stir in the heavy cream. Add the mascarpone cheese and stir to blend. Add the grated cheese and salt and pepper. Mix well and remove from the heat. Stir in the basil. Cover to keep the sauce warm.

In a large pot of boiling water, cook the pasta until al dente, no more than 2 to 3 minutes. Drain and toss with the sauce.

Frascarelli

SCATTERS

Frascarelli, a special type of pasta from Umbria, reminds me of the tiny pasta called *pastina* that my grandmothers put in soup. This pasta is made by sprinkling beaten eggs over flour and then gathering the mixture up and sifting it through a sieve or colander. I serve these little beads of pasta in a simple sage butter sauce.

SERVES 4 TO 6

½ pound (2 sticks) butter, melted

20 fresh sage leaves, torn into pieces

2 cups unbleached all-purpose flour

4 large eggs, beaten

In a skillet, melt the butter over medium-high heat. Add the sage leaves, reduce the heat to medium, and swirl the leaves in the butter for 2 to 3 minutes. Keep the sauce warm over very low heat, letting the sage leaves flavor the butter.

Spread the flour in a thin layer on a large work surface. Using your hands, sprinkle the beaten eggs evenly over the flour. Gently gather up the "scatters," or beads, that form and put them in a fine sieve or strainer. Shake the sieve to remove the excess flour—what you are left with are the *frascarelli*, little odd-shaped beads.

In a large pot of boiling water, cook the pasta for 1 minute. Drain well and serve tossed with the warm sauce.

Note: This is also very good with Salsa Arrabbiata (page 86).

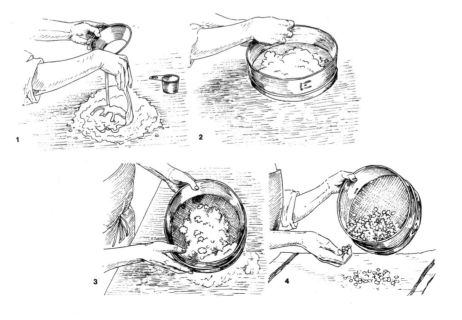

1

2

3

4

Rotolo di Pasta

PASTA ROLL

While most professional chefs in Italy are men, the one area that re-mains the domain of women is *pasta fatta a mano*, pasta made by hand. In most Italian restaurant kitchens, it is the women who produce the thinnest, sometimes almost translucent, sheets of pasta with only sev-eral forceful passes of the rolling pin—it takes me quite a bit longer. The *matterello*, or rolling pin, is thin and about two feet long, and the pasta dough yields in elastic submission to its sturdy shaping. My friend Maria, who makes all the pasta for Tre Vaselle in Torgiano, loves my version of a hand-rolled and stuffed pasta, which is first poached and then baked. I serve this spectacular dish as a first course or as a main course. You can make the filling and sauce a day ahead and refrigerate them until ready to use.

SERVES 8 TO 10

PASTA

1¾ cups unbleached all-purpose flour

¼ cup semolina flour

⅛ teaspoon salt

3 large eggs

FILLING

¼ cup pine nuts

¼ cup olive oil

1 medium red onion, thinly sliced

¼ pound prosciutto, diced

2½ cups chopped cooked spinach, well drained

1 cup ricotta cheese, well drained

⅔ cup grated Parmigiano-Reggiano cheese

1 large egg, beaten

Salt and freshly ground black pepper to taste

1 teaspoon grated nutmeg

CREMAZOLA SAUCE

2 cups heavy cream

½ cup (5 ounces) mascarpone cheese or cream cheese

¼ pound Italian Gorgonzola cheese, crumbled

Preheat the oven to 350°F.

To make the pasta, mix the flours and salt together and mound on a work surface. Make a well in the center of the flour. Crack the eggs into the well. Mix the eggs with your fingers or a fork. Then begin incorporating the flour from the inside of the well into the eggs, taking care not to break through the sides. Incorporate just enough of the flour to make a soft but not sticky dough. Brush away the excess flour and knead the dough until smooth, about 10 minutes. You may need to add a little warm water if the dough seems too dry or a little flour if it is too wet. Cover the dough with a damp towel and let it rest while you make the filling.

To make the filling, spread the pine nuts on a baking sheet and toast them in the preheated oven until lightly browned, about 5 minutes. Watch them carefully, as they burn easily. Set aside to cool.

In a skillet, heat the olive oil and sauté the onion until soft. Stir in the prosciutto and pine nuts and cook until the mixture is fairly dry. Stir in the spinach and cook for 1 minute. Remove the mixture to a bowl and let cool. Add the cheeses, egg, salt and pepper, and nutmeg. Mix well. Cover and refrigerate until ready to use.

On a well-floured surface, roll out the dough with a rolling pin to a large round about 22 inches in diameter. The dough should be very thin—no thicker than a sheet of typing paper.

Spread the filling evenly over the dough to within ½ inch of the edges. Roll up the dough like a jelly roll. Pinch the seam to seal it and to prevent the filling from coming out. Place the roll along a long edge of a large clean kitchen towel, roll the pasta up in the towel, and tie the ends of the towel with string.

Bring a large pot of water to a boil. Carefully lower the towel-encased pasta roll into the water, bending it gently to fit. When the water returns to the boil, partially cover the pot and poach the roll for 20 minutes. Remove the roll carefully with 2 spatulas, place it on a baking sheet, and let it cool.

Butter a 9- × -13-inch baking dish.

Untie and unwrap the towel and carefully transfer the roll to a cutting board. Cut the roll into 1-inch lengths and lay them on their sides in the baking dish in a single layer.

In a saucepan, combine all the sauce ingredients and bring to a slow boil over medium-high heat, stirring constantly with a wooden spoon. Lower the heat to medium and stir the mixture until smooth. Pour half the sauce over the rolls. Bake, uncovered, for 20 to 25 minutes, or until the pasta rolls are hot and the sauce is bubbling.

Reheat the remaining sauce to pass at the table, and serve immediately.

Spaghetti con Cavolfiore

SPAGHETTI WITH CAULIFLOWER

In this pasta dish, the vegetables are boiled with the spaghetti, and some of the cooking water is saved for the sauce. My grandmothers made this with broccoli as well as cauliflower. Humble as the dish is, it is good enough for company.

SERVES 6

1 medium head cauliflower	1 tablespoon anchovy paste
3 tablespoons plus ⅔ cup olive oil	Coarsely ground black pepper
1 cup toasted bread crumbs	1 pound spaghetti
2 cloves garlic, minced	½ cup grated Pecorino Romano cheese
1½ teaspoons crushed red pepper flakes	

Remove the leaves and core of the cauliflower and cut the head into small uniform florets. Set aside.

In a frying pan, heat the 3 tablespoons olive oil and brown the bread crumbs. Remove the bread crumbs and set aside. In the same frying pan, heat the remaining ⅔ cup olive oil. Add the garlic and sauté until the garlic is soft. Stir in the pepper flakes and cook for 1 minute. Stir in the anchovy paste and 1 tablespoon black pepper and cook for 1 minute longer. Keep the sauce warm over very low heat.

Meanwhile, in a large pot of boiling water, cook the cauliflower and spaghetti until the cauliflower is crisp-tender and the pasta is *al dente*. Drain, reserving ½ cup of the cooking water.

Lightly grease a serving platter with olive oil. Transfer the spaghetti and cauliflower to the platter and toss to coat with the oil. Add the reserved cooking water to the sauce and stir to blend. Pour the sauce over the spaghetti and cauliflower and toss well. Sprinkle with the cheese, black pepper to taste, and the bread crumbs. Serve immediately.

Frittata di Spaghetti

SPAGHETTI FRITTATA

There was always leftover spaghetti in the refrigerator at home. This was usually turned into an omelette of sorts that was good served hot, but even better at room temperature. Sometimes we'd take wedges of it to the park for a picnic. You can make this with any kind of leftover pasta, either sauced or plain. No leftovers? It's worth boiling some fresh.

SERVES 8 TO 10

1 teaspoon olive oil	Salt and freshly ground black pepper
4 slices (about ¼ pound) prosciutto or ham, diced	¼ cup chopped fresh basil or parsley
6 large eggs	2 cups cooked spaghetti
3 tablespoons grated Parmigiano-Reggiano cheese	1½ cups cubes mozzarella or other cheese (about 6 ounces)
	¼ cup olive oil
	4 tablespoons butter

In a frying pan, sauté the prosciutto or ham in the olive oil until crispy. Drain on brown paper.

In a large bowl, beat the eggs. Add the Parmigiano-Reggiano, salt and pepper, and basil or parsley. Add the spaghetti and mix well, then stir in the mozzarella cheese and prosciutto.

In a 9-inch frying pan, heat 2 tablespoons of the butter and 2 tablespoons of the olive oil. Add the spaghetti mixture and smooth the top with a spatula. Cook over medium-low heat until the frittata is browned on the bottom and set. Invert a plate larger than the frying pan over the pan and turn out the frittata. Heat the remaining butter and olive oil in the pan, and return the frittata to the pan to brown the other side. Shake the pan occasionally to keep the frittata from sticking.

Invert a serving plate over the frying pan and carefully turn out the frittata. Serve at room temperature, cut in wedges.

Note: This is even better the day after it is made. Serve it with Salsa Fresca di Pomodori e Basilico (page 87) spooned over the top.

Cavatelli

LITTLE CAVES

Cavatelli means "little caves" or quarries. This interesting pasta reminds me of gnocchi because of the little dents or ridges in the dough. I make these on a special cavatelli machine, but they can also be made by hand using a comb.

SERVES 6 TO 8

About 3¾ cups unbleached all-purpose flour

¼ cup semolina flour

1 teaspoon salt

1 large egg, beaten

1 pound whole-milk ricotta cheese, well drained

¼ cup water

In a large bowl, mix 3¾ cups all-purpose flour, the semolina and salt together. Add the egg, ricotta, and water and work the mixture with your hands until you can form it into a ball. If the dough seems too soft, add a little more unbleached flour; if the dough is too stiff, add a little more water.

Knead the dough on a well-floured surface until smooth, about 10 minutes. Cover the dough with a bowl and let rest for 10 minutes.

If using a cavatelli machine, shape the pasta following the manufacturer's directions. If shaping them by hand, break off small pieces the size of a marble and form into small ovals. Run each piece over the teeth of a clean unused comb or the tines of a fork to create parallel ridges. Place the cavatelli on a floured cloth to dry for 30 minutes to 2 hours before cooking.

In a large pot of boiling water, cook the cavatelli until they bob to the surface, about 4 minutes. Drain and top with a tomato or cream sauce of your choice.

Farfalle Piccanti

SPICY BUTTERFLIES

Farfalla, which means "butterfly," is the name of a type of macaroni that is shaped somewhat like a butterfly. I remember big soup bowls of farfalle being served at least once a week. I used a spoon to eat them because a fork just could not hold as many at one time. I like mine topped with a spicy sauce.

SERVES 4 TO 6

2	tablespoons olive oil	1/3	cup chopped fresh basil
1/2	cup thinly sliced onion	1	tablespoon chopped fresh oregano or mint
2	cloves garlic, chopped		Salt and freshly ground black pepper to taste
1	teaspoon crushed red pepper flakes		
1	cup diced prosciutto (about 1/4 pound)	1	cup shelled fresh peas
2	28-ounce cans plum tomatoes	1	pound farfalle (bowtie pasta)
			Grated Pecorino Romano cheese

In a large saucepan, heat the olive oil. Add the onion and sauté until very soft. Add the garlic and crushed red pepper. Sauté until the garlic is soft, but do not let it brown. Add the prosciutto and sauté until it begins to render its fat. Add the plum tomatoes, breaking them up with a wooden spoon, stir well, and simmer for 5 minutes. Add the basil, oregano or mint, and salt and pepper. Stir well and simmer, covered, over medium heat for 20 minutes. Add the peas and cook for 5 minutes more.

Meanwhile, in a large pot of boiling water, cook the farfalle until *al dente*. Drain well.

Place the farfalle in a bowl, add the hot sauce, and toss well to coat. Serve in individual soup bowls and pass grated cheese separately.

Gnocchi di Patate

POTATO GNOCCHI

No one in my family makes gnocchi as well as Aunt Nancy Scatorchie does. She can roll them off the tines of a fork with lightning speed. Perfect gnocchi depends on the use of mature potatoes and a minimal amount of flour; otherwise they will be too heavy. There are many variations of gnocchi; these little dumplings are covered with a zippy tomato sauce, dusted with Pecorino Romano cheese, and sprinkled with fresh basil.

SERVES 6

4   large baking potatoes
1   large egg, beaten
  1/8 teaspoon salt
3   tablespoons grated Pecorino Romano cheese

About 2 cups unbleached all-purpose flour
3   cups Fresh Tomato Basil Sauce (page 87)
Grated Pecorino Romano cheese

Put the unpeeled potatoes in a large pot, add water to cover, and bring to a boil. Boil until tender, about 30 minutes. The potatoes can also be cooked in a microwave for 20 minutes. Let cool.

Peel the potatoes. In a large bowl mash them fine; do not use electric beaters or a food processor, which would make the potatoes too smooth. Add the beaten egg, salt, and cheese. Mix well.

Put 2 cups of flour on a work surface and make a well in the center. Put the potatoes in the center of the well. Knead the flour into the potatoes until a soft and smooth dough is formed. Add a little more flour if the dough seems too sticky.

Break off a small piece of the dough about the size of an egg and, with floured hands, roll the chunk into a rope about 14 inches long and the width of your middle finger. Cut the rope into 1-inch pieces and roll each piece with your thumb down and off the front of the tines of a floured fork: This creates little ridges to trap the sauce. As you form the gnocchi, place them in a single layer on a floured cloth or baking sheet. Repeat with the remaining dough.

In a large pot of boiling water, cook the gnocchi, a few at a time, until they rise to the surface. Meanwhile, in a small saucepan, heat the tomato sauce. Spoon a thin layer of sauce over the bottom of a large serving platter. Transfer the cooked gnocchi with a slotted spoon to the platter. Spoon the remaining sauce over the gnocchi, sprinkle with grated Pecorino Romano cheese, and serve immediately.

Variation: To make spinach gnocchi, add 1 cup cooked spinach, squeezed dry and chopped, to the potato and egg mixture; add the flour. Then, instead of rolling the gnocchi on the tines of a fork, break off pieces of dough about the size of a marble and form them into small balls. Cook as directed above and serve with the tomato sauce.

Note: Uncooked gnocchi freeze well: Arrange them in a single layer on baking sheets, cover with foil, freeze until firm, and then transfer to plastic bags and freeze until needed. Boil them without thawing. My mother places frozen gnocchi directly into a baking dish, adds sauce, and bakes them, eliminating the boiling step: Bake at 350°F. for 30 to 35 minutes.

Gnocchi di Semolina

SEMOLINA GNOCCHI

One night in the Alto Adige region of Italy, I ordered *gnocchi di semolina*, and the waiter brought me a plateful of succulent little disks swimming in butter and topped with Parmigiano-Reggiano cheese. The whole affair had been quickly passed under the broiler to give the gnocchi a crisp crust. So enamored was I of their delicate flavor that I slipped the waiter a few thousand lire—and off he went in a flash to retrieve the recipe from the chef.

SERVES 6 TO 8

GNOCCHI

4   cups milk

7   tablespoons unsalted butter

1/8   teaspoon salt

1/2   teaspoon white pepper

1 1/2   teaspoons grated nutmeg

1   cup plus 2 tablespoons semolina flour

1   large egg

3/4   cup grated Parmigiano-Reggiano cheese

8   tablespoons (1 stick) unsalted butter

1/2   cup grated Parmigiano-Reggiano cheese

Grated nutmeg

Lightly grease a marble slab or a clean work surface with olive oil.

To make the gnocchi, in a large saucepan, preferably nonstick, combine the milk, 3 tablespoons of the butter, the salt, pepper, and nutmeg. Bring to just under a boil. Add the semolina in a steady stream, stirring all the while with a wooden spoon so no lumps form. Cook, stirring, until the mixture is thick, looks like cooked Cream of Wheat, and starts to come away from the sides of the pan, about 10 minutes. Remove the pan from the heat, add the remaining 4 tablespoons butter, the egg, and cheese. Stir vigorously to blend. Turn the mixture out onto the oiled slab and let cool for 20 minutes.

Preheat the oven to 350°F. Butter a large baking dish.

Place a sheet of oiled wax paper over the dough and roll the dough out with a rolling pin to an even 1/2-inch thickness. Remove the wax paper and cut out disks with a floured 1-inch cookie cutter. Arrange the disks in the buttered dish, overlapping them slightly. Gather the dough scraps, roll out, and cut out more disks; add these to the baking dish.

In a small pan, melt the butter. Pour it over the gnocchi and sprinkle with the Parmigiano-Reggiano cheese and a grating of fresh nutmeg. Bake for 15 minutes, or until hot, then run the dish under the broiler to brown the cheese. Serve at once.

Rigatoni con Salsa di Cipolla

RIGATONI WITH ONION SAUCE

Lard is often an important ingredient in traditional Italian cooking. It is used to brown and flavor meats and vegetables and in pastry crusts for added taste and flakiness. Whenever I'm in the teaching kitchens of Italy, I have to remind myself that Italian cooks do not see lard as an artery clogger, but as essential to their cooking. So many of my own students shudder when I use lard that I often make substitutions, but I notice the difference in taste right away. The lard my grandmothers and mother used was of a better quality then what we find today. The traditional recipe for this hearty macaroni dish calls for lard, but substituting lean salt pork works very well.

SERVES 4 TO 6

1 pound rigatoni

4 slices (about 1/4 pound) lean salt pork, finely diced

1 large white onion, thinly sliced

1 tablespoon unbleached all-purpose flour

1 to 1 1/2 cups Homemade Beef Broth (page 32)

6 tablespoons grated Parmigiano-Reggiano cheese

2 teaspoons coarsely ground black pepper

In a large pot of boiling water, cook the rigatoni for 10 to 12 minutes. They should still be somewhat firm and chewy; they will cook further in the sauce. Drain and cover to keep warm.

In a large skillet, sauté the salt pork with the onions until the salt pork is browned and has rendered its fat. Sprinkle over the flour and stir to blend. Stir in the rigatoni. Pour in half the beef stock, stirring all the while. Then add the cheese and the remaining stock, stirring well. Remove from the heat, stir in the pepper, and serve at once.

Rigatoni con Pomodori Secchi

RIGATONI WITH DRIED TOMATOES

In southern Italy, ripe, robust plum tomatoes are dried on long wooden boards in the hot Mediterranean sun until they are ready to be packed in olive oil or made into a tomato paste known as *conserva*. I dry my tomatoes in a dehydrator and then use them in salads, for antipasti, or in a quick and delicious sauce for pasta. If you have them on hand, you can have this dish on the table in a wink.

SERVES 6

1   cup dried tomatoes packed in olive oil, homemade (page 218) or store-bought

1   clove garlic, minced

1   pound rigatoni

3   tablespoons minced fresh basil

⅓   cup grated Parmigiano-Reggiano cheese

⅓   cup grated Asiago cheese

Drain the tomatoes, reserving 2 tablespoons of their oil. Place the tomatoes and the reserved oil in a food processor or blender and pulse until coarsely ground. Or chop the tomatoes very fine by hand. Transfer the tomatoes to a nonreactive saucepan, stir in the garlic, and cook for 2 to 3 minutes. Remove from the heat and set aside.

In a large pot of boiling water, cook the rigatoni until *al dente*. Drain, reserving ⅓ cup of the cooking water.

Place the rigatoni in a serving bowl and add the tomato mixture, reserved cooking water, and the basil. Toss to coat well. Add the cheeses and toss again. Serve immediately.

Note: A generous grinding of fresh black pepper adds to the spiciness of this dish.

Frittata di Spaghetti al Forno

BAKED SPAGHETTI FRITTATA

Another way to make *frittata di spaghetti* is to bake it instead of trying to flip it out of a frying pan. Here's a version that uses vegetables and all those bits and pieces of cheeses that have been hiding in the back of the refrigerator. Other vegetables and cheeses can be added—just be sure to cut them all the same size.

SERVES 8 TO 10

1 tablespoon butter

1 tablespoon olive oil

1/2 cup diced onion

1 cup diced bell peppers

1/2 cup diced zucchini

6 large eggs

3 tablespoons grated Pecorino Romano cheese

3 tablespoons minced fresh parsley or basil

Salt and freshly ground black pepper to taste

1 1/2 cups cubed mixed cheeses (Swiss, Italian Fontina, mozzarella, and/ or Provolone)

1/2 cup oil-cured olives, pitted and diced

2 cups cooked spaghetti

Preheat the oven to 350°F. Lightly butter a 9-×-10-inch or 9-×-12-inch baking dish.

In a large skillet, heat the butter and olive oil. Add the onion, peppers, and zucchini and sauté for 3 to 4 minutes, until the vegetables are softened. Let cool slightly.

In a large bowl, beat the eggs, until light colored. Add the Pecorino Romano, parsley or basil, and salt and pepper. Add the vegetables to the egg mixture, along with the cheeses and olives. Mix well. Add the spaghetti and mix well.

Spread the mixture in the buttered dish and smooth the top with a spatula. Bake for 25 minutes, or until a knife inserted into the frittata comes out clean. Cut into squares to serve.

Note: This can be made ahead and eaten either warm or at room temperature. It also makes great picnic fare because it travels well.

Tortelli di Zucca alla Raffaella

RAFFAELLA'S PUMPKIN TORTELLI

A few years ago I had the good fortune to meet a group of Italian students who were visiting the States. Among them was Raffaella Neviani, a vivacious young woman from Cavriago, in the north of Italy. When she left to return home, I helped her load her belongings on the bus for the long ride to the airport. Hugging me goodbye, she slipped into my hand her mother's heirloom recipe for pumpkin-filled tortelli, a specialty of Reggio-Emilia. These rectangular ravioli are fun to make and the crushed amaretti cookies in the filling are a subtle but delicious addition. This recipe makes a lot, so you can freeze some for later use.

MAKES ABOUT 100

FILLING

1   1-pound butternut squash or pumpkin

¼ cup crushed amaretti cookies

½ teaspoon grated nutmeg

½ teaspoon salt

4   teaspoons grated Parmigiano-Reggiano cheese

PASTA

4   large eggs

3   cups unbleached all-purpose flour

⅛ teaspoon salt

To make the filling, preheat the oven to 350°F.

Cut the squash or pumpkin in half, scoop out the seeds, and discard. Place the halves cut side down in a small baking dish, add ½ cup water, and cover the dish with foil. Bake for 35 minutes, or until the squash is easily pierced with a fork. Let cool.

With a spoon, scoop out the flesh of the squash. Put it in a colander and let it drain for 45 minutes.

Transfer the squash to a bowl and mash it well. Add the amaretti, nutmeg, salt, and Parmigiano-Reggiano cheese and mix well. Cover and refrigerate until ready to use.

To make the pasta, combine the eggs, flour, and salt following the directions for Basic Egg Pasta on pages 46 to 47. Cover the dough and let rest for 10 minutes.

Knead the dough well and cut it into 4 pieces. Work with 1 piece at a time, keeping the rest covered. Roll each piece out to the thinnest setting on a pasta machine, or roll it out with a rolling pin on a floured surface to a thickness of ⅛ inch.

Cut 4-×-2½-inch rectangles from the sheets of dough. Place 1 tea-spoon of the filling in the center of each rectangle, fold the rectangles in half lengthwise, making sure to pinch the edges well to seal in the filling, and place on a floured towel. Gather the dough scraps into a ball and reroll them to make more tortelli. (You can also make round, half-moon, or square-shaped tortelli.)

To cook, bring a large pot of water to a boil. Cook the tortelli, about 2 dozen at a time, for 1 to 2 minutes, or until they rise to the surface. Drain them carefully, sauce, and serve. Raffaella's mother serves these tossed with a generous amount of melted butter and sprinkled with grated Parmigiano. They are also good with sage butter—add a small handful of fresh sage leaves to the melted butter and press them into the butter with a wooden spoon to release their flavor.

To freeze, arrange the tortelli in a single layer on floured baking sheets, cover with foil, and freeze until hard. Transfer them to plastic bags and freeze for up to 3 months. Do not defrost them before boiling (they will take a little longer to cook).

Ravioli con Aragosta

LOBSTER RAVIOLI

It is interesting to conjecture as to how ravioli came to be. These plump little pillows of pasta hold a variety of traditional savory fillings, depending on where in Italy you are. My Grandmother Galasso used to make ravioli out of leftover pasta dough that was too small to do anything else with. She filled them with a mixture of bits and pieces of meats, cheeses, and herbs. Then they were gently placed on a clean blanket until the cooking water was boiling. When I make ravioli and I really want to splurge, I fill them with lobster. I like to serve them with Salsa di Peperoni Rossi (page 88). This recipe makes a lot: Cook what you need and freeze the rest.

MAKES 150 TO 200

LOBSTER FILLING

2 cups cooked lobster meat (about 12 ounces)

1 large egg, beaten

1 teaspoon fine sea salt

1 teaspoon white pepper

¼ cup grated Parmigiano-Reggiano cheese

2 tablespoons finely minced fresh parsley

1 recipe Basic Egg Pasta (page 46)

To make the filling, with a knife, mince the lobster meat fine. Put it in a bowl, add all the remaining filling ingredients, and mix well. Refrigerate, covered, until ready to use.

To make the ravioli using a form, first roll the dough through a pasta machine to the finest setting and cut into 13-inch lengths, or roll it out with a rolling pin on a floured surface as thin as possible and cut into strips approximately 5 inches by 13 inches. Place one strip of dough over the bottom section of the ravioli form, making sure that the dough overlaps all the edges of the form by about ½ inch. Use the top part of the form to make slight impressions in the dough. Put 1 teaspoon of filling in each impression and cover with another sheet of dough. Roll over the form with a rolling pin several times to seal the edges. Trim the excess dough from around the form and save to reroll. Shake the ravioli out through the holes in the form and place them in a single layer on a floured baking sheet or a clean towel.

If you prefer to make the ravioli without a form, roll each piece of dough through a pasta machine to the finest setting and cut each strip of dough in half; or roll the dough out on a floured surface as thin as possible and cut in 5-inch-wide strips. Place teaspoons of the filling about 2 inches apart on one strip of dough, and cover with another strip of dough. Press down around the mounds of filling to seal the dough, and cut in ravioli squares with a pasta wheel or sharp knife. Place the ravioli in a single layer on a floured baking sheet or clean towels as you make them.

To cook, bring a large pot of salted water to a boil. Cook the ravioli, about 2 dozen at a time, just until they bob to the top, about 3 minutes. Drain and serve with a sauce of your choice.

To freeze, arrange the ravioli on baking sheets in a single layer, cover with foil, and freeze until solid. Place them in plastic bags and freeze for up to 3 months. Do not defrost before boiling.

Note: Ravioli forms can be purchased in cookware shops or through catalogs.

Lasagne Bianche con Pignoli

WHITE LASAGNA WITH PINE NUTS

I have spent a good part of the last few years translating a fourteenth-century manuscript on Italian food of the Renaissance called *Libro della Cucina del Secolo XIV*. One of the recipes in the book is for *laganum*, or lasagna. The sauce called for inspired me to create this *lasagne bianche*, very light-tasting lasagna. The recipe makes enough for a crowd. This also freezes beautifully, so you can bake one pan and freeze the other for another meal.

SERVES 16

FILLING

1	cup pine nuts
6	10-ounce packages fresh or frozen spinach, thawed if frozen
6	cups ricotta cheese
5	large eggs
6	tablespoons minced fresh parsley
3	cups diced mozzarella cheese (about ¾ pound)
4	tablespoons butter, at room temperature
½	pound prosciutto, diced
2	teaspoons grated nutmeg
2	teaspoons salt

2	teaspoons white pepper

WHITE SAUCE

8	cups milk
½	pound (2 sticks) unsalted butter
1	cup unbleached all-purpose flour, sifted
2	teaspoons salt
1	teaspoon grated nutmeg
3	tablespoons finely minced fresh sage

1	recipe Basic Egg Pasta (page 46)
1	cup grated Parmigiano-Reggiano cheese

To make the filling, preheat the oven to 350°F. Spread the pine nuts on a baking sheet and bake until lightly browned, about 5 minutes. Set aside to cool.

If using fresh spinach, remove the stems and wash it. Place it in a large dry pot, cover, and cook over medium-high heat until it is wilted, about 4 minutes. Drain in a colander. Squeeze out the excess moisture and chop fine. If using frozen spinach, squeeze out the excess moisture and chop fine.

In a large bowl, combine the spinach and pine nuts. Beat in the eggs. Then add all the remaining filling ingredients, mixing well. Cover and refrigerate until ready to use.

To make the sauce, in a large saucepan, scald the milk (bring to just under a boil). Remove from the heat and set aside.

In a large heavy saucepan, melt the butter over medium-high heat. Add the flour and stir with a wooden spoon until smooth. Stir in the milk, salt, and nutmeg and cook, stirring, until the mixture comes to a boil. Then cook, stirring, until the sauce thickens, 5 to 10 minutes. Remove the sauce from the heat and stir in the sage. Cover to keep warm.

Cut the pasta dough into 4 pieces. Work with 1 piece at a time, keeping the rest covered with a damp towel. Roll out the dough through a pasta machine to the second-finest setting, or roll it out on a floured surface to a thickness of ⅛ inch. Cut the sheets of dough into 3- × -6-inch strips and lay them flat on clean towels.

Preheat the oven to 350°F.

In a large pot of boiling water, cook the lasagna strips a few at a time for 2 to 3 minutes, or until *al dente*. Drain them on a towel.

Spread ½ cup of the White Sauce over the bottom of a 9- × -13-inch pan. Cover with a layer of lasagna strips and spread about 2 cups of the filling over the lasagna. Spoon on a thin layer of sauce. Repeat two more times, and top with a layer of lasagna. Spread 1 cup of sauce over the lasagna, sprinkle with ½ cup of the cheese, and cover with foil. Repeat with the remaining ingredients to fill another pan. Bake for 30 minutes. Let stand for 10 minutes before cutting and serving.

Salse

SAUCES

ITALIANS MAKE many very good sauces, both cooked and uncooked, and it is a misconception to think that every region of Italy uses tomato sauce exclusively. That was the sauce my grandmothers put on most of their dishes because it was what they had made in Avellino and Caltanissetta. But every region of Italy has its special sauces, from the *ragù* of Bologna to the *pesto* of Genoa to the *saor* of Venice.

Another common misconception about Italian sauces is that food is generously covered with them, when, in fact, Italians use sauces very sparingly, even on pasta. A perfect example of this practice is the exceptional dish of tortelli I ordered at Ristorante Cesari on Via de Carbonesi in Bologna. The oval-shaped pasta, stuffed with a savory filling of fresh ricotta cheese and red peppers, was topped with an ethereal sauce of butter and Parmigiano-Reggiano cheese. The sauce seemed as if it were hardly there, but it was just the perfect balance for the pasta and allowed all the individual flavors to come through.

Most Italian sauces are very simple to prepare and do not require tedious reducing to get the right consistency. The key to making good sauces is to start with the best seasonal ingredients. It is no sin to use canned tomatoes when fresh are not available, but it is a sin to try and make pesto sauce from dried basil leaves, when only fresh will do. In the case of herbs, using only fresh is a commandment for me, as it was for my grandmothers. It would have been foreign to them to use dried basil or parsley in their sauces. The only dried herb they ever gave their blessing to for sauce making was oregano, because it maintained some of its flavor and smell, but most dried herbs do not bear any resemblance to their fresh counterparts. They are oiless, odorless, and flavorless—you are defeated even before you begin.

There is no set formula to follow when making Italian sauces. You can travel from region to region in Italy and the cooking style for making sauces will vary from cook to cook. The one common thread is the use of what is readily available.

Ragù Napoletano

NEAPOLITAN MEAT SAUCE

A ragù is a meat sauce made with pork or beef. It starts with a *soffritto*, sautéed aromatic vegetables, to which the rest of the ingredients are added. It is a hearty sauce that is perfect over chunky types of macaroni, as well as over slices of polenta. Don't be put off by the lard; it gives a subtle flavor to the sauce. However, you can substitute olive oil if you prefer.

MAKES ABOUT 8 CUPS

2 tablespoons olive oil	1 pound beef round or chuck steak, cut into ½-inch cubes
1 clove garlic, chopped	
1 onion, coarsely chopped	½ cup dry red wine
1 rib celery, coarsely chopped	2 28-ounce cans plum tomatoes
1 large carrot, coarsely chopped	1 bay leaf
1 tablespoon lard	1 tablespoon coarse salt

In a large saucepan, heat the oil. Add the garlic and sauté until soft. Add the onion, celery, and carrot and sauté for 5 to 7 minutes, or until soft. Using a slotted spoon, remove the vegetables from the pan; set aside.

Add the lard to the saucepan and melt it over medium-high heat. Pat the meat dry with paper towels, add it to the pan, and brown it well. Add the wine and simmer for 5 minutes. Add the tomatoes, bay leaf, and salt. Return the vegetables to the pan. Simmer the ragù, covered, over low heat until the meat is tender, about 45 minutes. Remove the bay leaf and discard. Process the ragù in a food processor until smooth.

Use immediately or freeze for up to 3 months.

Pesto

The word *pesto* comes from *pestare,* to pound. Pesto is made with fresh basil leaves and is the signature sauce of the region of Liguria and, in particular, Genoa. Its sweet, slightly peppery flavor marries well with many ingredients. Pesto is delicious on pasta but it's equally good on fish and pizza and a great addition to hearty soups. Try it in Torta di Pesto (page 26).

MAKES 2 CUPS

1½ cups packed fresh basil leaves

3 cloves garlic, peeled

3 tablespoons grated Parmigiano-Reggiano or Pecorino Romano cheese

½ cup extra-virgin olive oil

¼ cup pine nuts

Salt and freshly ground black pepper, optional

Extra-virgin olive oil

In a food processor, combine the basil and garlic and process to a coarse puree. Add the cheese and process to blend. With the motor running, add the olive oil in a thin steady stream through the feed tube. Add the pine nuts and blend the mixture until smooth. Season with salt and pepper if you wish.

To store, transfer to a jar and pour a thin layer of extra-virgin olive oil over the top to preserve the pesto. Refrigerate.

Note: You can also make this the traditional way using a mortar and pestle. Grind the basil and garlic together to a coarse puree. Add the nuts and grind to a smooth puree. Blend in the cheese. Blend in the oil a little at a time. Season to taste.

Salsa di Aglio e Olio

GARLIC AND OIL SAUCE

Garlic and olive oil, two staples of the Mediterranean diet for centuries, provide the flavorings for a simple sauce used over spaghetti. When I'm in a hurry, this is the sauce I make. The secret to this sauce is to use a good-quality virgin olive oil and to mix it with a little of the water the spaghetti was cooked in. This recipe makes enough sauce for ½ pound spaghetti.

2/3 cup virgin olive oil

2 cloves garlic, finely minced

1 teaspoon salt

1 teaspoon coarsely ground black pepper

1/3 cup reserved spaghetti cooking water

In a frying pan, heat the oil. Add the garlic and sauté until soft. Add the salt and pepper. Add the reserved pasta cooking water and blend well. Cook over low heat for 1 minute. Pour the sauce over hot spaghetti and toss to coat. Serve immediately.

Note: Grandma Galasso often sprinkled over the pasta a fistful of toasted bread crumbs that had been sautéed in olive oil.

Salsa Cinque Minuti

FIVE-MINUTE SAUCE

I concocted this pasta sauce one hot summer day when my garden said "deal with me now." I spent the entire day marinating eggplant, drying tomatoes, making pesto, and wondering what to do with the golden yellow hybrid tomatoes my husband had planted. These tomatoes are very plump and juicy and have a mild flavor. The very first Italian tomatoes were yellow too; they were called *pomodori*, or apples of gold. So it seemed appropriate to make a sauce out of my yellow tomatoes; if you can't find yellow tomatoes, use red plum tomatoes.

6 tablespoons olive oil

1 large clove garlic, chopped

1 1/2 teaspoons crushed red pepper flakes

1/2 cup diced unpeeled eggplant

1 1/2 cups coarsely chopped yellow tomatoes (about 3 medium)

1/4 cup dried tomatoes, homemade (page 218) or store-bought

1/2 cup chopped fresh basil

1 teaspoon sugar

Salt and freshly ground black pepper to taste

In a large skillet, heat the olive oil. Add the garlic and sauté until soft. Stir in the red pepper flakes. Add the eggplant and sauté until lightly browned. Add the yellow tomatoes, dried tomatoes, basil, sugar, and salt and pepper and stir well. Cook over medium-high heat for 5 minutes. Use immediately.

Note: Serve this sauce over cooked rotelle, sprinkle with grated Pecorino Romano cheese.

CHEESE, LIKE bread, is one of man's most basic foods. The farmers of Italy have been making it for centuries, transforming the rich milk of cows, sheep, goats, and buffalo into distinctive cheese, both fresh and aged.

Today, making cheese has become mechanized in many places in Italy, but some local areas still adhere to the old methods of production. This became evident to me during my recent stay in the culinary city of Reggio Emilia in the region of Emilia Romagna, where the king of all Italian cheeses, Parmigiano-Reggiano, is made. There I received a personalized tour of a cheese factory from Alessandro Lori, a man who knows a lot about Parmigiano-Reggiano's history and production. The making of this particular cheese is controlled by law and its name testifies to the fact that it must be produced in the Emilia-Romagna region, which includes the cities of Parma, Modena, Bologna, Mantua, and Reggio Emilia. The cheese must be made from cow's milk, from both a morning and evening milking, and it must be made between April and November each year, when the best milk is obtainable.

Alessandro Lori is not a cheesemaker, but a high-ranking, well-respected banker. He was born in Reggio Emilia and grew up near the pasturelands that feed the cows that yield the rich milk for this famous cheese. Parmigiano-Reggiano is so prized that the bank where Alessandro works owns huge warehouses full of aged golden wheels of the cheese, stacked floor to ceiling. Alessandro says that the bank's attitude is summed up by the words "Cheese is money."

Cheese is nothing more than the coagulated heated portion of milk, called *curds*. What causes the milk to coagulate is rennet, an enzyme produced from the stomach lining of sheep or from plants. The *whey* is the liquid left after the curds are removed. It is used to make soft fresh cheeses like ricotta.

The principles of cheese making may be simple but the quality of the end product is determined by a number of things: The type of milk used, its fat content, and the temperature it is cooked at; the amount of aging time; the time of year the cheese is made; whether or not it has undergone a brine bath; and the ability of an experienced cheese maker to know when the cheese is ready for consumption.

The uses of cheeses in Italian cooking have antique origins that have continued on to today. Almost every region of Italy boasts a locally made cheese and it would be a tremendous task to try to describe all of them. But mention should be made of the more familiar ones, their particular characteristics and usage.

Asiago   A semihard cow's milk cheese made in the province of Vicenza, and one of my favorites. It has a pale yellow color and a nice nutty flavor that gets sharper as it ages. Good for eating, grated over pasta, in *frittate,* and in cream sauces.

Bel Paese   A semisoft cow's milk cheese with a mild taste. Wonderful with crusty bread and fresh pears.

Caciocavallo   A cow's milk cheese from southern Italy that is molded into a round or pear shape with a little knob on the top. A good eating cheese with a hint of smokiness. It makes a good grating cheese once it ages.

Fior di Latte   A cow's milk cheese from southern Italy that is similar to fresh water buffalo mozzarella. Creamy white, it is best eaten fresh. Excellent with ripe summer tomatoes and basil.

Fontina   A cow's milk cheese with a distinctive brown rind. It comes from a particular breed of cow in the Valle d'Aosta in northern Italy. It has a slightly nutty taste and a creamy texture. Good as an eating cheese and mixed with other cheeses as a filling for *crespelle.*

continued

Gorgonzola A cow's milk cheese with green mold running through it, made in Gorgonzola, Lombardy, in northern Italy. It has a distinct flavor that becomes sharp as it ages. Wonderful with crusty bread and in cream sauces.

Mascarpone A very rich cow's milk cheese from Lombardy, with the texture of cream cheese. Used mainly in desserts like *tiramisù*, it is very perishable. I like it with fresh figs or pears.

Mozzarella A soft delicate cheese made in the Campania region of southern Italy. It comes from the milk of the water buffalo and is both very perishable and expensive. Wonderful fresh with bread and a drizzle of olive oil. There is also a cow's milk version that is less rich tasting.

Parmigiano-Reggiano The king of Italian cheeses. The production of this cow's milk cheese is controlled by law. Both a young and an aged type are made. The young is table ready in less than a year and is white in color. The aged is yellow and drier and granier in texture. An excellent table and grating cheese.

Pecorino A sheep's milk cheese made in almost every region of Italy. The best known is Pecorino Romano, from the Lazio region. It has a salty taste and sharp flavor and is wonderful grated on tomato-based pasta dishes. Equally good as table cheese, and I love it on pizza.

Provolone Originally made from water buffalo milk, this cheese from southern Italy is now made from cow's milk. It develops a sharp flavor as it ages and can be used as a table cheese and in recipes with eggplant, pasta, and breads. In Sardegna, this cheese is grilled on hot stones.

Ricotta The word means "recooked," and this cheese is made from the whey produced in the cheese-making process. The whey is cooked to produce this soft white cheese. Ricotta can be made from sheep's or cow's milk whey; sheep ricotta has a sharper taste. Used in lasagna, for tortes, and in desserts like cannoli. We often had it fried in butter with a grinding of black pepper over the top.

Scamorza   A southern Italian cheese made from cow's milk or a mixture of cow's and sheep's milk. It has a brownish color and a rounded shape. Good as a table cheese or grilled.

Taleggio   A cow's milk cheese from Lombardy. Creamy, white, and soft, it is good with fresh fruit or crusty bread.

Most of these cheeses are available in grocery stores or specialty cheese shops; the more unusual ones are often obtainable through mail-order catalogues. Be wary of imitation Italian cheeses. A good case in point is Parmigiano-Reggiano. The real thing has the words "Parmigiano-Reggiano" embedded in the rind of the cheese as well as the seal of the province where it is made. This trademark guarantees that you are getting the real thing. Many people buy imitation Parmesan cheese from Argentina, thinking it is authentic.

For grated cheese, it is best to buy Parmigiano in a chunk, bring it to room temperature, and grate what you need. Do not remove the rind of the cheese, as this helps to preserve its freshness. To keep grating cheese for future use, wrap it well and keep it in a cool but not too cold place.

When I was served Parmigiano-Reggiano at the Lori house, I watched as Lorenza Lori cut it with a special little cheese knife with an almost triangular-shaped blade no more than 2 inches long. She drew a line with the blade down the side of the cheese wedge and, as if by magic, it split apart to reveal its yellow color, grainy texture, and clean nutty taste.

Salsa Arrabbiata

MAD TOMATO SAUCE

My grandmothers and mother made tomato sauce every week and firmly believed that you had to cook the tomatoes all day long in order to produce a good sauce. What made a lengthy cooking time necessary were the tough cuts of meat, such as chuck and pork butt, that were put in to simmer and flavor the sauce. I don't have all day to cook sauce, but I'd bet a bushel of tomatoes that even my grandmothers and mother would like tomato sauce done my way.

MAKES 3½ CUPS

3   pounds fresh plum tomatoes

3   tablespoons extra-virgin olive oil

3   large cloves garlic, finely chopped

1½ teaspoons crushed red pepper flakes

1½ teaspoons salt

½   teaspoon freshly ground black pepper

⅓   cup minced fresh basil

Preheat the oven to 400°F.

Cut the tomatoes in half. Place them cut side down on a baking sheet and bake for 10 to 15 minutes, or until they are just slightly soft. Transfer the tomatoes to a food processor or blender and pulse until very smooth. Set aside.

In a medium saucepan, heat the olive oil. Add the garlic and red pepper flakes and cook until the garlic is soft. Add the pureed tomatoes and cook for 10 minutes. Pour the sauce into a sieve set over a bowl and strain, using a wooden spoon to press on the solids to extract as much liquid as possible; discard the solids. Add the salt, pepper, and basil; stir to blend. The sauce is best when freshly made but can be refrigerated for up to 1 week.

Note: This sauce is great over any type of short, chunky macaroni. I like it with orecchiette.

Salsa Fresca di Pomodori e Basilico

FRESH TOMATO BASIL SAUCE

September usually finds me up to my elbows in fresh tomatoes and basil as I prepare a basic tomato sauce that I use on everything. I no longer bother to skin the tomatoes; I just use my food processor to pulverize them into a pulp. There are many variations on Italian tomato sauce, some simmered all day and some ready after a couple stirs of the spoon. If you don't want to bother with fresh tomatoes, this recipe works with canned plum tomatoes. Look for the San Marzano variety: They are sweet and juicy.

MAKES 9¹/₂ TO 10 CUPS

5 pounds ripe plum tomatoes or 3 28-ounce cans crushed plum tomatoes	1¹/₂ cups dry red wine
¹/₂ cup extra-virgin olive oil	Coarse salt and freshly ground black pepper to taste
¹/₂ cup diced onion	4 or 5 large sprigs basil
3 cloves garlic, minced	

If using fresh tomatoes, core them, cut them into coarse chunks, and puree in a food processor until smooth. Strain the fresh or canned tomatoes through a fine sieve to remove the seeds. Set aside.

In a deep heavy pot, heat the olive oil. Add the onion and sauté until soft. Add the garlic and sauté until soft. Add the tomatoes and stir to blend. Add the wine, salt and pepper, and basil and stir well. Bring to a boil, lower the heat, and simmer for 25 minutes. The sauce is ready to use, or it can be refrigerated for up to 1 week or frozen for up to 3 months.

Salsa di Gorgonzola

GORGONZOLA SAUCE

The following is an adaptation of the Gorgonzola sauce that I use for Rotolo di Pasta (page 60). Since a sauce of just Gorgonzola cheese would be too heavy and too overpowering in taste, I add some creamy, mild mascarpone to the recipe.

MAKES ABOUT 3 CUPS

2 cups heavy cream

¹/₂ cup (5 ounces) mascarpone cheese

¹/₄ pound Italian Gorgonzola cheese

In a medium saucepan, combine all the ingredients. Bring to a low boil and stir with a wooden spoon over low heat until the cheeses are melted and smooth. Use immediately.

Salsa di Peperoni Rossi

RED PEPPER SAUCE

Peperoni means "peppers," not the dried sausage used on pizza. Peppers are everywhere in Italian cuisine: stuffed, fried, baked, marinated, and eaten raw. I like to make a sauce out of red bell peppers and cream that is wonderful on pasta and fish. Try it on Ravioli con Aragosta (page 74).

MAKES ABOUT 3¹/₂ CUPS

4 large red bell peppers

4 tablespoons butter

2 cloves garlic, minced

1 cup heavy cream or half-and-half

1 teaspoon grated nutmeg

1¹/₂ teaspoons salt

¹/₄ teaspoon freshly grated black pepper

¹/₄ cup minced fresh basil or thyme

Place the peppers on a lightly greased broiler pan and broil, turning occasionally, until blackened all over, about 15 minutes. Place the peppers in a large paper bag, close the bag tightly, and let cool for 20 minutes.

Peel the peppers and remove the seeds and cores. Rinse the peppers well, place them in a food processor or blender, and puree until smooth. Set aside.

In a large frying pan, heat the butter and sauté the garlic over medium heat until soft. Add the pepper puree and mix well. Lower the heat and gradually stir in the heavy cream. Add the nutmeg, salt, and pepper and cook, stirring, for 5 minutes. Remove from the heat and stir in the basil or thyme. Serve immediately over hot pasta or refrigerate for up to 3 days.

Salsa Tartufo Nero

BLACK TRUFFLE SAUCE

I have to admit that when I was growing up in an Italian household, there was only one sauce to be taken seriously, and that was tomato sauce! Both my grandmothers were from the southern regions of Italy where tomato plants were revered almost as much as the local patron saints, so I can hardly blame them for putting tomato sauce over everything from macaroni to eggplant.

My library of Italian sauces is more encompassing and shows the versatility of the Italian cook and the simple approach to making tasty sauces. One favorite is black truffle sauce from Norcia, in Umbria, where the prized black *funghi* grow deep in the ground around the roots of oak trees. Their wrinkled look belies their exquisite aroma and taste. Pigs and dogs are trained to sniff out the "black gold," and each farmer keeps his truffle turf a deep secret. I usually use black truffles from a jar for this recipe because fresh ones are available only in specialty stores from fall to mid-winter; if you can get fresh truffles, this will be better still.

MAKES ⅔ CUP

2   fresh or bottled black truffles, about 2 ounces total

½   cup virgin olive oil

2   cloves garlic, peeled

Salt and freshly ground black pepper, optional

Slice the truffles paper-thin.

In a frying pan, heat the olive oil. Sauté the garlic until it is golden brown; remove and discard it. Turn off the heat and add the truffles to the pan. Do not let the truffles sit in the hot pan for too long—you want them just to flavor the oil. Add salt and pepper to taste if you wish. Serve this sauce immediately, on pasta, gnocchi, or roasted veal.

Polenta e Riso

POLENTA AND RICE

NORTHERN ITALIANS would be as lost without their *polenta* as southern Italians would be without their *maccheroni*. It has been a staple of northern Italian cooking for generations. So important is polenta, in fact, that most northern households have a special copper pot called the *paiolo* and a long-handled spoon to do the job of quick and vigorous stirring. There is even a special day honoring polenta, called the *Polentone* (Big Polenta).

In northern Italy, polenta often takes the place of pasta or bread. It can be made from either coarse or finely ground cornmeal according to personal taste. Polenta's image, until just recently, has been rather negative. But now it has found favor with imaginative cooks who pair it with everything from vegetables to soups; layer it for lasagne, and cut it into pieces and fry it for antipasti. Traditionally, the hot polenta is poured out onto a wooden board, a shallow depression is made down the middle of the polenta with a spoon, and tomato sauce is poured into it. Cold polenta is cut into slices, usually with a string or wire, and used as bread to make a sandwich. It can be served with stews or under wild birds that have been roasted on a spit. Polenta can be made ahead and refrigerated, ready to use.

One of the particular joys of Italian travel is learning about the regional differences in food. Rice is found all over Italy, but the northern regions of Lombardy, Piedmont, and the Veneto, are well known for their classic rice dishes. Northern cooks transform rice into delicate first courses as well as desserts. There are three types of rice to be found in Italy: common rice, used for soup and desserts; fine rice, used for pilafs; and superfine, or Arborio, rice used for the classic risotto. The recipes in this section all use Arborio rice, which is a short, starchy rice that can absorb a lot of liquid. When it is cooked, it expands to two or three times its original size.

Risotto is rice that has been sautéed briefly in fat, usually butter, and then stirred constantly as broth or water is added in small amounts, allowing the rice to absorb each addition before another is added. The rice swells as it is cooked, and the final product must be fluid and flow off the spoon almost in ribbons.

As for pasta, rice should always be cooked *al dente*, that is, it should still have a bite to it. Most grocery stores carry Arborio rice. Do not try to make risotto with quick-cooking rices; they do not have the same starch content. A general formula to use when cooking Italian rice is: ½ cup Arborio rice cooked in 1½ cups water yields 1 cup of cooked rice.

Polenta

Polenta, or cornmeal cooked in milk or water, is to be found in the northern Italian regions of Lombardy, Piedmont, the Trentino, and Friuli-Venezia-Giulia. Polenta requires constant vigorous stirring to achieve its characteristic smooth consistency.

SERVES 8 TO 10

4½ cups water

1½ teaspoons salt

1½ cups coarsely ground cornmeal

In a large heavy pot, bring the water to a boil. Add the salt. Add the cornmeal in a thin stream, stirring vigorously all the while with a wooden spoon. Cook, stirring constantly, over medium heat until the mixture thickens and begins to leave the side of the pan, about 15 to 25 minutes, depending on the coarseness of the cornmeal.

Immediately pour the polenta onto a lightly oiled wooden board or platter. Let it cool for 15 minutes, then cut into slices. Serve with Salsa Fresca di Pomodori e Basilico (page 87), or use in any of the following recipes or in place of bread, noodles, or lasagna.

Polenta con Formaggio e Verdure

POLENTA WITH CHEESE AND VEGETABLES

Northern Italians are sometimes referred to as *mangia polenta*, mush eaters, because of the amount of cornmeal they eat. There are many ways to prepare it and some Italians say polenta made with coarse-ground cornmeal is better than that from fine-ground. Some prefer to use white cornmeal as opposed to yellow, as is the custom in Montalcino, Tuscany. As a child, I did not like polenta, but Nonna Galasso made it every so often, even though she was a southern Italian. Whenever she served it, I developed a stomachache that would quickly disappear when she offered me a pack of Lifesavers—after I ate my polenta.

SERVES 8

¼ cup olive oil	1 recipe Polenta (page 91), chilled
2 cloves garlic, minced	8 thin slices of Italian Fontina cheese (½ pound)
1½ cups thin strips (matchsticks) zucchini	
1½ cups thinly sliced mushrooms	

In a skillet, heat the oil. Add the garlic and sauté until soft. Add the vegetables and sauté until soft. Cover to keep warm and set aside.

Cut the cold polenta into 8 slices and place them on a greased broiler pan. Divide the vegetable mixture evenly among the slices, and top each slice with a slice of cheese. Broil just until the cheese begins to melt. Serve immediately.

Polenta con Porcini Secchi

POLENTA WITH DRIED PORCINI

A good polenta dish is enhanced by a balance of flavors. By itself, polenta is rather bland, but when you match it with an ingredient with a definite flavor, like woodsy-tasting *porcini*, then you have a real culinary marriage.

SERVES 10

2 cups dried porcini mushrooms (about 2 ounces)	Salt and freshly ground black pepper to taste
6 tablespoons olive oil	1 recipe Polenta (page 91), chilled

In a small bowl, soak the porcini in water to cover for 1 hour.

Drain the porcini, reserving the soaking liquid, and cut into dice. Strain the soaking liquid and set aside.

In a skillet, heat the olive oil. Add the garlic and sauté until soft. Add the porcini and ¼ cup of the reserved soaking liquid, cover, and simmer for 5 minutes. Add salt and pepper.

Meanwhile, cut the cold polenta into 10 thick slices. Place them on a lightly greased broiler pan or grill rack and broil or grill them until lightly browned. Carefully transfer the slices to a serving platter, top with the porcini mixture, and serve.

Polenta con Salsa di Pomodoro

POLENTA WITH TOMATO SAUCE

Polenta with tomato sauce is very common in the northern regions of Italy and can be likened to the southern favorite dish of pasta with tomato sauce. Southern Italians also have their own version of polenta with tomato sauce, known as *polentina;* it is a little soupier than its northern cousin.

SERVES 8

¾ cup olive oil

2 cloves garlic, chopped

3 cups peeled and diced fresh tomatoes (about 6 medium tomatoes)

2 tablespoons dry red wine

4 tablespoons chopped fresh basil

Salt and freshly ground black pepper to taste

1 recipe Polenta (page 91), chilled

In a saucepan, heat ¼ cup of the olive oil. Add the garlic and sauté until soft. Add the tomatoes and red wine and simmer for 5 minutes. Add the basil and salt and pepper and simmer for 5 minutes more.

Meanwhile, cut the polenta into 8 thick slices. In a frying pan, heat the remaining ½ cup olive oil and fry the polenta slices on both sides until lightly browned. Place the slices in individual soup bowls.

Pour the sauce over the polenta slices and serve immediately.

Polenta in Carrozza

POLENTA SANDWICHES

Polenta is very versatile. When it is cold, it can be sliced and layered into a type of lasagna or used like bread. My favorite way to have it is as a sandwich, stuffed with cheese and ham and then fried in butter. With a salad and a glass of wine, this makes a very satisfying meal.

MAKES 6

1	recipe Polenta (page 91), chilled	3	large eggs
¼	pound prosciutto, thinly sliced	1½	cups fresh bread crumbs
½	pound Fontina cheese, thinly sliced	5	tablespoons butter

Cut the polenta into 12 slices. Top 6 of the slices with the prosciutto and then the cheese. Top each sandwich with another polenta slice.

In a shallow bowl, beat the eggs. Spread the bread crumbs on a plate. Dip both sides of each sandwich in the eggs and then dredge in the bread crumbs to coat both sides. Set the sandwiches aside on a baking sheet to dry slightly.

In a frying pan, heat the butter. Add the sandwiches and fry on both sides until golden brown and the cheese is melted. Serve immediately.

Arancini di Siciliani

SICILIAN RICE BALLS

When my grandmothers arrived in this country, they had to make many changes in the way they cooked. Many things they were used to in Italy were not available in America, such as the short-grain, starchy rice known as Arborio—so they made do with "American rice." Today we can find Arborio and other Italian rices in the grocery store. Because Arborio rice contains so much starch, it can absorb a lot of liquid and therefore is the rice used to make not only creamy risotto, but also *arancini,* Sicilian rice balls that resemble small oranges. Serve these with lemon wedges or with Salsa Fresca di Pomodori e Basilico (page 87).

1   cup Arborio rice

3   large eggs

¹/4   cup grated Pecorino Romano
     cheese

3   tablespoons finely minced fresh
     parsley

¹/4   cup homemade tomato sauce

Salt and freshly ground black
pepper to taste

¹/4   cup diced mozzarella cheese

¹/2   cup diced prosciutto or ham
     (about 2 ounces)

2   cups fresh bread crumbs, toasted

Peanut oil for deep-frying

In a saucepan, bring 2¹/2 cups water to a boil. Add the rice and cook for 15 minutes. The rice should still be quite firm. Drain and transfer to a bowl.

Lightly beat 1 of the eggs and add to the rice, along with the grated cheese, parsley, 2 tablespoons of the tomato sauce, and salt and pepper. Mix well. Chill the mixture in the refrigerator for about 15 minutes.

In another bowl, mix the mozzarella cheese, prosciutto or ham, and the remaining 2 tablespoons tomato sauce.

With floured hands, divide the rice mixture into 8 or 10 portions and roll each portion into a ball the size of a small orange. Poke a hole into the center of each ball with your finger and insert about 1¹/2 table-spoons of the mozzarella mixture. Reshape and smooth the balls to en-close the filling.

In a shallow dish, beat the remaining 2 eggs. Spread the bread crumbs on a plate. Dip the balls into the eggs, turning to coat them well. Roll the balls in the bread crumbs to coat them evenly. Then let them dry on a plate for about 45 minutes.

In a deep fryer or deep heavy pan, heat the peanut oil to 375°F. Fry the balls until they are golden brown on all sides. Drain them on brown paper and serve immediately, with lemon wedges or the fresh tomato sauce.

Risotto alla Lorenza

LORENZA'S RISOTTO

Reggio-Emilia is home to my friend Lorenza Lori, who cooks her risotto in a flavorful combination of a meat ragù and the soaking liquid from the porcini mushrooms used in the dish, instead of the traditional broth and wine. The only addition I have made to Lorenza's recipe is the grated Parmigiano-Reggiano at the end. Serve this risotto as an accompaniment to Spiedo Misto (page 138) or as a first course.

SERVES 8 AS A FIRST COURSE

1   cup dried porcini mushrooms (about 1 ounce)

RAGÙ

¼ cup olive oil

1   white onion, thinly sliced

½ pound sweet Italian sausage, casings removed

2   cups chopped fresh or canned plum tomatoes (about 4 medium tomatoes)

½ cup water
Salt to taste

6   tablespoons butter

2   cups Arborio rice

2   tablespoons heavy cream

1   cup grated Parmigiano-Reggiano cheese

Put the porcini in a large bowl and add 4 cups cold water. Set aside to soak until soft, about 30 minutes.

To make the ragù, in a large skillet, heat the oil. Add the onion and sauté until golden brown and almost caramelized. Add the sausage, breaking up the meat, and brown it. Stir in the tomatoes, ½ cup water, and salt, mixing well. Let simmer until thickened, about 15 minutes. Transfer to a food processor and blend until smooth. Put the ragù in a bowl and set aside.

Drain the porcini mushrooms in a colander set over a bowl. Dice the porcini and set aside. Strain the porcini liquid several times to remove any sediment. Pour it into a saucepan and bring it to just under a boil. Keep warm over very low heat.

In a large heavy saucepan, melt the butter over medium heat. Add the rice and cook it for 1 to 2 minutes, stirring to coat it well with the butter. When the rice begins to make a crackling sound, lower the heat to medium low and add ¼ cup of the reserved porcini liquid. Cook, stirring, until all the liquid is absorbed. Add ¼ cup of the ragù and cook, stirring, until the rice has absorbed the liquid. Then slowly add the remaining porcini liquid and sauce to the rice in alternate additions, ¼ cup at a time, letting the rice absorb all the liquid each time before adding more. You may not need to add all the porcini liquid; the rice should be *al dente,* not mushy. Stir in the heavy cream. Remove the rice from the heat and stir in the cheese. Serve immediately.

Risotto con la Frutta

RICE WITH FRUIT

No one was more surprised than I when I was served a blueberry risotto in the Alto Adige region of Italy, close to the Swiss border. Not only was it attractive to look at, but its taste was a fine example of Italian *alta cucina,* or innovative high-style cuisine.

SERVES 6

4½ to 5 cups Homemade Chicken Broth (page 30)	2 cups Arborio rice
6 tablespoons butter	1 cup dry white wine
½ cup finely minced white onion	1 cup fresh blueberries

In a saucepan, bring the chicken broth just to a simmer. Keep warm over low heat.

In a large heavy saucepan, melt the butter over medium heat. Add the onion and sauté until very soft; do not allow to brown—it should remain colorless and almost seem to dissolve. Add the rice and cook 1 to 2 minutes, stirring to coat each grain with the butter-onion mixture. Lower the heat to medium low and add ½ cup of the white wine. Cook, stirring constantly, until all the wine is absorbed. Add ½ cup of the chicken broth and cook, continuing to stir, until the rice has absorbed the liquid. Add the remaining ½ cup wine and then add 4 cups of the broth ½ cup at a time, continuing to stir and allowing the rice to absorb each addition of liquid. The rice should be *al dente,* not mushy. If necessary, add up to ½ cup more broth. Reduce the heat to low and add the blueberries. Cook, stirring to mash the berries slightly, for 3 to 4 minutes, or until the berries are softened. Serve at once.

Variation: Substitute Asti Spumante or other sparkling white wine for the dry white wine.

Risotto alla Milanese

RICE MILAN STYLE

One of the traditional rice dishes of northern Italy is risotto, made with a starchy rice. The little pearls are first quickly sautéed in butter, and then liquid is added to finish the cooking process and plump up the grains of rice. The Venetians like to say the rice should be *all'onda*, or on the wave crest. That is, the rice should not be lumpy, but wavy and creamy and flow easily off the spoon. There are many variations of the classic *risotto alla Milanese*; this one is my favorite. The saffron gives a subtle flavor, and a yellowish hue, to the rice.

SERVES 6

1 teaspoon saffron threads	½ cup finely minced white onion
2 tablespoons warm water	2 cups Arborio rice
4½ to 5 cups Homemade Chicken Broth (page 30)	1 cup dry white wine
6 tablespoons butter	¾ cup grated Parmigiano-Reggiano cheese

Put the saffron threads in a small bowl and add the warm water. Set aside to soak.

In a saucepan, bring the chicken broth just to a simmer. Keep warm over low heat.

In a large heavy saucepan, melt the butter over medium heat. Add the onion and sauté until very soft; do not allow to brown—it should remain colorless and almost seem to dissolve in the butter. Add the rice and cook 1 to 2 minutes, stirring to coat each grain with the butter-onion mixture. When the rice begins to make a crackling sound, reduce the heat to medium low and add ½ cup of the white wine. Cook, stirring constantly, until all the wine is absorbed. Add ½ cup of the hot chicken broth and cook, continuing to stir, until the rice has absorbed the liquid. Add the remaining ½ cup wine and then add 4 cups of the broth ½ cup at a time, continuing to stir and allowing the rice to absorb each addition of liquid. Test the rice for doneness: It should be just *al dente*, not at all mushy, and hold its shape. If necessary, add up to ½ cup more broth and cook, stirring, until the liquid is absorbed and the rice is *al dente*. Add the saffron threads with the water and mix well.

Remove the rice from the heat and stir in the Parmigiano-Reggiano cheese. Serve at once.

Risi e Bisi con Prosciutto

RICE AND PEAS WITH PROSCIUTTO

Risi e bisi, or rice and peas, is another classic rice dish from the north. The best place to have this is in the Veneto, when the first spring peas appear. They are very delicate and sweet and are a succulent addition to the rice. I also like to add prosciutto, but there are limitless versions of this dish.

SERVES 6

2 cups shelled fresh peas	1 cup dry white wine
4½ to 5 cups Homemade Chicken Broth (page 30)	2 cups Arborio rice
6 tablespoons butter	¾ cup grated Parmigiano-Reggiano cheese
½ cup finely minced white onion	1 teaspoon white pepper
½ cup diced prosciutto (about 2 ounces)	

If the peas are large, cook them in boiling water until just tender, about 5 to 7 minutes. Drain and set aside. Small tender peas do not need precooking.

In a saucepan, bring the chicken broth just to a simmer. Keep warm over low heat.

In a heavy saucepan, melt the butter. Add the onion and prosciutto and sauté until the proscuitto is golden brown, about 3 to 4 minutes. Add the rice and stir to coat well with the butter-onion mixture. Add the wine and 4½ cups of the chicken broth to the rice, in alternate additions, ½ cup at a time, stirring each addition and allowing the rice to absorb all the liquid before adding more. Add the peas to the rice about 5 minutes before the rice is cooked. The rice should be creamy and just *al dente*. If necessary, add up to ½ cup more broth and cook, stirring, until the liquid is absorbed and the rice is *al dente*.

Remove the rice from the heat, stir in the Parmigiano-Reggiano cheese and white pepper, and serve at once.

Insalata di Riso

COLD RICE SALAD

One of the dishes we had in the summertime was a cold rice salad that was filling enough to serve as the main course. There was no rhyme or reason as to what went into this dish; it just evolved as various leftovers were taken out of the refrigerator.

SERVES 6 TO 8

2   cups Arborio or long-grain rice

1   3½-ounce can tuna packed in olive oil

½   cup dried tomatoes packed in oil, homemade (page 218) or store-bought, drained and diced

1   red bell pepper, diced

¼   cup chopped pitted Kalamata olives

1   small sweet white or red onion, finely chopped

¼   cup chopped fennel bulb

3   fresh basil leaves, finely chopped

Salt and freshly ground black pepper, optional

Sliced tomatoes

Fresh basil leaves

In a medium saucepan, bring 6 cups of water to a boil over high heat. Add the rice and bring back to the boil. Cover, lower the heat to medium, and cook the rice until *al dente*, about 20 minutes. Drain the rice and let cool.

In a large bowl, combine the rice, tuna, dried tomatoes, red pepper, olives, onion, fennel, and chopped basil. Add salt and pepper to taste, if you wish, and mix well. Pack the mixture tightly into a 6-cup round mold or an elongated 12- × -4-inch loaf pan. Cover the mold with foil. Refrigerate for 4 to 6 hours, or overnight.

Unmold the rice onto a platter and garnish with sliced fresh tomatoes and basil leaves.

Pane

BREAD

Iɴ ɪᴛᴀʟʏ, where bread making is a time-honored craft, each region has its own particular bread. Some of the best known ones are *panettone* and the *rosetta* of Milan, *ferrarese* from Emilia Romagna, *pane Toscano* from Tuscany, *malfalda* from Sicily, and *carta di musica* from Sardinia. There are hundreds more, some made only at certain times of the year, such as Christmas, Easter, festivals, and saints' feast days.

Bread making is an honorable part of my cooking too. When I make dough and work it with my hands, I take great satisfaction and comfort in knowing that I am continuing to practice an ancient craft. Unfortunately, Italian breads are hard to duplicate here. In Italy, the flours vary in absorbency and bread is baked in stone ovens, but with some helpful hints, and the right equipment, you can make respectable Italian bread here. Following are a few tips for making the recipes in this chapter:

1. To "proof the yeast" means to dissolve the yeast in warm water, about 110° to 115°F., until it swells and becomes foamy, to prove that it is alive. Some claim that this step is no longer necessary since the yeast industry prints an expiration date on the package, but I always take this step to ensure that the yeast is fresh and active. Do check the package for freshness. If you buy fresh dry yeast loose, store it in a tightly sealed jar in the refrigerator.

2. Unless otherwise stated, all ingredients should be at room temperature when added to dissolved yeast. Do not add cold flour stored in the refrigerator or freezer to the yeast mixture, as it will surely kill the yeast.

3. Unbleached all-purpose flour has a higher gluten content than bleached flour. Gluten is wheat protein and it is what gives elasticity to dough. It enables you to knead the dough successfully and also helps the bread to retain its shape when baked. I use unbleached flour exclusively for my baking.

4. Semolina, the central core of the wheat berry, is used to make many Italian breads and pasta. Coarse-ground semolina is used for commercially prepared macaroni products. It is difficult to work with because it does not absorb liquids well. Fine-milled semolina is wonderful for certain pastries. I mix it with unbleached flour in some of my bread recipes.

5. Many Italian breads, like *pane Toscano* and *panettone*, require a "sponge," or starter dough, made from yeast, water, and flour and sometimes a little sugar. The sponge must be made in advance and left to brew and bubble for about 8 to 24 hours. Using a sponge produces a bread with a definite tang, a result of the long and slow fermenting, and also allows the bread to rise impressively and still hold its shape. Making an Italian sponge (*la madre*), the mother dough that will breathe life into the flour and water, is very similar to making a sourdough starter.

6. To simulate the stone ovens of Italy, I bake my breads on a clay baking stone. Breads baked on a stone have a wonderful crust and cook more uniformly. You can purchase baking stones in any good cookware store, or you can use unglazed quarry tiles, set in the bottom of your oven.

7. Dough is very forgiving. If you prepare the dough but cannot bake it the same day, lightly coat it with olive oil or a little butter, put it in a plastic bag, seal it, and refrigerate. When you are ready to proceed, remove it from the bag, put it in a lightly oiled bowl, cover with a towel, let rise until doubled in size, and continue with the recipe. It will take a little longer to rise since it is cold, but that will not affect the taste or texture.

8. I find a baker's peel very useful for bread making. A peel is a wooden paddle with a long handle that allows you to transfer the risen loaf to the hot baking stone. I use it for pizza as well. Baker's peels are available in housewares stores or through specialty catalogues.

9. Successful bread depends in large part on the amount of liquid you add to the flour; this may be milk, water, eggs, melted butter, flavorings, and/or juices. Too much liquid will produce a sticky affair; too little liquid and you will wind up with a crumbly mess. You'll also find that if you bake bread on damp, humid days, you'll use more flour than usual, because the flour absorbs the additional moisture in the air. For these reasons, it is important to really "feel" the dough. After you have been making bread as long as I have, you will intuitively know if you have the right proportions of flour to liquid. You should be able to work the dough with your hands without straining to move it. It should be satiny smooth and soft before the final rise. Trial and error is the only way.

Once you make homemade bread, there will be no going back to store-bought. At one time, I thought store-bought bread was better than what was made at home. Grandma Galasso used to make our school lunches and she knew how much we hated the whole wheat bread my mother made—so she kept a loaf of spongy white store-bought bread hidden in her bedroom, and made our lunches early in the morning before my mother got up. I felt so relieved when I opened my lunch bag that Grandma understood that my sandwich had to look just like the other kids'. Of course, now I know better!

Pasta Basica

BASIC DOUGH

I used to make one dough for pizza, another for bread, and yet another one for other baked goods. Each was a little different: One contained sugar, another used bread flour, and still another was made from un-bleached all-purpose flour. Then I got smart and developed one dough that could be used to make bread, *focacce*, breadsticks, or whatever. The recipe is an old family favorite that I've changed a little to make it versatile enough to do all the things I want it to do. The beauty of this dough is that you can easily double and triple the recipe, and it freezes beautifully too. Once you've tried this recipe, simple as it is, there will be no going back to anything else.

MAKES 1¾ POUNDS DOUGH

1 tablespoon (1 package) active dry yeast	4 to 5 cups unbleached all-purpose flour
1¾ cups warm (110° to 115°F.) water	Extra-virgin olive oil
1 teaspoon salt	

In a large bowl, dissolve the yeast in ¼ cup of the warm water. Allow the yeast to proof until it is foamy, about 10 minutes. Add the remaining 1½ cups water and the salt. Add the flour 1 cup at a time; you may not need to add all of it. Work the mixture until it comes together in a ball. Place the dough on a floured work surface and knead it for 5 to 10 minutes, folding the dough over on itself several times, until it is shiny and elastic.

Grease a bowl generously with olive oil. Put the dough in it and turn the dough a few times to coat with the oil. Cover the bowl tightly with plastic wrap, place it in a warm place away from drafts, and let the dough rise for 3 to 4 hours, or until doubled in size. The more slowly and the longer the dough rises, the tangier the flavor will be. Punch the dough down, turn it out onto a floured surface, and knead a few times. Then proceed as directed in the recipes that follow.

Focaccia

A *focaccia* is a rustic flat bread. Sometimes it is topped with olive oil and black pepper, cheese, or herbs and slivers of garlic, which is my favorite version. This makes a great snack for a picnic or antipasto before dinner.

MAKES 2 13-INCH FOCACCE

1   recipe Basic Dough (page 104)
    Cornmeal (if using a baking stone)
3   tablespoons extra-virgin olive oil
3   large cloves garlic, slivered

2   tablespoons fresh rosemary or 1 teaspoon dried, or to taste
    Coarsely ground black pepper to taste
½   cup grated Pecorino Romano cheese

Preheat the oven to 400°F. and lightly grease 2 pizza pans; or preheat the oven to 450°F. and set a baking stone on the bottom rack of the oven to preheat.

If baking on pizza pans, divide the dough in half and roll out each piece on a lightly floured surface to a 13-inch circle. Place each round on a pizza pan and spread 1½ tablespoons of the olive oil all over each round. Press half the garlic slivers into each round, then sprinkle evenly with the rosemary, pepper, and grated cheese. Bake for 15 to 20 minutes, or until the bottoms are crisp and the tops golden brown. Cut into wedges and serve hot.

If using a baking stone, bake 1 focaccia at a time: Divide the dough in half, and set one half aside. Roll out the dough on a lightly floured surface to a 13-inch circle and place on a baker's peel dusted with cornmeal. Spread 1½ tablespoons of the oil all over the dough, press half the garlic slivers into it, and sprinkle with half the rosemary, pepper, and half the cheese. Bake for 10 to 12 minutes, or until the crust is very crisp and the top lightly browned. While the first focaccia is baking, prepare the second one and place it on the baker's peel ready to bake. Cut each focaccia into wedges and serve warm or at room temperature.

Note: Throw away your old pizza wheel! I use kitchen shears to cut this and other types of pizza. No struggling, just nice even slices.

Pizza Fritta

FRIED DOUGH

I always looked forward to weekends and holidays when my mother and Grandmother Galasso would make *pizza fritta*, fried dough. Usually they did this early in the morning before anyone else was awake. The smell of those little rounds of dough cooking and the sound of them being shaken up in cinnamon and sugar would coax me out of my warm bed every time.

MAKES 14

1 recipe Basic Dough (page 104)	1 cup sugar
Vegetable oil for deep-frying	1 tablespoon cinnamon

Divide the dough into 14 equal pieces about the size of a small lemon. With your hands, shape each piece into a 3-inch round and place on floured towels. Let rise until doubled in size, about 30 minutes.

Heat the oil to 375°F. in a deep fryer or deep heavy pot. Put the sugar and cinnamon in a large brown paper bag, close the bag, and shake well. Set aside.

Test the oil by dropping in a small piece of dough; if it puffs immediately, the oil is ready. Add 2 or 3 rounds at a time to the oil and fry until golden brown, about 3 or 4 minutes. Remove the rounds with a slotted spoon and drain on brown paper. While they are still hot, put the rounds in the paper bag with the sugar and cinnamon, close the bag, and shake to coat them. Remove to a serving plate and serve hot.

Pane Italiano

ITALIAN BREAD

This easily made loaf of Italian bread is good for *panini gravidi*, or sandwiches.

MAKES 1 LARGE LOAF

1 recipe Basic Dough (page 104)	Cornmeal (if using a baking stone)

Preheat the oven to 400°F. and set a baking stone on the bottom rack to preheat for 30 minutes; or preheat the oven to 375°F. and lightly grease a baking sheet.

Shape the dough into an oval or round loaf. Place the dough on a baker's peel dusted with cornmeal, if using a baking stone, or on the greased baking sheet. Cover with a towel and let rise for 30 minutes, or until doubled in size.

Cut several parallel slashes about ½-inch deep in the top of the dough with a razor blade or make an X with scissors. If using a baking stone, sprinkle the preheated stone with cornmeal and carefully slide the bread onto it. Bake for 30 to 35 minutes, or until the crust is golden brown and the loaf is hollow-sounding when the bottom is tapped with your knuckles. If baking on a baking sheet, bake for 35 to 40 minutes. Transfer to a wire rack and let cool completely.

Grissini

BREADSTICKS

Turin, located in the Piedmont region in northern Italy, is famous for its *grissini*, pencil-thin breadsticks. Throughout Italy, restaurants offer these grissini to munch on while waiting for your meal.

MAKES 18 TO 24

1 *recipe Basic Dough (page 104)*	*Coarse salt, optional*
1 *large egg beaten with 1 teaspoon water for egg wash*	*Dried oregano, optional*

Preheat the oven to 375°F. Lightly grease 2 baking sheets.

Pinch off 1-inch pieces of the dough. With the palms of your hands, roll out each piece on a lightly floured surface to a thin rope about the thickness of a pencil, 10 to 12 inches long. Carefully transfer the grissini to the baking sheets, spacing them about 1 inch apart. Brush each one with the egg wash. If you wish, sprinkle the grissini with coarse salt and oregano. Bake for 10 minutes, or until crisp and nicely browned. Transfer to wire racks to cool completely.

To serve, stand the grissini upright in a pottery crock or basket.

Note: These are fun to make with children. They are also a great hostess gift. Tie a bundle together with a pretty ribbon.

Pangrattati

BASIC BREAD CRUMBS

Bread crumbs can be made from any type of homemade or store-bought bread. If you do use leftover store-bought bread, be aware that a firm peasant-type bread produces far better crumbs than a soft, spongy loaf.

MAKES 2 CUPS

2   cups stale bread pieces

½ cup olive oil or 8 tablespoons (1 stick) butter, optional

2   tablespoons chopped fresh herbs, optional

Preheat the oven to 300°F.

Put the bread on a baking sheet and toast it in the oven until it is dry and hard, about 25 to 30 minutes. Place the bread in a food processor or in a paper bag and process or roll out with a rolling pin to the desired texture.

To make flavored crumbs, heat the olive oil or butter in a frying pan. Add the crumbs and sauté them until lightly browned, 2 to 3 minutes. Add the herbs and mix well.

Store in airtight containers in the refrigerator or freezer.

Bread Crumbs

Bread was never wasted at home. Even the smallest piece could be used for something. Stale bread was always saved, and when there was enough for *pangrattati,* or bread crumbs, the bread was toasted in a 300°F. oven, to dry it out slowly without burning it. Then my Grandmother Galasso would put the pieces in a paper bag, close it up, and roll over it with her rolling pin until she had the consistency she wanted.

Fine crumbs were used to bind fillings for stuffings for vegetables or to coat meat or fish for frying. Coarse crumbs often took the place of cheese in a pasta dish. The crumbs were sprinkled over the pasta before it was served. I often wondered aloud why bread crumbs were sprinkled over so many dishes and my grandmother would say, *"Perchè non c'è formaggio!"* ("Because there is no cheese!")

The toasted crumbs were kept in jars in the refrigerator and when my grandmother or mother wanted flavored crumbs, a little olive oil or butter was put in a frying pan and the crumbs were browned in the fat to give them flavor. Sometimes garlic or fresh herbs were also added.

Many of the recipes in this book call for bread crumbs. Homemade ones made from bread you have baked yourself are far superior to store-bought and you will notice the difference immediately, but that doesn't mean that you cannot use commercially prepared ones when necessary. I still smash them by hand with a rolling pin, but you can also grind them in a food processor or blender. Take care not to overprocess them. Toasted fresh bread crumbs can be stored in containers in the refrigerator for several weeks or frozen for several months.

Pane Toscano

TUSCAN BREAD

Bread has always had historical and symbolic, as well as practical, meaning for mankind. Somewhere in antiquity the idea of making food from grain and water took hold and literally changed the way in which people interacted with one another. Human suffering, wars, and the course of history have been determined by whether or not there was bread to eat.

One of the many breads that has its roots in historical events is Tuscan bread. Its main characteristic is that it has always been made without salt because of a tax on salt imposed by the popes in the thirteenth and fourteenth centuries. To show their displeasure, the townspeople went without salt, and the bakers refused to put it in their bread. To this day, this saltless bread is eaten daily in Tuscany and is a reminder of the steadfastness of a proud people. Some people say that the saltless bread is the perfect foil for the many kinds of flavorful foods tradition-ally made with it. Cooked cannellini beans, flavored with dark green Tuscan olive oil, are wonderful on this bread. The bread is equally good in soup or as the base for *fettunta*, Tuscan bread grilled and rubbed with garlic, then drizzled with dense extra-virgin olive oil. Making Tus-can bread requires a starter dough, known as a sponge, which needs at least a day to develop its sour tang.

MAKES 1 LARGE LOAF

SPONGE

1   tablespoon (1 package) active dry yeast

½ cup warm (110° to 115°F.) water

1   cup unbleached all-purpose flour

1½ teaspoons (½ package) active dry yeast

1¼ cups warm (110° to 115°F.) water

4   to 4½ cups unbleached all-purpose flour

Cornmeal (if using a baking stone)

To make the sponge, in a small bowl, sprinkle the yeast over the warm water. Let stand to proof until foamy, about 10 minutes, and then add the flour. Stir well to mix; the mixture should have the consistency of a soft dough. Cover the bowl with plastic wrap and allow to rise in a warm draft-free place for 24 hours.

In a large bowl, sprinkle the yeast over ¼ cup of the water and let proof until foamy, about 10 minutes. Add the remaining 1 cup water. Add the sponge and mix well with your hands. Add 3½ cups of the flour and mix well, then add enough of the remaining flour to make a soft ball. Turn the mixture out onto a floured surface and knead until smooth. Place the dough in a lightly greased bowl, turn to coat the dough, cover with plastic wrap, and let rise for 3 to 4 hours, or until doubled in size.

Turn the dough out onto a floured surface and gently form it into a rectangular or round loaf. Place the loaf on a baker's peel that has been dusted with cornmeal if using a baking stone, or place on a greased baking sheet. Let rise for about 35 minutes, or until doubled in size.

Preheat the oven to 400°F. If using a baking stone, set it on the bottom rack of the oven to preheat for 30 minutes.

If using a baking stone, sprinkle the preheated stone with cornmeal and carefully slide the bread onto the stone. Bake for 30 to 35 minutes, or until the bread is evenly browned and the bottom crust is hard. If baking on a baking sheet, bake for 35 to 40 minutes, or until the bread is nicely browned and hollow sounding when tapped on the bottom.

Note: This is the perfect bread to use for the small toasted bread appetizers called *crostini,* as well as for *fettunta.* If planning to use the bread for crostini, shape the dough into 2 or 3 long narrow loaves and adjust the baking time accordingly.

Pane di Mamma

MAMMA'S BREAD

Not a speck of bread was ever wasted; when it was stale, it was toasted for bread crumbs; if a slice fell on the floor by accident, it was picked up, kissed, and used. Nothing was more sacred in our home than bread.

MAKES 1 LARGE LOAF OR 2 SMALLER LOAVES

1	tablespoon (1 package) active dry yeast	4	to 4½ cups unbleached all-purpose flour
2	cups warm (110° to 115°F.) water	1½	cups fine semolina flour
½	teaspoon sugar	1	teaspoon salt

In a large bowl, dissolve the yeast in ½ cup of the water and stir in the sugar. Let proof, covered, in a warm place, until foamy, about 10 to 15 minutes. Add the remaining 1½ cups water and stir well. Mix 4 cups of the all-purpose flour, the semolina flour, and salt and add to the yeast mixture about 1 cup at a time. Mix with your hands until a ball of dough is formed. If necessary, add additional all-purpose flour until the dough is no longer sticky. Knead the dough on a floured surface until smooth, about 5 minutes. Place it in a lightly oiled bowl, turn to coat the dough, cover the bowl tightly with plastic wrap, and set aside to rise for 1½ hours, or until doubled in bulk.

Punch the dough down and knead it for 5 minutes. Shape it into a long rectangular loaf or divide in half and make 2 small round loaves. Place the bread on a baker's peel that has been dusted with cornmeal, if using a baking stone, or on a greased baking sheet. Cover and let rise again for about 30 minutes, or until doubled in bulk.

Preheat the oven to 400°F. and set a baking stone on the bottom oven rack to preheat for 20 minutes. Or, if using a baking sheet, preheat the oven to 375°F.

If using a baking stone, dust the stone with cornmeal and slide the bread onto the stone. Bake the large loaf for 30 minutes, the smaller loaves for 25 minutes, or until the bread is nicely browned and hollow-sounding when tapped on the bottom with your knuckles. If baking on a baking sheet, bake the large loaf for about 40 minutes, the smaller loaves for 25 to 30 minutes. Transfer to a wire rack to cool.

Note: This recipe can be doubled. The bread freezes well if wrapped in foil and then in a plastic bag. To serve, let defrost at room temperature.

Panini di Pepe alla Grazia

GRACIE'S PEPPER ROLLS

Gracie La Puma, a good friend of my family's, never arrived empty-handed on her frequent visits to our house; there was always just-baked bread or cookies "for the kids." Her spicy, black pepper–flecked rolls were my favorite. I could never eat just one; I doubt you will either. I recently called her to get the recipe for those rolls. She is almost 90 years old, but her familiar voice came riveting over the phone as if she were standing right next to me. "Honeee, justa putta somma farina ina the wella; adda leetle yeast anda water and putta as mucha anice anda pepper youa wanta. Goda blessa honee. Howsa you maddar?"

MAKES ABOUT 3 DOZEN

2   tablespoons (2 packages) active dry yeast

2½ cups warm (110° to 115°F.) water

1   tablespoon olive oil

1   tablespoon salt

1   tablespoon coarsely ground black pepper

¼   cup anise seeds

6½ to 7 cups unbleached all-purpose flour

1   large egg beaten with 1 teaspoon water for egg wash

Sesame seeds

In a large bowl, dissolve the yeast in the water. Let proof until the yeast is foamy, about 10 minutes. Add the oil, salt, pepper, and anise seeds. Add the flour about a cup at a time, mixing it with your hands, until a ball is formed; you may not need all the flour. Turn the dough out onto a floured surface and knead until elastic, 10 to 15 minutes. Put the dough in a lightly oiled bowl, cover with a clean towel, and let rise in a warm draft-free place for about 1 hour.

Preheat the oven to 375°F. Grease 2 baking sheets.

Punch the dough down. Break off 2-inch pieces of dough and shape them into round rolls. Place them 2 inches apart on the baking sheets and brush the tops with the egg wash. Sprinkle the tops with sesame seeds. Cover loosely with clean towels and let rise for 20 minutes, or until doubled in size.

Bake for 15 to 20 minutes, or until golden brown. Serve warm.

Note: To freeze, wrap the rolls individually in foil and seal them in plastic bags. They can be frozen for up to 3 months. Defrost in the refrigerator and reheat to serve.

Torta sul Testo

FLAT BREAD ON A STONE

When I was in Umbria, in central Italy, I learned the ancient way of making simple peasant bread on a stone, or *testo*. The bread is shaped into a flat round, like a small pizza, and then cooked on a hot stone. You can achieve the same results by cooking the bread on a hot griddle or in an electric frying pan. Here the bread is cut into wedges and filled with a savory spinach mixture to make little sandwiches.

MAKES 6 ROUNDS, OR 12 SMALL SANDWICHES

FILLING

2   10-ounce packages fresh or frozen spinach

2   tablespoons extra-virgin olive oil

1/4 pound prosciutto, sliced and cut in thin strips

Freshly ground black pepper

DOUGH

3 1/2 cups unbleached all-purpose flour

1   teaspoon baking soda

1   large egg

3   tablespoons extra-virgin olive oil

6   tablespoons grated Pecorino Romano cheese

Warm water

To make the filling, if using fresh spinach, trim and wash it thoroughly, but do not drain. Place the spinach in a large pot, cover, and cook over medium-high heat until the spinach is wilted, about 5 minutes. Drain well and squeeze out the excess liquid. Chop fine. If using frozen spinach, cook as directed on the package, drain, and squeeze out the excess liquid. Chop fine.

In a frying pan, heat the olive oil. Add the prosciutto and sauté it until it just begins to brown. Add the spinach and a good grinding of black pepper and mix well. Set aside.

To make the dough, in a large bowl, mix the flour and baking soda together. In another bowl, beat the egg, olive oil, and cheese together. Add to the flour mixture and stir to blend well. Add the warm water 2 tablespoons at a time, mixing with your hands until a smooth dough is formed. Turn the dough out onto a floured surface and knead for 10 minutes, or until elastic and very smooth. Let it rest, covered, for 10 minutes. Divide the dough into 6 pieces and roll out each piece into a 6-inch circle; set aside on a floured surface.

Heat a cast-iron griddle or an electric frying pan until hot. Prick the dough pieces all over with a fork and then make light overlapping circle imprints all over each piece with a small glass. These marks are decorative, but they also speed the cooking process. Place 1 or 2 of the breads on the griddle or in the hot pan; do not cook more than 2 at a time. Cook until the breads have browned slightly on the bottom, about 3 to 4 minutes, then turn them over and brown them on the other side. Transfer to a wire rack to cool completely. Repeat with the remaining pieces.

Cut each torta into 4 wedges. Divide the filling evenly among 12 of the wedges and top with the remaining wedges to make sandwiches. Serve immediately.

Pane di Spinaci alla Nonna

GRANDMA'S SPINACH BREAD

Every morning, rain or shine, Grandma Galasso would get up early and walk the mile or so to attend mass at Our Lady of Pompeii Church. On Saturdays, when the spirit moved me, I would go with her. She always sat in the first pew and read from a fragile thumb-smudged Italian prayer book. On the way home, I'd ask her what she was going to cook, but I already knew the dreaded answer: On Saturdays we always had liver and onions and *zagoots*, or zucchini mixed with scrambled egg. Sometimes it was even worse, when she tried to serve us her spinach concoctions, such as her spinach bread. It's funny how I now gravitate to making so many of those dishes that I hated so as a kid. This is a great company appetizer served in slices with fresh mozzarella cheese and glasses of hearty red wine.

MAKES 1 RING-SHAPED LOAF

1   recipe dough for Mama's Bread (page 112)

FILLING

1¼   pounds (2 10-ounce packages) fresh spinach

2   tablespoons extra-virgin olive oil

1   clove garlic, minced

½   cup oil-cured black olives, pitted and cut in pieces

⅛   teaspoon salt

Freshly ground black pepper to taste

1   large egg white beaten with 2 teaspoons water for egg wash

Sesame seeds

Prepare the dough as directed on page 104 and set aside to rise until doubled in size.

To make the filling, trim the spinach and wash and drain it thoroughly. Put it in a pot, without any additional water, cover, and cook over medium heat until the spinach is wilted. Drain the spinach and let cool. Squeeze it as dry as possible and chop fine.

In a frying pan, heat the olive oil. Add the garlic and sauté until soft. Add the spinach and cook for 2 to 3 minutes. Add the olives, salt, and pepper and stir well. Remove from the heat and let cool.

When the dough has risen, punch it down and roll it into a circle about 16 inches in diameter. Lift the dough onto a greased baking sheet; don't worry if it doesn't quite fit for the moment. Spoon on the spinach filling, spreading it to within 1 inch of the edges.

Roll the dough up tightly like a jelly roll. Turn the ends under to seal and pinch the seam to seal. Bring the 2 ends together to form a circle. Make random 1/2-inch-deep slits with a knife or scissors in the top of the dough. Brush the top with the egg wash and sprinkle generously with sesame seeds. Let the bread rise, covered, for about 30 minutes, or until doubled in size.

Preheat the oven to 375°F.

Bake for 35 to 40 minutes, or until nicely browned. Let cool slightly on the baking sheet, then remove to a wire rack. Serve warm.

Pane di Zucca

PUMPKIN SEED BREAD

I liked to visit our neighbor Mrs. Belurgi, because there was always something good to eat in her kitchen like her *taralli*, or hard biscuits, and her pumpkin seed bread, which she made with toasted pumpkin seeds saved from harvested pumpkins. Sometimes she added raw slivers of pumpkin to the dough.

MAKES 1 LARGE LOAF OR 2 SMALLER LOAVES

²/₃ cup hulled pumpkin seeds

1   tablespoon (1 package) active dry yeast

1¹/₂ cups warm (110° to 115°F.) water

¹/₈ teaspoon salt

3¹/₂ to 4 cups unbleached all-purpose flour

Olive oil

1   large egg white beaten with 2 teaspoons water for egg wash

Preheat the oven to 350°F.

Spread the pumpkin seeds on a baking sheet and toast them in the oven for 10 minutes. Set aside to cool.

In a large bowl, dissolve the yeast in ¹/₂ cup of the warm water and let it proof until foamy, about 10 minutes. Add the salt and the remaining 1 cup water and stir to mix. Add the flour about ¹/₂ cup at a time, mixing it in with your hands, until you have a ball of dough that holds together.

Turn the dough out onto a floured surface and knead with floured hands until smooth and elastic, about 10 minutes. Grease a large bowl generously with olive oil. Put the dough in the bowl and turn to coat it with oil on all sides, cover with a towel and place it in a warm draft-free place to rise until doubled in size, about 1 hour.

Preheat the oven to 375°F.

Punch the dough down and turn it out onto a floured surface. Roll out the dough into a 16-inch circle. Brush with a little olive oil and scatter the pumpkin seeds over the dough. Roll the dough up like a jelly roll and fold the roll in half. Knead the dough for 5 minutes; some of the seeds will pop through the surface, which will give the bread a nice look when it is baked.

Form the dough into a large round loaf or 2 smaller loaves. Place on a greased baking sheet and let rise, covered, for about 30 minutes, or until doubled in size. Brush the loaf (loaves) with the egg wash. Make a slash about ¹/₂ inch deep in the top of the dough with scissors or a razor blade. Bake for 45 minutes, or until the bread is nicely browned and hollow-sounding when tapped on the bottom.

Note: I also like to bake this on a preheated baking stone at 425°F., which produces a harder crust.

Torta di Spinaci

SPINACH PIE

My mother made a very good spinach pie that was often served for lunch. Sometimes Grandma would insist on using Swiss chard instead of spinach. Raisins and pine nuts give it almost a sweet and sour quality. This pie is best eaten while still warm.

SERVES 8

1 recipe *Basic Dough (page 104)*	¹/₄ *cup pine nuts*
	¹/₄ *cup raisins*
FILLING	*Salt and freshly ground black*
¹/₄ *cup olive oil*	*pepper to taste*
2 *cloves garlic, minced*	
4 *cups cooked spinach (4 10-ounce packages, fresh or frozen), drained, squeezed dry, and chopped*	1 *large egg beaten with 1 teaspoon water for egg wash*
	Coarse salt, optional

Prepare the dough as directed on page 104 and set it aside to rise until doubled in size.

To make the filling, in a frying pan, heat the olive oil. Add the garlic and sauté until soft but not browned. Add the spinach, pine nuts, and raisins, and sauté for 5 minutes. Season with salt and pepper. Remove the mixture to a bowl and let cool.

Punch down the dough and divide it into 2 pieces. Roll out 1 piece on a floured surface to an 11-inch circle and fit it into a greased 9-inch round cake pan. Spoon the filling over the dough, spreading it evenly. Roll out the second piece of dough and place it on top of the filling; seal the edges by pinching the doughs together. Trim off any excess dough and use the trimmings to make a pattern on top of the pie.

Brush the top with the egg wash and sprinkle with coarse salt if desired. Cover with a towel and let rest for 25 minutes.

Preheat the oven to 375°F.

Bake the pie for 45 minutes, or until the top is nicely browned. Let cool slightly, then cut in wedges to serve.

Pane di Pasqua di Signora Condello

MRS. CONDELLO'S EASTER BREAD

One of the Easter breads my mother made had colored eggs nestled in the dough before it was baked. The recipe came from her friend Mrs. Condello, who made sure this bread was blessed by the priest on Holy Saturday. The bread has a coarse texture, is not overly sweet, and can be dressed up with a thin vanilla icing and gaily colored sprinkles after it is baked. (The eggs will not be edible.)

MAKES 2 9-INCH ROUND BREADS

DOUGH		
6	large eggs	6 cups unbleached all-purpose flour
8	tablespoons (1 stick) butter, softened	5 teaspoons baking powder
1¼	cups sugar	8 colored hard-boiled eggs
2	teaspoons vanilla	1¼ cups confectioner's sugar
¼	cup plus 2 teaspoons vegetable oil	2 to 3 tablespoons milk
		Colored sprinkles

Preheat the oven to 350°F.

In a large bowl, beat the eggs, butter, sugar, vanilla, and vegetable oil with a rotary beater or a wooden spoon until well blended. Sift the flour and the baking powder together and add to the egg mixture about a cup at a time, mixing with your hands until a soft but no longer sticky dough is formed.

Transfer the dough to a well-floured surface and knead until smooth and pliable, about 5 minutes. Divide the dough into 4 pieces. Roll each piece into a rope 22 inches long and 1 inch thick. Cut a 2-inch piece off each rope and reserve. Loosely braid 2 of the ropes together and bring the ends together to form a circle; pinch the ends together. Repeat with the remaining 2 ropes.

Place each braid on a greased baking sheet. Space 4 eggs evenly around the circles, nestling them in the braided dough. Divide each of the reserved 4 pieces of dough into 4 pieces. Roll each piece into a 3-inch-long rope. Using 2 ropes of dough per egg, place a cross over each egg, tucking the ends into the dough.

Bake the braids for 35 to 40 minutes, or until the bread is nicely browned. Transfer to wire racks to cool.

In a small bowl, combine the confectioner's sugar and 2 tablespoons of the milk. Mix well. Add enough additional milk to make a thin icing, stirring until smooth. Drizzle the icing over the braids and scatter colored sprinkles over them.

Pane di Signora Belurgi

MRS. BELURGI'S BREAD

Mr. and Mrs. Belurgi were recent immigrants from Veroli, Italy. They were related to us by marriage. Whenever I passed their house on my way to church, I would stop in, because Mrs. B was always cooking something wonderful. One of the things I remember most was her lemon yeast bread. It was a rustic round loaf with a rich mahogany shine and smelled like a bagful of tangy lemons.

MAKES 2 ROUND LOAVES

2 tablespoons (2 packages) active dry yeast	2 tablespoons vanilla
	Juice of 1 large lemon
1 cup warm (110° to 115°F.) water	2 tablespoons grated lemon zest
3 tablespoons plus 1 cup sugar	9 to 10 cups unbleached all-purpose flour
6 large eggs	
12 tablespoons (1½ sticks) butter or margarine, melted	1 large egg beaten with 1 teaspoon water and 1 tablespoon sugar for egg wash
½ cup warm milk	

In a bowl, dissolve the yeast in the warm water. Sprinkle the 3 tablespoons sugar over and stir to dissolve. Let proof in a warm place until foamy, about 10 minutes.

In a large bowl, beat the eggs with a whisk or hand mixer until very pale yellow. Beat in the 1 cup sugar, the butter, milk, vanilla, lemon juice, and lemon zest and beat for 5 minutes with a whisk, 3 minutes with a mixer. Stir in the yeast mixture and mix well. Add the flour 1 cup at a time, mixing with your hands, until you have a dough that holds together; you may not need all of the flour.

Turn the dough out onto a floured surface and knead it until smooth, about 5 minutes. Place the dough in a lightly buttered deep bowl, turn to coat, cover with plastic wrap, and let rise for 2 hours, or until doubled in size.

Turn the dough out onto a floured surface. Divide the dough in half and shape it into 2 freeform round loaves. Place each loaf on a greased baking sheet, cover with a towel, and let rise in a warm place for 30 minutes.

Preheat the oven to 375°F.

Brush the tops of the loaves with the egg wash. Bake for 45 minutes, or until the bread is nicely browned and hollow-sounding when tapped on the bottom with your knuckles. Let cool completely on wire racks.

Torta Pasqualina

STUFFED EASTER TORTA

Easter was a holiday that I can remember anxiously anticipating. After a Lenten season of fasting, I was ready for some kind of extravaganza. Preparations included the making of various yeast breads, which were taken to the church the day before Easter Sunday and blessed by the parish priest. My job was to decorate the twelve lamb cakes that were baked in old molds and given away as Easter gifts. Why twelve cakes? Because that's how many apostles there were at table at the Last Supper, and the lamb was the symbol of love and sacrifice. The day before Easter, an army of aunts came over to our house to help my grandmother and mother prepare the roast capon, as well as the deep-dish *torta pasqualina*, an elaborate pastry *torta* stuffed with cheese, spinach or artichokes, and, sometimes, cured meats.

SERVES 10

PASTRY DOUGH

6   cups unbleached all-purpose flour

1   teaspoon salt
    About 2½ cups ice water

2   tablespoons olive oil

4   cups cooked spinach (4 10-ounce packages, fresh or frozen), drained, squeezed dry, and chopped

½   cup grated Parmigiano-Reggiano cheese

3   cups ricotta cheese, well drained

¾   cup heavy cream

⅛   teaspoon salt

2   tablespoons chopped fresh marjoram
    Olive oil

10 large eggs
    Salt and freshly ground black pepper to taste

5   tablespoons butter

2   tablespoons grated Pecorino Romano or Parmigiano-Reggiano cheese

1   large egg yolk beaten with 1 teaspoon water for egg wash

To make the dough, in a large bowl, mix the flour and salt together. Add 1½ cups ice water, a little at a time, and mix the ingredients with your hands to form a rough ball of dough. Add the olive oil and mix well. Add just enough additional ice water to form a smooth ball; the dough should not be sticky. Transfer the dough to a floured surface and knead it until very smooth and elastic, about 5 minutes. Divide the dough into 10 equal pieces. Set aside, covered, on a floured surface.

In a bowl, mix the spinach with the ½ cup grated Parmigiano-Reggiano. Set aside. In another bowl, mix the ricotta cheese with the heavy cream, salt, and marjoram. Set aside.

Preheat the oven to 375°F. Butter a 10-inch springform pan.

On a floured surface, roll a piece of dough to a 12-inch circle. Brush with a little olive oil; and fit into the bottom of the springform pan. Repeat with 4 more of the pieces of dough, brushing each one with a little olive oil.

Spread the spinach mixture evenly over the dough. Spread the ricotta cheese mixture evenly over the spinach. Use a whole egg to make 10 shallow impressions in the ricotta layer and carefully crack 1 egg into each impression. Sprinkle the eggs with salt and pepper and put about ½ tablespoon of the butter on each. Sprinkle over the 2 tablespoons grated Pecorino Romano or Parmigiano-Reggiano cheese.

Roll out the remaining 5 pieces of dough and layer them over the filling, making sure to brush each circle of dough with olive oil. Trim off the excess dough, leaving a 1-inch overhang. Tuck it in around the edges of the pan to seal it.

Brush the top of the dough *torta* with the egg wash. Bake for 1 hour, or until the top is nicely browned. Let cool.

Release the sides of the springform and cut the *torta* into wedges to serve.

Pitta

STUFFED ITALIAN SANDWICH

I don't know why there is no word in the Italian language for *picnic*—if ever there were people who loved to eat outdoors, it's Italians. Wander by any piazza in any Italian town or city and you will see people congregating to eat and to people-watch. They eat on trains, in parks, outside bars, and on hillsides, underneath graceful olive trees. *Pitta* is perfect picnic food: a large hollowed-out round loaf of bread, stuffed with salad, cured meats, and cheeses, that, when cut, has a wonderful striped look. Make it the day before your picnic.

SERVES 8 TO 10

1 cup oil-cured Sicilian olives, chopped	1 tablespoon extra-virgin olive oil
1 cup Kalamata olives, chopped	½ pound Genoa salame, thinly sliced
3 anchovies packed in oil	
½ cup marinated artichoke hearts, drained	½ pound prosciutto, thinly sliced
½ cup marinated whole pimentos, drained	½ pound capicola, thinly sliced
	½ pound mozzarella cheese, sliced
2 cloves garlic, minced	½ pound Provolone cheese, sliced
½ cup mixed chopped fresh basil, parsley, and fennel leaves	1 2-pound round loaf (9- to 10-inch diameter) Italian bread (see Note)

Place the olives, anchovies, artichokes, and pimentos in a food processor and pulse to coarsely chop. Transfer the mixture to a bowl, add the garlic, herbs, and olive oil, and mix well. Cover the bowl and let this salad marinate at room temperature for 1 hour.

With a bread knife, cut a ½-inch slice off the top of the bread and set aside. With your fingers, hollow out the inside "crumb" of the bread, leaving a ½-inch wall and base. Reserve the crumbs for another use.

Place half of the marinated salad in the hollowed-out bread, spreading it as evenly as possible. Then place alternating layers of the meats and cheeses on top of the salad until all the ingredients are used. Press down on each layer with your hand as you add it. Spread the remaining salad evenly on top of the last layer. Replace the bread top. Wrap the loaf tightly in foil and place a 3-pound weight on top. Refrigerate the loaf for at least 6 hours, or overnight.

Remove the weight and foil, cut the loaf into wedges, and serve.

Note: Either Pane Toscano (page 106) or Pane di Mamma (page 112), shaped into a round loaf, would be a good choice here.

Rotolo di Broccoli

BROCCOLI ROLL

Sometimes I get carried away with my family's cooking ethic: Never throw any food away, and always cook more than you think you will need just in case the doorbell rings. I always worry that company will appear unannounced and I will have nothing to feed them. If you have my broccoli roll on hand, you won't have to worry.

SERVES 8

1 recipe Basic Dough (page 104)	½ pound pepperoni, diced
¼ cup olive oil	¼ pound mozzarella cheese, diced
2 cloves garlic, minced	¼ pound Provolone cheese, diced
2 cups finely chopped cooked broccoli	Salt and freshly ground black pepper to taste
2 tablespoons red wine vinegar	1 large egg beaten with 1 teaspoon water for egg wash
2 teaspoons minced fresh basil	
1 teaspoon dried oregano	Coarse salt
	Sesame seeds

Prepare the dough as directed on page 104 and set aside to rise until doubled in size.

In a large frying pan, heat 3 tablespoons of the oil. Add the garlic and sauté until soft. Add the broccoli and sauté for 2 to 3 minutes. Add the wine vinegar, basil, and oregano and cook for 2 to 3 minutes. Remove the mixture to a bowl and let cool.

Punch the dough down, turn it out onto a floured surface, and knead for 5 minutes. Roll the dough out to a 12- × -14-inch rectangle. Lift the dough onto a lightly greased baking sheet; don't worry if the edges hang over the sides of the sheet at this point.

Brush the top of the dough with the remaining 1 tablespoon olive oil. Spread the broccoli mixture over the dough to within ½ inch of the edges. Scatter the diced pepperoni and cheeses over the dough and sprinkle with salt and pepper. Starting with a long side, roll the dough up tightly like a jelly roll. Pinch the seam to seal and position the roll so the seam is on the bottom; tuck the 2 ends under the roll.

Brush the top with the egg wash and sprinkle with coarse salt and sesame seeds. Cover with a towel and let rise for about 30 minutes.

Preheat the oven to 375°F.

Bake for 25 to 30 minutes, or until nicely browned. Let cool and cut into thick slices.

Panettone

There are many folktales surrounding the origin of panettone, a sweet fruit bread from Milan. *Panettone* means "big bread," which indeed it is, since it is baked in a high-sided mold. One of the stories surrounding its origins is that there once was a struggling baker named Antonio, who made a sweet bread very much loved by the Grand Dukes of Milan. Tony had a daughter, and one of the dukes became infatuated with her. To win her hand, the Duke provided Antonio with all the expensive ingredients he needed to continue baking his bread, the *pan di Tonino*.

Today panettone is sold in many Italian pastry shops and is infrequently made at home because it needs to be started the day before it is baked and requires several long risings to give it its characteristic airy texture. It is a highlight of the Christmas season and if you happen to be in Milan then, stop to see the panettone and other wonderful breads, cookies, and pasta at the Motta store near the Galleria.

MAKES 1 LARGE BREAD OR 2 SMALLER BREADS

SPONGE

1 tablespoon (1 package) active dry yeast	4 large egg yolks
1/4 cup warm (110° to 115°F.) water	3/4 cup sugar
	1 tablespoon vanilla
1/2 cup unbleached all-purpose flour	1/4 cup warm water
	4 1/2 to 5 cups plus 1 tablespoon unbleached all-purpose flour
2/3 cup golden raisins	Grated zest of 1 medium orange
1/4 cup grappa or brandy	Grated zest of 1 medium lemon
5 tablespoons butter, softened	1/2 cup chopped citron
2 large eggs	

To make the sponge, in a small bowl, dissolve the yeast in the water. Add the flour and stir with a spoon or your fingers to make a loose, almost liquid, dough. Cover with plastic wrap and let rise in a warm place for at least 6 hours, or overnight.

In a small bowl, combine the raisins and grappa or brandy, and let marinate for at least 6 hours, or overnight.

In a large bowl, beat the butter, whole eggs, egg yolks, sugar, vanilla, and water together. Drain the raisins in a small strainer set over a bowl, pressing on the raisins with a spoon to remove as much of the liquid as possible. Add the liquid to the egg mixture, and refrigerate the raisins until needed. Add the sponge to the bowl and mix well with your hands.

Add the flour about 1½ cups at a time and mix until a ball of dough is formed; you may not need all of the flour. Turn the dough out onto a floured work surface and knead for 5 to 10 minutes, until the dough is smooth and elastic, adding additional flour as needed. Place the dough in a lightly buttered bowl, turn to coat it with butter, cover it with a clean cloth, and let rise for 6 hours.

Butter and flour a panettone mold or other high-sided mold at least 6½ inches tall and 7 to 8 inches wide. (The ceramic insert to a crockpot is ideal, or you can use two 2-pound coffee cans to make smaller loaves. Panettone can also be baked in 2 greased and floured 6-by-6-inch clay flowerpots.)

Punch the dough down and turn it out onto a floured surface. Flatten the dough out with your hands and sprinkle over the lemon and orange zest. In a small bowl, mix the reserved raisins and the citron with the 1 tablespoon flour and sprinkle this mixture over the dough. Fold the dough in half, press the edges to seal, and knead it to distribute the fruits. Knead for 5 to 10 minutes, or until the fruits are well distributed and the dough is smooth; add additional flour as necessary. Place the dough in the mold(s), cover with a clean cloth, and let rise for 35 minutes.

Preheat the oven to 400°F.

Cut an X in the top of the bread with scissors or a razor blade. Bake for 5 minutes, reduce the heat to 375°F., and bake for 10 minutes. Then reduce the heat to 350°F. and bake for 30 to 35 minutes, or until a metal or bamboo skewer inserted into the center of the bread comes out clean; if the top of the bread begins to brown too much, cover the bread loosely with foil. Let cool for about 30 minutes on a rack before removing the bread from the mold.

Note: There are many versions of panettone. Some use Vin Santo, a sweet dessert wine, instead of grappa; some are made with olive oil instead of butter; and others use pine nuts and anise seed instead of raisins and citron—try these variations.

Orsi Piccoli

LITTLE BEARS

My children have fond memories of making little dough bears from sweet bread dough at Christmastime. Early on the day we made them, I would get out everything we would need to bring the bears to life and give them personality: currants for the eyes, coarse sugar for the body, and pieces of colorful ribbons to tie as bows around their necks. What a time we had! I still make the sweet-tasting dough at holiday time, but I don't have my children beside me to help. Still, every Christmas morning, I lay an army of little bears on the table and Beth and Chris are *bambini* once again.

MAKES 6 6-INCH-HIGH BEARS

1 1/3 cups milk

1 tablespoon (1 package) active dry yeast

5 1/4 cups unbleached all-purpose flour

1 teaspoon salt

2/3 cup sugar

8 tablespoons (1 stick) butter, cut into pieces

Raisins or currants

1 large egg beaten with 1 tablespoon milk for egg wash

Turbinado or coarse natural brown sugar

In a saucepan, scald (bring almost to a boil) the milk. Remove from the heat and let cool to tepid (110° to 115°F.). Pour the milk into a large bowl and add the yeast. Stir to blend and let proof until the yeast is foamy, about 10 minutes.

In another bowl, mix the flour, salt, and sugar together. Add the butter and work it into the flour mixture until it resembles coarse meal. Slowly add the milk-yeast mixture to the flour, mixing with your hands until a ball of dough is formed. Turn the dough out onto a floured surface and knead until smooth, about 10 minutes. Place the dough in a lightly buttered bowl, turn to coat with butter, cover with a towel, and let rise until doubled in size, about 1 hour.

Punch the dough down and divide it into 24 equal pieces.

Use 4 pieces for each bear: Roll 3 pieces into balls about 2 inches in diameter. Place the 3 balls of dough on a greased baking sheet, arranging them in a line as if making a snowman (1 for the head, 1 for the upper body, and 1 for the lower body). Divide the fourth piece of dough into 7 pieces for the ears, nose, feet, and hands and attach to the bear.

Repeat with the remaining dough, placing the bears 3 inches apart on the baking sheet(s).

Cover with a towel and let rise for 20 minutes.

Preheat the oven to 350°F.

Insert raisins or currants into the heads for the eyes. Brush the bears with the egg wash and sprinkle with sugar. Bake for 20 to 25 minutes, or until golden brown. Let cool on wire racks, then tie ribbons around the necks.

Note: You can make more bears by using smaller pieces of dough. These freeze beautifully and can be made weeks ahead. Wrap them individually in foil, place in plastic freezer bags, and freeze for up to 3 weeks. They are great treats for children's birthday parties, too.

Calzoni

Calzone means "pant leg," and *calzoni* are pizza turnovers—little half-moons of dough that house savory fillings of meat, cheeses, and/or vegetables. When shaped, they are said to resemble the wide billowing trousers that the men of Naples wore in the eighteenth and nineteenth centuries. There are four fillings to choose from here.

MAKES 8

DOUGH

1 tablespoon (1 package) active dry yeast

1 cup warm (110° to 115°F.) water

1/8 teaspoon sugar

2 tablespoons warm milk

1 tablespoon olive oil

3 to 3 1/2 cups unbleached all-purpose flour

1 teaspoon salt

Cornmeal

olive oil

1 recipe Filling (recipes follow)

1 large egg beaten with 1 tablespoon water for egg wash

To make the dough, in a large bowl, dissolve the yeast in the warm water. Stir in the sugar and mix well. Let proof until the yeast is foamy, 5 to 10 minutes. Add the milk and olive oil and stir to blend. Mix 3 cups of the flour and the salt and add to the yeast mixture. Mix with your hands until a ball of dough is formed. If the dough seems sticky, add up to 1/2 cup additional flour.

Turn the dough out onto a well-floured surface and knead it until it is very smooth. Place the dough in a lightly oiled bowl, turn to coat with the oil, cover with a clean towel, and let rise in a warm draft-free place for about 1 1/2 hours, or until doubled in size.

Punch the dough down. Turn it out onto a floured surface and knead for 5 minutes, or until smooth and elastic. Cut the dough into 8 pieces. Roll each piece out with a rolling pin to a 7-inch circle. Place the circles on floured towels as you make them and keep covered as you work with the remaining dough.

Preheat the oven to 375°F. Grease 2 baking sheets and sprinkle with cornmeal.

Brush each circle of dough lightly with olive oil. Divide the filling among the circles, placing it on the lower half of each circle. Bring the other half over to enclose the filling, like a turnover, and seal the edges closed by pressing on them with the tines of a fork.

Place the calzoni 2 inches apart on the prepared baking sheets. Brush the tops with the egg wash and make a small slit with scissors in the top of each calzone. Let rise for 20 minutes.

Bake the calzoni for 20 to 25 minutes, or until golden brown. Let cool slightly before serving.

Note: To freeze calzoni, let cool completely and wrap them individually in aluminum foil. Defrost in the refrigerator and reheat in a 350°F. oven for 20 minutes, or until warm.

Variation: To make mini calzoni divide the dough into 24 pieces, roll out into 2 inch circles, and fill as directed above. Bake at 375°F. for 15 minutes, or until golden brown. Makes about 2 dozen.

MAKES 3½ TO 4 CUPS

SAUSAGE FILLING

- ¾ pound sweet Italian pork sausage, casings removed
- 1 small red bell pepper, cored, seeded, and cut into thin strips
- 1 small yellow bell pepper, cored, seeded, and cut into thin strips
- 2 cloves garlic, peeled and mashed
- 1 small red onion, diced
- 1½ teaspoons fennel seeds
- 1 cup diced mozzarella cheese (about ¼ pound)

  Salt and freshly ground black pepper to taste
- ½ cup Fresh Tomato Basil Sauce (page 87)

In a skillet, sauté the sausage (in its own fat) until browned, crumbling it with a fork. Transfer the sausage with a slotted spoon to a bowl, and drain off all but 1 tablespoon of the fat from the skillet. Add the peppers, garlic, and onion and sauté for 5 minutes, or until the vegetables are soft. Add to the sausage along with the fennel seeds, cheese, salt and pepper, and sauce. Stir to mix well. Let cool.

MAKES 3½ TO 4 CUPS

VEAL-RICE FILLING

- 1 tablespoon butter
- ¾ pound ground veal
- 1 cup thinly sliced mushrooms
- ½ cup cooked rice
- 1 cup diced Italian Fontina cheese (about ¼ pound)
- 1 tablespoon grated lemon zest
- 1 teaspoon fresh lemon juice
- 2 teaspoons minced fresh parsley

In a large skillet, melt the butter over medium-high heat and brown the veal. Remove the veal to a bowl with a slotted spoon. Add the mushrooms to the skillet, and sauté until soft. Add the mushrooms to the veal along with the remaining ingredients, and mix well. Let cool.

continued

EGGPLANT-CHEESE FILLING

¼ cup peanut oil

2 cups peeled and cubed eggplant

1 anchovy packed in oil, mashed

1 cup Fresh Tomato Basil Sauce
   (page 87)

1 cup diced pepperoni (about ¼
   pound)

1 cup diced Provolone cheese (about
   ¼ pound)

1 tablespoon minced fresh basil

1 tablespoon freshly cracked black
   pepper

In a large skillet, heat the peanut oil and sauté the eggplant for 5 minutes, or until soft. Add the anchovy and cook for 2 minutes. Add the tomato sauce, stirring to blend well, and simmer the mixture for 5 minutes. Transfer the mixture to a bowl and add the pepperoni, cheese, basil, and pepper. Stir to mix well. Let cool.

PROSCIUTTO-BROCCOLI FILLING

1 tablespoon olive oil

¼ pound prosciutto, diced

1½ cups chopped cooked broccoli

½ teaspoon freshly ground black
   pepper

1 cup diced Asiago cheese (about ¼
   pound)

¼ cup oil-cured olives, pitted and
   chopped

In a skillet, heat the olive oil and sauté the prosciutto until browned and crisp. Remove the prosciutto to a bowl. Add the broccoli to the skillet and sauté for 1 minute. Add the broccoli to the prosciutto, along with the pepper, cheese, and olives. Stir to mix well. Let cool.

Carne e Pollame

MEAT AND POULTRY

THE FIRST time I went to Italy, I had on my agenda of what to see the sights most tourists see: the Vatican, the Roman Forum, Michelangelo's *David*, the Sistine Chapel, the Piazza del Populo, the Baptistry, and the Pantheon. Also on my list was a visit to *il mercato publico*, the public market, and *il supermercato*, the supermarket. Saturday is the big market day all over Italy, but every town also has a market day during the week. All the best that Italy has to offer in the way of fresh foods can be seen on these days.

Going to market is serious business. Elderly women in black dresses, carrying string shopping bags, walk arm in arm from stall to stall commenting on the freshness of the fruits and vegetables. A stylishly dressed young couple argues with the meat vendor about the size of the *scallopine*. The fishmonger has all he can do to keep up with the scores of people waiting to take home fresh-caught eels, shrimp, spiny lobster, squid, trout and more. The men stand around and talk about the latest soccer game with their *amici intimi* (buddies), and the *bambini* (children), are hugged and kissed by everyone.

The meats for sale look good enough to eat raw. The cuts are lean and with good color. You can find lamb, pork, beef, veal, and goat, and there are even signs that direct you to *carne per i gatti e cani,* meat for cats and dogs. There is a special section where you can pick out your own rabbit, pigeon, chicken, duck, or turkey and it will be freshly prepared and dressed while you wait.

There are many regional meat specialties in Italy. Some of my favorites include *bistecca alla fiorentina,* the famous steak dish of Florence; *vitello,* or young calf, in Milan; superb lamb, or *agnello,* in Rome and Sardinia; and the *porchetta,* or roast suckling pig, for which Umbria is noted.

Veal is the signature meat of Italy. The animals are milk-fed and sent to market when only a few months old. Because of its blandness, veal marries well with wine sauces, all sorts of stuffings, and breading. I find it very difficult to get the same quality veal here and when I prepare a veal dish, it is always with a certain feeling of trepidation.

Domestic pigeons and tiny birds that are cooked on a spit and served with polenta or hearty bread to catch the drippings are all part of Italy's rich cuisine. And it would take an entire book to discuss the many cured meat products of Italy, from *prosciutto crudo,* the prized salt- and air-cured ham from Parma and San Daniele, to the endless varieties of *prosciutto locale* and superior *salame* one finds in almost every region.

Bue in Umido

STEWED BEEF

When I was a child, we ate a lot of stews because they were less expensive than other meat dishes and could be stretched to feed a large family. Lard was always inserted into the raw meat before cooking, to give it added flavor, but I use pancetta, Italian bacon, which is leaner and just as flavorful.

SERVES 6 TO 8

3 tablespoons lard or 2 slices pancetta

1 3-pound rump roast

1/2 cup sliced celery

1/2 cup sliced carrots

1/2 cup thinly sliced onion

1 sprig each rosemary, thyme, and sage, tied together with string

1 cinnamon stick

1 bay leaf

4 cups dry red wine

3 tablespoons olive oil

Salt and freshly ground black pepper to taste

3 tablespoons butter

1/2 cup diced pancetta

1 1/2 cups button mushrooms

12 small pearl onions, peeled

Dice the lard or pancetta. With a small knife make 1-inch-deep incisions all over the roast and insert the lard or pancetta. Put the roast in a deep nonmetal dish, and scatter the celery, carrots, and onion around the meat. Add the herb sprigs, cinnamon stick, and bay leaf and pour the wine over the meat. Cover and let marinate in the refrigerator for at least 8 hours, or overnight, turning the meat occasionally.

In a large Dutch oven, heat the olive oil. Remove the meat from the marinade, reserving the marinade, wipe it with paper towels, and brown it on all sides in the olive oil. Add all the marinade ingredients and salt and pepper to the pan. Bring to a boil, lower the heat, and simmer, covered, for about 2 hours, until the meat is very tender.

Meanwhile, in a saucepan, melt the butter. Add the 1/2 cup pancetta and sauté until crisp. Add the onions and sauté for about 5 minutes, turning to glaze them in the fat, until browned. Add the mushrooms and sauté until soft. Set aside.

Remove the meat to a cutting board. Strain the cooking juices through a strainer into a bowl, pressing on the solids with the back of a spoon to extract all the juices. Discard the solids. Add the pancetta mixture to the cooking juices and cover to keep warm.

Slice the meat into serving pieces, arrange on a platter, and spoon the vegetables and some of the meat juices over it.

Braciolone della Nonna Galasso

GRANDMA GALASSO'S STUFFED ROLLED BEEF

Grandma Galasso's *braciolone*, or rolled stuffed beef, was a great favorite in our house. Round or flank steak was sprinkled with slivers of garlic, then stuffed, rolled and tied, browned, and cooked in tomato sauce. The only thing I did not like was the hard-boiled eggs Grandma put in the center; when I make the dish, I leave them out.

SERVES 6 TO 8

2   *pounds top round steak or flank steak, cut about 1/4 inch thick*

Salt

1   *tablespoon coarsely ground black pepper*

4   *cloves garlic, 3 cloves cut in thin slivers and 1 clove chopped*

1/4   *cup chopped fresh parsley*

1/2   *cup grated Pecorino Romano cheese*

1   *small red onion, thinly sliced*

3   *hard-boiled eggs, shelled, optional*

2   *tablespoons olive oil*

1   *tablespoon lard or butter*

4   *cups crushed fresh (about 8 medium tomatoes) or canned plum tomatoes*

1/2   *cup water*

1   *cup dry red wine*

1   *bay leaf*

Freshly ground black pepper to taste

Lay the meat out flat and pound it with a meat hammer to flatten it slightly to a uniform thickness. Be careful not to tear the meat. (It will be a little more difficult to do this with flank steak.)

Wipe the meat dry with paper towels. Rub it all over with 1 teaspoon salt and the coarse pepper. Sprinkle the slivers of garlic evenly over the meat, then scatter over the parsley, cheese, and onion. Place the eggs lengthwise down the center of the meat so they are touching each other. Starting at a long side, roll up the meat like a jelly roll. Tie the roll with string at 1-inch intervals.

In a large deep saucepan, heat the olive oil and lard or butter over medium-high heat. Add the chopped garlic and sauté until soft. Remove the garlic with a slotted spoon and discard. Add the meat to the pan and brown it on all sides. Lower the heat to medium low and add all the remaining ingredients; add salt to taste. Stir to blend well. Simmer the meat, covered, for 1 1/2 hours, or until tender.

Remove the meat from the sauce and let rest for 5 to 10 minutes. Remove the strings and cut into 1/2-inch slices. Arrange on a serving platter, spoon the sauce over, and serve immediately with pasta.

Abbacchio al Forno

ROAST LAMB

Roast baby lamb, considered a delicacy, takes the place of honor on the Italian Easter table. The word *abbacchio* refers specifically to baby lamb weighing between 15 and 25 pounds and milk-fed. Lamb is prepared in many ways in Italy: grilled on a spit, braised, stewed, and roasted in the oven. The Romans take particular pride in their method of cooking lamb.

SERVES 8

1	4-pound leg of lamb	1	tablespoon salt
3	cloves garlic, slivered	1½	teaspoons coarsely ground black pepper
3	sprigs fresh rosemary, leaves only, or 2 tablespoons dried	1	cup dry white wine
½	cup olive oil		

Wipe the meat dry with paper towels. With a small knife make slits about 1 inch deep all over the meat and insert the slivers of garlic and rosemary.

In a small bowl, combine the olive oil, salt, and pepper and mix well with a fork. Rub the mixture all over the lamb, coating it well. Place the meat in a deep dish, cover it, and let it marinate in the refrigerator for 2 to 3 hours.

Preheat the oven to 350°F.

Place the lamb on a rack in a roasting pan and add the wine to the pan. Roast for 1 to 1½ hours or until the internal temperature reaches 170°F., basting the meat every 15 minutes with the pan juices. Remove the roast to a cutting board and let cool slightly.

Carve into pieces, arrange on a platter, and pour the pan juices over the meat. Serve immediately.

Spiedo Misto

MIXED GRILL

At a rustic outdoor *ristorante* called La Stalla (the name means "stable"), everything on the menu was cooked in the classic Umbrian style, *alla griglia*, grilled on an open fire. We sat under a grape arbor at tables covered with red-and-white-checked cloths. When the *spiedo misto* came to the table smelling of fresh herbs and wine, it was the perfect ending to a long day.

SERVES 8

1   pound boneless pork loin

1   pound boneless beef or veal loin

1   pound skinless boneless chicken breasts

Coarse salt to taste

Coarsely ground black pepper to taste

3   cloves garlic, peeled and crushed

2   tablespoons minced fresh sage

2   tablespoons chopped fresh rosemary

¼   cup olive oil

3   medium bell peppers (an assortment of red, green, and/or yellow), cored, seeded, and cut into 2-inch squares

¼   cup dry white wine

4   thick slices pancetta or prosciutto, cut in 1-inch squares

Small bunch of fresh sage, leaves only

¾   pound sweet or hot Italian sausage, cut into chunks

½   cup fresh lemon juice

Olive oil

Cut the meats and chicken into 1-inch cubes. Season the pork with coarse salt and pepper and rub with the garlic; season the beef or veal with salt and pepper and sprinkle with the sage; season the chicken with salt and pepper and sprinkle with the rosemary. Set aside.

In a skillet, heat the olive oil and sauté the peppers until just crisptender. Add the wine and cook until the liquid is reduced by about half.

Thread the skewers in this order: pork, bell pepper, chicken, pancetta, sage leaf, veal, bell pepper, and sausage. Do not crowd the pieces. Place the skewers in a nonmetal dish large enough to hold them in a single layer and drizzle the lemon juice and olive oil over them. Let them marinate for several hours in the refrigerator, basting and turning them often.

Heat the grill and lightly oil the grill rack. Remove the skewers from the marinade, place them on the grill, and baste with the marinade. Grill, turning and basting the skewers, until done to taste, about 8 to 12 minutes.

Maiale con Aceto Balsamico

PORK IN BALSAMIC VINEGAR

Umbria, the central region of Italy, is noted for its *porchetta*, or suckling pig, grilled on an open spit with fresh rosemary until the skin crackles and is almost bronze-colored. When I was studying the food of Umbria, I was inspired by the many ways pork is prepared, including this dish, which uses pork tenderloin. It is so easy to prepare and it can be cooked up to 3 days ahead. The marinade, which includes balsamic vinegar, gives the pork a flavor that is hard to beat.

SERVES 4

MARINADE

1   medium white onion, thinly sliced
1/4 cup cider vinegar
3   tablespoons fresh rosemary
2   tablespoons minced fresh sage
1   tablespoon chopped fresh parsley
2/3 cup balsamic vinegar
    Juice of 1/2 lemon

1   tablespoon pink peppercorns
1/2 cup extra-virgin olive oil

1 1/2 pounds boneless pork tenderloin
    Salt and coarsely ground black
    pepper to taste
2   tablespoons olive oil
2/3 cup dry white wine (preferably
    Frascati)

To make the marinade, in a skillet, combine the onion and cider vinegar and simmer until the onion is soft. Add the rosemary, sage, parsley, balsamic vinegar, lemon juice, peppercorns, and extra-virgin olive oil. Stir well, remove from the heat, and set aside.

Preheat the oven to 375°F.

Pat the meat dry with paper towels and rub it all over with 1 tablespoon of the olive oil. Sprinkle with salt and black pepper.

In a frying pan, heat the remaining 1 tablespoon olive oil over medium-high heat and brown the meat on all sides. Transfer the meat to a baking dish and add 1/3 cup of the wine to the dish. Roast for 20 to 25 minutes, or until cooked to 155° to 160°F.; midway through the cooking add the remaining 1/3 cup wine to the pan.

Transfer the meat to a deep nonmetal dish just large enough to hold it. Pour the marinade over the meat, and let it marinate, covered, in the refrigerator for at least 3 hours, or up to 3 days.

Bring the meat, in the marinade, to room temperature before serving. Cut it in thin slices, arrange on a serving platter, and spoon some of the marinade over the slices.

Note: This dish can also be reheated in the marinade and served warm. Either way, it is a winner.

Salsiccia Fresca

FRESH SAUSAGE

I remember my mother and father grinding what seemed like mountains of fresh pork butt for Italian sausage. Their philosophy was if you were going to make sausage, you might as well have plenty on hand. It was nothing for them to spend a Saturday stuffing 25 to 50 pounds of sausage meat into hog casings. Whenever I make sausage, I see my parents mixing huge tubs of fresh ground pork, perfuming it with fennel seeds and hot red pepper flakes.

When you buy pork butt, pick one that is not too lean, or the meat will be dry. If you don't have a meat grinder, have the butcher grind the pork for you.

MAKES 5 POUNDS

5 pounds boneless pork butt, with some fat, ground once on coarse grind, and once on medium grind

2 tablespoons coarse salt, or more to taste

2 tablespoons coarsely ground black pepper, or more to taste

3 tablespoons fennel seeds

1 tablespoon crushed red pepper flakes, or more to taste

1 package natural hog casings (available in the meat section of the grocery store or in butcher shops)

In a large bowl, combine the pork and all the seasonings; mix well. Test for seasoning by frying a small patty in a frying pan; taste and add seasoning if necessary.

In another bowl, soak 4 casings in several changes of cold water to remove the salt. Cut the casings into 12- to 14-inch lengths if necessary. (Keep the remaining casings, still packed in salt, in the refrigerator for future use.)

Slip one end of a casing onto the throat of a sausage funnel. Place the funnel under the kitchen faucet and run cold water through it. With the water running, slide the casing up onto the funnel, leaving about 3 inches free at the end. Turn off the water and tie a knot in the end of the casing.

Push the sausage meat, a little at a time, through the funnel with your thumbs. Fill the casing, leaving about 2 inches free at the end to knot; do not pack too tightly. Tie the end and poke holes with a toothpick in the casing to release any air bubbles. Repeat with the remaining sausage meat and casings. Cook immediately, or refrigerate for up to 2 days.

To bake the sausages, preheat the oven to 350°F. Place the sausages in a baking dish and add just enough water to cover the bottom of the pan. Bake uncovered for 25 to 30 minutes, or until nicely browned; as excess water and fat accumulates in the pan, drain it off. Drain on paper towels and serve.

To fry, place the sausages in a large frying pan and add just enough water to cover the bottom of the pan. Cook over medium heat, turning occasionally, for 25 to 30 minutes, or until browned; as excess water and fat accumulates in the pan, drain it off. Drain on paper towels and serve.

Note: These are great cooked on an outdoor grill.

Pezzettini di Vitello

VEAL IN LEMON SAUCE

Veal is very popular in Italy, especially in the northern regions. Calves are milk-fed and then butchered when only a few months old. This accounts for its tenderness. Young veal is almost flavorless. The success of a veal dish depends on the sauce, or the seasonings and stuffings used. I cook veal at home for important occasions, and it is always very good, but I must admit that there is just no comparison with Italian veal. In this dish, veal is served in a very light lemon sauce.

SERVES 4

2 tablespoons butter	4 large eggs, beaten
1 pound veal cutlets, cut in ¹/₂-inch-wide strips	Juice of 2 lemons
Salt and freshly ground black pepper to taste	¹/₄ cup finely chopped fresh parsley

In a large skillet, melt the butter over medium-high heat. Season the veal strips with salt and pepper and fry until they are browned. Remove the veal strips and cover to keep warm.

Whisk the eggs and lemon juice together in the top of a large double boiler, and set over simmering water. Cook, whisking constantly, for about 8 minutes, or until the mixture is thick enough to coat the back of a spoon; take care not to let the mixture get too hot or the eggs will scramble. Lower the heat, add the veal strips, and cook, stirring, for about 2 minutes, or until heated through. Season with salt and pepper. Transfer the meat and sauce to a serving platter and sprinkle with the parsley. Serve immediately.

Note: This dish is good with risotto.

Scallopine alla Pizzaiola

VEAL SCALLOPS WITH TOMATO SAUCE

It was not enough to grow up in an Italian household with my Neapolitan and Sicilian grandmothers, two great cooks: I still had to make those trips to Italy to see for myself how the natives cooked. My destination on one trip was the Bellevue Syrene in Sorrento, where I had enrolled in cooking classes. The journey south from Rome takes about 4½ hours and winds along a breathtaking coastline. Jagged cliffs, hairpin turns, and aquamarine water are everywhere. Once I arrived, it was no-nonsense, down-to-business cooking, from early in the morning to late in the afternoon. I was very proud of the dishes I created in class, especially the veal with fresh tomato sauce. It was tender as a cloud and just spicy enough. This dish is a favorite for company, because it can be prepared in just a few minutes.

SERVES 4

TOMATO SAUCE

¼ cup olive oil

3   cloves garlic, finely chopped

4   cups coarsely chopped fresh plum tomatoes (about 8 medium tomatoes), drained of their juices

2   teaspoons salt

1½ tablespoons chopped fresh oregano or 1 tablespoon dried

¼ cup chopped fresh basil

1   pound veal cutlets
    Salt and freshly ground black pepper to taste

2   tablespoons butter

¼ cup chopped fresh parsley

To make the sauce, in a large skillet, heat the oil and sauté the garlic until soft. Add the tomatoes, salt, and oregano. Simmer over low heat for about 15 minutes, until slightly thickened. Remove from the heat, stir in the basil, and set aside.

Season the veal on both sides with salt and pepper. In a large skillet, melt the butter. Add the veal and sauté until lightly browned on both sides, about 2 minutes. Add the tomato sauce and simmer for about 5 minutes. Stir in the parsley and serve immediately.

Note: This sauce is also good over thin-sliced pan-fried sirloin steaks.

Vitello alla Marsala

VEAL MARSALA

When I am planning to make veal Marsala, I phone my butcher and tell him exactly what I want. He always tries to accommodate me, especially when I promise him a sampling of the dish. When making this dish, remember not to overcook the veal. It will only take a minute or two to cook on both sides. I prefer sweet Marsala for the sauce, but dry can be used.

SERVES 6

2 pounds veal cutlets (cut from the saddle), about ⅛ inch thick	⅔ cup Marsala wine, sweet or dry
½ cup flour	½ cup fresh lemon juice
Salt	Lemon wedges
White pepper	Parsley sprigs
6 to 8 tablespoons butter	

If the veal slices are more than ⅛ inch thick, pound them thin with a meat hammer, but be careful not to rip them. Cut any large pieces in half.

Mix the flour, 1½ teaspoons salt, and 1 teaspoon pepper together and spread it on a plate. Dredge each cutlet in the seasoned flour, shaking off the excess.

In a large frying pan, heat 4 tablespoons of the butter. Add 4 or 5 of the veal cutlets, making sure not to crowd them, and cook for about 1 minute on each side, or until they are no longer pink. Remove them to a warm platter. Repeat with the remaining veal, adding more butter to the pan as needed.

Add the Marsala wine and lemon juice to the juices in the pan and simmer over medium heat, scraping the bottom of the pan with a wooden spoon to release all the browned bits. Correct the seasoning if necessary, return the veal to the pan, and heat until hot. Transfer the meat to a serving platter, pour the pan juices over, and garnish with lemon wedges and parsley sprigs. Serve immediately.

THE CELEBRATION of Christmas holds special memories for me. I look into my mind's eye and see the huge upstairs back room where the dried cherry cookies were stored as well as some of the presents. I see my father trying to "secretly" paint a used two-wheeler bike, which would be my Christmas present.

In the kitchen below, frantic preparations were going on for the Christmas Eve feast. The meal for the vigil of Christmas was always a meatless one that included smelts that were lightly floured and fried in oil; baccalà, or dried, salted cod, that was either made into a stew or cooked simply with butter and lemon juice; and squid that was cut into rings and fried, or served cooked in tomato sauce and as part of a marinated seafood salad. Vegetables included slices of raw fennel mixed with cooked chickpeas and fava beans and coated in olive oil; cauliflower that was rolled in flour, beaten egg, and bread crumbs and fried; and roasted peppers marinated in olive oil and vinegar.

There were bowlfuls of roasted chestnuts, bright red apples, pears, figs, and oranges. One of my favorite treats was *torrone*, a sweet nougat confection from Benevento that came in little blue boxes. A huge tray displayed Italian cookies, including *cucidati* from Sicily.

By the time all this was consumed, we were ready for midnight mass. The celebration of Christmas continued after that with a hearty breakfast of homemade Italian sausage and *pizza fritta*.

Before we went to bed in the early morning of Christmas Day, we hung our stockings and opened the window, because in our family, besides the expected visit of Santa Claus, this was the night that Santa Lucia came on a donkey to deliver presents to good children. She was covered in snowy white lace but couldn't see in the darkness; the donkey, by magic, knew where to go. Children left their windows open so she could get in to deliver her gifts. I remember Grandma Saporito telling

Christmas Dinner

this story, as well as my friend Lorenza, who said that in Italy, Santa Lucia, whose feast day is celebrated on December 13, is more popular than Christmas trees and Santa Claus.

On Christmas Day, Grandma Galasso's eight children came to pay their respects and stayed to enjoy *cappelletti in brodo*, roast capon, Grandma's stuffed potatoes, and my mother's spectacular whiskey cake. When dinner was over, I took my stocking down from the mantle and shook out the bright plump oranges, the little blue boxes of *torrone*, and the shiny quarters that seemed to glisten as much as the tinsel on the tree. Santa Lucia and Santa Claus had been generous.

Cappelletti in Brodo (page 31)
LITTLE HATS IN BROTH

Cappone al Forno (page 156)
ROAST CAPON

Cavolfiore Fritto (page 175)
FRIED CAULIFLOWER

Patate della Nonna (page 190)
GRANDMA'S POTATOES

Insalata Rinforzata (page 198)
REINFORCED SALAD

Pane di Mamma (page 112)
MAMA'S BREAD

Castagne al Forno (page 247)
ROASTED CHESTNUTS

Panettone (page 126)

Torta di Whisky alla Mamma (page 222)
MAMA'S WHISKEY CAKE

Filetto di Vitello ai Tartufi Neri

VEAL WITH BLACK TRUFFLES

Although I like to prepare traditional Italian food, there are some *alta cucina* dishes, or new innovations, that are very successful. The following recipe comes from the kitchen of Mario Ragni, my cooking teacher in Perugia. It uses two unique ingredients: tiny artichokes and black truffles. Italian artichokes are tender enough to eat raw. I have used the small California artichoke for this recipe, but if you can find only large artichokes, boil them until tender, drain, and remove the leaves, scrape out the fuzzy chokes, and slice the artichoke hearts before adding to the dish. This is an extravagant dish, but the results are outstanding.

SERVES 6

8 ripe strawberries	1 tablespoon unbleached all-purpose flour
4 tablespoons butter	
3 ounces pureed black truffles (see Note)	½ cup thin shavings mild Pecorino Romano cheese
6 veal cutlets, about 8 ounces each	2 small artichokes, trimmed and cut in paper-thin slices
Salt and freshly ground black pepper to taste	1 fresh black truffle, cut in paper-thin slices (see Note)
½ cup dry white wine	

Preheat the oven to 350°F.

In a small bowl, mash the strawberries to a paste. In a large frying pan, melt the butter over medium heat. Add the berries and stir well to blend. Heat for 1 minute. Stir in the truffle puree and heat until hot.

Season the veal with salt and pepper. Raise the heat to high and add the cutlets, without crowding them; cook the veal in batches if necessary. Cook, turning once, until the meat is no longer pink. Return all the veal to the pan, add the wine, and simmer for about 3 minutes.

Remove the cutlets to a baking dish and season with salt and pepper. Stir the flour into the cooking liquid in the frying pan and cook, stirring until slightly thickened. Spoon the sauce over the meat and cover with the thin cheese shavings.

Bake for 5 minutes, or until the cheese is melted. Sprinkle the artichoke slivers and black truffle slices over the veal and serve at once.

Note: Pureed truffles can be purchased in gourmet food stores and through food catalogues. Fresh truffles are sold by the ounce—and can cost up to fifty dollars per ounce! Do not despair if you cannot find fresh truffles to shave over the top of the dish; simply omit them.

Vitello con Radicchielle

VEAL WITH DANDELION GREENS

In the spring, Grandma Galasso picked dandelion greens, which grew near our house. She would wash and cut them and boil them forever it seemed. They were served plain with olive oil drizzled over the top, or sometimes mixed with other vegetables or meat. Their sharp flavor is a good contrast to the mild veal. If dandelion greens are unavailable, Swiss chard or broccoli rabe would be a good alternative.

SERVES 4

1   pound dandelion greens, washed, trimmed, and cut crosswise into 2-inch-wide strips

6   large eggs

¼   cup grated Parmigiano-Reggiano cheese

2   tablespoons olive oil

1   clove garlic, finely minced

1   pound veal cutlets, cut into ½-inch-wide strips

Salt and freshly ground black pepper to taste

Put the dandelion greens in a saucepan and add water to cover. Bring to a boil and boil until the greens are tender, 5 to 8 minutes. Drain in a colander and set aside.

In a bowl, beat the eggs with the cheese. Set aside.

In a large skillet, heat the olive oil. Add the garlic and sauté for about 1 minute. Add the veal strips and brown them in the oil. Add the dandelion greens to the veal, season with salt and pepper, and toss to mix. Slowly pour the egg mixture over the veal and greens and cook over medium heat until the eggs are set, about 6 to 7 minutes. Serve immediately, with crusty bread.

Scallopine alla Salsa Verde

VEAL IN GREEN SAUCE

The secret of this veal dish is the sauce, which is similar to pesto, but uses butter and parsley in addition to oil and basil leaves. Do not try to make this sauce with dried herbs; it just won't work.

SERVES 6

GREEN SAUCE

1/2 pound (2 sticks) butter

4 cloves garlic, chopped

1/2 cup coarsely chopped walnuts

3/4 cup parsley leaves

1/4 cup basil leaves

Salt and freshly ground black pepper to taste

1 to 2 tablespoons extra-virgin olive oil

4 to 6 tablespoons butter

1 1/2 pounds veal cutlets

1/2 cup sliced mushrooms

Salt and freshly ground black pepper to taste

To make the sauce, in a food processor, or a mortar, combine all the sauce ingredients except the olive oil. Process, or grind with a pestle, to a smooth paste. With the motor running, slowly pour the olive oil through the feed tube, adding just enough oil to give the paste a very creamy consistency; or add the oil to the mortar drop by drop, blending until very creamy. Set aside.

In a large frying pan, melt 2 tablespoons of the butter. Sauté the veal cutlets in batches if necessary, adding more butter as needed, until lightly browned on both sides, about 2 to 3 minutes. Remove the veal to a warm platter and add 2 tablespoons of the remaining butter to the skillet. Sauté the mushrooms until soft and glazed with butter. Return the veal to the pan to reheat. Add the sauce and carefully stir to mix. Serve immediately.

Note: This sauce is also good served over fresh pasta or mixed into risotto.

Fricco di Pollo all'Eugubina

CHICKEN GUBBIAN STYLE

Gubbio is a quiet ancient hill town in the region of Umbria. I love it because people there take time for the important things: work, reflection, and the pleasure of another's company. The winding streets offer surprises at every turn, such as the craftsmen who still fashion by hand the much-coveted ceramic ware the area is noted for. Around *mezzogiorno* (noon), the smell of lunch being prepared begins to waft its way down the shady *strade*. The food is simple peasant fare that reflects old traditions.

SERVES 4

1	3-pound chicken, cut into 8 pieces	2	sprigs fresh rosemary or 1 teaspoon dried
1/4	cup olive oil	1	cup dry white wine
1	large white onion, coarsely chopped	1 1/2	cups pureed fresh plum tomatoes (3 to 4 medium tomatoes), strained to remove seeds
1/4	cup red or white wine vinegar		Salt and freshly ground black pepper to taste
4	fresh sage leaves or 1 teaspoon dried		

Wash and dry the chicken pieces. Set aside.

In a large skillet, heat the olive oil over medium-low heat. Add the onion and sauté slowly for 5 minutes, or until tender. Raise the heat to medium high, add the chicken pieces, and brown on all sides. Add the vinegar and boil until it has evaporated. Lower the heat, add the sage and rosemary, and cook for 20 minutes.

Raise the heat, add the wine, and boil until it has evaporated. Add the tomato puree and salt and pepper, reduce the heat to medium low, and cook for 25 minutes, or until the sauce has thickened and the chicken is easily pierced with a fork.

Transfer the chicken to a platter and spoon some of the sauce over the top. Serve immediately.

Note: Sometimes I serve this with polenta on the side or penne.

Pollo con Vino alla Pierrette

PIERRETTE'S CHICKEN IN WINE

What luck! On a recent trip to Italy I had dinner at La Grotta, a small, rustic *ristorante* in Fiesole, a small town outside Florence. What a surprise awaited me when I ordered the house chicken in wine. When I took my first bite, I knew that I had found the exact taste of my Grandmother Saporito's lost chicken in wine recipe (see Pollo con Vino, page 152). With fork flying, I motioned the *camerière* (waiter) to my table to tell me how the dish was made. He said he'd bring out the chef. Her name was Pierrette Mathieau; she was French but married to an Italian! She seemed amused by my excitement but proudly gave me the following recipe—and now I sleep much better at night knowing that Grandma would be pleased.

This dish must be started two days in advance.

SERVES 4

3 pounds chicken pieces

MARINADE
1 large onion, thinly sliced
2 tablespoons fresh rosemary
2 tablespoons minced fresh parsley
2 tablespoons minced fresh sage
2 tablespoons minced fresh basil
1 bay leaf
1 rib celery, diced
1 large carrot, diced
2 cloves garlic, minced

2 cups dry red wine, preferably Barbaresco or Chianti
   Salt and freshly ground black pepper to taste

2 tablespoons butter
6 tablespoons olive oil
3 tablespoons unbleached all-purpose flour
   Red wine to cover the chicken
8 slices Italian bread

Wash and dry the chicken pieces. Set aside.

In a deep nonmetal rectangular dish large enough to hold the chicken pieces in a single layer, combine all the marinade ingredients. Add the chicken pieces to the marinade, cover the dish, and refrigerate for 2 days, occasionally turning the chicken in the marinade.

Remove the chicken pieces from the marinade and set aside. Strain the marinade through a strainer lined with cheesecloth into a bowl, pressing on the solids with a spoon to extract all the juices; reserve. Discard the solids.

In a large skillet, heat the butter and 2 tablespoons of the olive oil over medium-high heat and brown the chicken on all sides. Sprinkle the chicken with the flour and add the reserved marinade. Add additional red wine to completely cover the chicken. Cover the skillet and simmer over low heat for 35 minutes.

Meanwhile, in a skillet, heat the remaining ¼ cup olive oil and fry the bread slices a few at a time until browned on both sides. Drain the bread on brown paper.

Uncover the skillet and cook the chicken, turning the pieces occasionally, until the liquid has reduced by half and the sauce is thickened. To serve, put 2 slices of the bread on each plate, arrange the chicken on top, and spoon the sauce over . . . thank you, Pierrette!

Pollo con Vino

CHICKEN WITH WINE

I once admitted on national television that I could not remember how to make my Grandmother Saporito's chicken in wine dish; never mind that I had eaten that dish so many times. I even called my Aunt Phoebe, who lived with Grandma her entire life, to find out the secret. . . . Sadly, she had no clue. So we put this recipe together from memory, Aunt Phoebe remembering one thing, me another. What follows is not exactly like Grandma's (see Pollo con Vino alla Pierrette, page 150) but it's good in its own right; I still get letters from viewers who tell me they've made this and they like it. They also tell me I should have paid more attention to what Grandma did. Enough said.

SERVES 8 TO 10

1½ cups unbleached all-purpose flour	2 teaspoons chopped garlic
2 teaspoons salt	½ cup diced red bell pepper
1 teaspoon coarsely ground black pepper	½ cup diced onion
2 3-pound chickens, each cut into 8 pieces	¼ cup red wine vinegar
	2 cups dry red wine
6 to 8 tablespoons olive oil	
6 to 8 tablespoons butter	

Mix the flour, salt, and pepper and spread it on a plate.

Rinse and dry the chicken pieces. Dredge each piece in the seasoned flour, shaking off the excess.

In a large frying pan, heat 2 tablespoons each of the oil and butter and sauté the garlic until soft. Remove the garlic to a bowl. Add the red pepper and onions to the frying pan and sauté until soft. Add to the garlic, and set aside.

Add 2 tablespoons each of the olive oil and butter to the frying pan and brown the chicken pieces in batches, adding more oil and butter as needed, until golden on all sides, about 10 minutes. Return all the chicken to the pan and splash on the red wine vinegar and cook until the liquid has evaporated. Add the onions and garlic and 1 cup of the red wine and cook the chicken over medium-high heat until most of the wine has evaporated and the chicken is beginning to take on a glaze.

Lower the heat to medium, add the remaining 1 cup wine, and cook the chicken until it is a dark rich color and well glazed and most of the wine has evaporated, about 15 minutes.

Transfer the chicken to a serving platter and spoon the pan juices and vegetables over. Serve immediately.

Pollo e Limone

CHICKEN AND LEMON

When I am in a hurry and don't want to spend a lot of time fixing a meal, I make this chicken dish and a simple vegetable like Broccoli Casalinghi (page 176).

SERVES 4

2 pounds chicken pieces	2 fresh sage leaves
¼ cup olive oil	Coarse salt and freshly ground black pepper to taste
1 large garlic clove, peeled	
2 sprigs rosemary	Juice of 1 large lemon

Wash and dry the chicken pieces; set aside.

In a large deep skillet, heat the olive oil over medium heat. Add the garlic, rosemary, and sage. Sauté until the garlic is soft and the herbs are wilted. Remove and discard the garlic and herbs.

Add the chicken pieces to the skillet and brown on all sides. Sprinkle the chicken with the coarse salt and pepper and pour over the lemon juice. Cover the pan and simmer over medium-low heat for 45 minutes, or until the chicken is tender.

Transfer to a serving platter and serve immediately, with the pan juices spooned over.

Prosciutto

PROSCIUTTO, one of Italy's most famous exports, is salt-cured ham. The best *prosciutti* come from San Daniele, in the Friuli-Venezia-Giulia region, and from Parma, in the Emilia-Romagna region. Those from Tuscany and Umbria are good too, though they are saltier, drier, and less pink than their northern counterparts. Some people claim that it is the diet of acorns that the pigs feed on and the clean northern mountain air that makes the San Daniele and Parma *prosciutti* exceptional.

Prosciutto comes from the leg portion of the pig and is aged slowly, first by frequent rubbing with salt over a period of several days, and then by air-drying in a well-ventilated place under specific conditions of temperature and humidity. The curing process takes twelve to eighteen months, overseen by quality-control groups such as the Consortium of Prosciutto di Parma and the Consortium of Prosciutto di San Daniele.

In Reggio Emilia, where some of the best *prosciutti* are to be found, my friends Alessandro and Lorenza Lori took me to the basement of their home to see how they store their prized ham. It sits on an old wooden shelf with a cloth loosely draped over it. When they need some prosciutto, they bring the entire ham up to the kitchen, slice off almost see-through slices, and return the rest to the basement. The taste is mild, the texture is smooth as velvet, and there is just a slight hint of saltiness.

Prosciutto crudo, or raw ham, is eaten as a first course with melon or figs. It is used in soups, or in stuffings for veal and chicken, in sauces, to flavor *risotti*, and with pasta. *Prosciutto cotto* is cooked ham, similar to our boiled ham, but much leaner and sweeter tasting.

Until recently prosciutto crudo di Parma could not be imported into the United States, but now that the ban has been lifted, you can buy authentic prosciutto di Parma in food stores. Purchase the ham just before you are going to use it. It is usually sliced paper-thin, so it will dry out fast if not wrapped properly. To keep it as fresh as possible, wrap each piece in a sheet of plastic wrap, then wrap these in foil and store in the meat tray of your refrigerator.

Pollo e Coniglio con Ginepro

CHICKEN AND RABBIT WITH JUNIPER BERRIES

Pungent and peppery juniper berries grow wild in the woods and on the mountainsides of Italy. They are used commercially to make gin. When they are ground in a mortar with a pestle, their fragrant and distinctive oils are released, adding a wonderful surprise to this dish. If rabbit is difficult to find, you can use all chicken.

SERVES 8

2   pounds chicken pieces

2   pounds rabbit pieces

2   tablespoons butter

¼ cup olive oil

3   tablespoons unbleached all-purpose flour

1   teaspoon salt, or more to taste

1   teaspoon coarsely ground black pepper, or more to taste

2   cups dry white wine

3   tablespoons crushed juniper berries

½ cup Homemade Chicken Broth (page 30)

2   cups seedless grapes

Preheat the oven to 350°F.

Wash the chicken and rabbit pieces and pat dry.

In a large skillet, heat the butter and olive oil over medium-high heat. When the fats are hot, add the chicken and rabbit pieces, in batches if necessary, and brown quickly on all sides. Transfer to a baking dish. Sprinkle the flour over the cooking juices in the skillet, add the salt and pepper, and cook over low heat, stirring and scraping up any browned bits with a wooden spoon, until the flour is dissolved, about 1 minute. Add 1 cup of the wine and half the juniper berries and stir until smooth. Pour the mixture over the chicken and rabbit pieces, cover the dish with foil, and bake for 25 minutes.

Uncover the dish, add the remaining 1 cup wine, juniper berries, and the chicken broth. Bake, uncovered, for 20 minutes more, or until tender, basting frequently with the pan juices. Ten minutes before the meat is done, sprinkle the grapes over. Serve in the baking dish or transfer the meat to a serving platter and spoon the pan juices over.

Note: Juniper berries are available in the spice section of the grocery store.

Cappone al Forno

ROAST CAPON

We always had roast capon for Easter and just about every other holiday. Nobody in my family liked lamb, even though it is traditional on many an Italian table. Capon is a castrated young male chicken with very flavorful meat. We had it prepared in much the same way as chicken. When roasted, filled with a savory meat stuffing, it is delicious.

SERVES 8

STUFFING

1½ cups shredded day-old bread

3 tablespoons milk

2 tablespoons olive oil

¾ pound ground veal

¾ pound ground pork

¼ cup diced prosciutto (about 1 ounce)

⅔ cup hazelnuts, finely chopped

½ cup chopped fresh parsley

¼ cup grated Pecorino Romano cheese

1 large egg, beaten

⅔ cup dry white wine

Salt and freshly ground black pepper to taste

1 5-pound capon

2 tablespoons olive oil

1½ teaspoons coarse salt

2 tablespoons fresh rosemary

½ cup dry white wine

To make the stuffing, put the bread in a small bowl and add the milk. Crumble the bread in the milk and set aside.

In a large frying pan, heat the olive oil and brown the ground veal and pork. Add the prosciutto and sauté for 2 to 3 minutes, or until browned. Transfer to a large bowl, add the soaked bread and all the remaining stuffing ingredients, and mix well.

Preheat the oven to 350°F.

Wash and dry the capon inside and out. Stuff the filling loosely into the body cavity with your hands. Sew or skewer the opening closed and truss the capon. Put the capon on a rack in a roasting pan, brush all over with the olive oil, and rub the coarse salt over the breast. Scatter the rosemary over the capon. Roast the capon for 2½ hours, or until the meat is tender, and the internal temperature registers 180°F., basting occasionally with the wine.

Carve the capon into serving pieces and serve with the stuffing.

Coniglio Contadino

RABBIT FARMER STYLE

Southern Italians are very fond of country-style rabbit dishes. In Sorrento, you begin the preparation for the following dish by making a visit to the market to pick out a fresh rabbit. Then it must be cleaned, cut into pieces, and soaked to remove some of its gaminess. We do not have the same demand for rabbit as in Italy, but if you can find it fresh rather than frozen, you will be surprised at how delicate this dish is.

SERVES 6

2 pounds rabbit pieces	1/4 pound pancetta or salt pork, diced
Juice of 1 large lemon	
1/2 cup unbleached all-purpose flour	1 1/2 cups coarsely chopped onions
Salt and freshly ground black pepper	1 tablespoon fresh rosemary or 1 teaspoon dried
3 tablespoons olive oil	1 cup dry white wine, preferably Soave
	1 cup shelled fresh peas

Place the rabbit pieces in a bowl and add cold water to cover. Add the lemon juice and refrigerate, covered, overnight.

Preheat the oven to 375°F.

Remove the rabbit pieces from the water and dry well. Combine the flour, 1 teaspoon salt, and 1 teaspoon pepper and lightly flour the rabbit pieces.

In a large skillet, heat the olive oil over medium-high heat. Add the rabbit pieces and brown them on all sides. Add the pancetta or salt pork and sauté for 2 minutes. Sprinkle with the rosemary and remove from the heat.

Spread the onions in the bottom of a baking dish. Arrange the rabbit pieces, with the pancetta or salt pork, on top. Add the wine, peas, and salt and pepper to taste. Cover the dish with foil and bake for 35 minutes, or until the rabbit pieces are tender.

Serve in the baking dish or transfer the rabbit to a serving platter and spoon the vegetables and pan juices over.

Rollato di Tacchino

ROLLED TURKEY BREAST

What do you do when no one in your family will eat dark meat? I used to have this problem at Thanksgiving, but now our holiday table features a *rollato*, a rolled and stuffed turkey breast. This is a very popular way of preparing turkey in Italy, although the stuffing varies from region to region. In my version, I use roasted chestnuts. The nice thing about this dish is that it can be prepared and cooked up to two days ahead.

SERVES 6 TO 8

STUFFING

½ pound whole chestnuts

1 cup fresh bread crumbs

5 tablespoons olive oil

¼ pound prosciutto, diced

1½ tablespoons fresh rosemary or 2 teaspoons dried

2 tablespoons chopped fresh parsley

2 cloves garlic, finely chopped

¼ cup grated Parmigiano-Reggiano cheese

1 3- to 3½-pound turkey breast

Salt and freshly ground black pepper to taste

2 tablespoons olive oil

1 tablespoon fresh rosemary or 1 teaspoon dried, optional

½ to 1 cup dry white wine

To make the stuffing, preheat the oven to 450°F.

With a knife, make a slit or an X in the top of each chestnut. Place them on a baking sheet and roast for about 25 minutes. Remove and let cool; reduce the oven temperature to 400°F.

Crack the chestnuts open with a nutcracker and remove the nutmeats. Chop the nutmeats coarsely and put them in a large bowl.

In a skillet, heat 3 tablespoons of the olive oil and fry the bread crumbs until lightly browned. Add the bread crumbs to the bowl with the chestnuts. Add 1 tablespoon of the olive oil to the skillet and sauté the prosciutto until crispy. Add to the bread crumbs. Add all the remaining stuffing ingredients and the remaining 1 tablespoon olive oil, mix well, and set aside.

Remove the skin from the turkey and butterfly the breast: Keeping the knife horizontal, slice the breast lengthwise almost, but not quite, all the way through so it opens like a book. Lay the breast out flat and rub it all over with salt and pepper. Spread most of the stuffing mixture evenly over the turkey to within 1 inch of the edges. Starting with a long edge, roll the meat up like a jelly roll. Tie the roll with string in 3 or 4 places to hold it closed.

In a large skillet, heat the olive oil and brown the turkey roll well on all sides.

Place the turkey on a rack in a roasting pan and sprinkle it with salt and pepper, the rosemary, if you wish, and the remaining filling. Add ½ cup of the wine to the pan and roast for about 1 hour, or until the meat is tender and the internal temperature registers 175° to 180°F. Baste the breast occasionally with the pan juices, adding additional wine to the pan as necessary.

Remove the meat from the oven, and let it rest for 15 minutes before slicing it. Remove the strings and cut the roll into ½-inch slices. Or let cool completely; this is good hot or cold.

Note: I serve this with fresh cranberries cooked with rosemary sprigs. The rosemary gives a wonderful flavor to the cranberries and compliments the turkey very nicely. To make the sauce, combine 6 cups cranberries, ¼ cup water, ½ cup sugar, and 2 rosemary sprigs in a saucepan. Cook until mixture thickens, about 10 to 12 minutes. Discard the rosemary.

Pesce

FISH

WHERE DOES one begin to talk about the fish in the Italian diet? From ancient times, the nets of Mediterranean fishermen have been laden with a rich variety and abundance of fishes. Italians know intuitively what to do with fish. Even squid, which we considered not so long ago to be good only for bait, is turned into wonderful classic fish dishes in Italy. Fish is boiled, baked, fried, breaded, stuffed, stewed, and grilled. The classic *fritto misto di pesce* gives the hungry fish lover an opportunity to try different kinds of fish dipped in flour and then quickly fried in olive oil and served with tangy lemon wedges. Marinated cold fish dishes are an integral part of antipasti. Fish stews are popular and vary with the local catch all over Italy.

Successful fish cookery is dependent upon a few basic rules. Always use fresh fish. The way to determine this is by using your senses—sight, smell, touch—and getting to know someone in a good retail fish store. Fish should never smell "fishy." Check to make sure that the eyes are not sunken into the head, a sure sign of old fish. If buying filleted fish, look for fillets with good color; in the case of flounder or sole, do not buy fish that has a gray look to it. Feel the fish. Fish that seems limp or soggy has been frozen and defrosted.

Go to a fish market that has a good reputation and will get you what you want. We can't always duplicate a fish dish as it would appear on an Italian table, but we can come fairly close by making substitutions with other kinds of fish.

Pesce in Carta

FISH IN PAPER

This is my favorite way to cook fish. It's both healthful and very quick. Wrapping the fish in parchment paper keeps it moist and creates tasty juices. Paper-thin slices of vegetables are cooked along with the fish, and you have a complete meal with no cleanup. In the summer, I wrap the fish in foil and put it on the grill. This dish is impressive enough for company. Any firm-fleshed white fish, such as cod, haddock, or catfish, or even monkfish, will do.

SERVES 4 TO 6

3 tablespoons olive oil

2½ pounds fish fillets

4 cups fresh spinach, washed and well drained

2 to 3 fennel sprigs

1 onion, sliced paper-thin

1 carrot, sliced paper-thin

½ fennel bulb, sliced paper-thin

½ cup dried tomatoes packed in oil, homemade (page 218) or store-bought, drained and diced

Sea salt and freshly ground black pepper to taste

Parchment paper or aluminum foil

Preheat the oven to 450°F.

Place a large sheet of parchment paper or aluminum foil on a baking sheet large enough to hold the fish. Brush the paper or foil with 1 tablespoon of the olive oil. Make a bed of the spinach and place the fish on top. Place the fennel sprigs on the fish and scatter the vegetables over. Sprinkle with the remaining 2 tablespoons oil and salt and pepper. Bring the paper or foil up around the fish to enclose it and turn the edges over to seal. Fasten with paper clips or just fold the edges over two or three more times. Bake the fish for 10 to 12 minutes, depending on thickness.

Carefully transfer the fish to a serving dish. Open up the parchment or foil. Cut the fish into serving pieces and serve with some of the vegetables and juices spooned over.

Note: To grill, wrap the fish and other ingredients in foil and place on a hot grill for 10 to 12 minutes, depending on thickness.

Variation: Prepare individual servings in parchment paper or foil packets and let each person open his own.

Baccalà alla Bolognese

DRIED COD BOLOGNESE STYLE

I could never understand the fascination dried cod, or baccalà, held for my family. It didn't look very appealing to me, all shriveled and gray-looking, but it seemed to be one of the kingpin fishes for Italian families. Most people don't want to bother with the several soakings of the fish, which plump it up before it is cooked, but if prepared right, baccalà is worthy of praise. You will need to soak the cod for 2 days before making this dish, but then it goes together very quickly.

SERVES 4

1³/4 pounds dried codfish
  Flour for dredging
4 tablespoons butter
2 tablespoons olive oil
1 clove garlic, minced

3 tablespoons minced fresh parsley
  Salt and freshly ground black pepper to taste
  Juice of 1 lemon

Put the cod in a deep dish, add cold water to cover, and let it soak for 2 days in the refrigerator, changing the water several times.

Rinse and dry the fish and cut it into 2-inch chunks. Dredge the fish in the flour, shaking off the excess.

In a large skillet, heat 2 tablespoons of the butter and the olive oil. Add the fish pieces and brown them well on all sides over medium-high heat. Sprinkle the fish with the minced garlic and parsley and stir the mixture gently. Cut the remaining 2 tablespoons butter into bits and add it to the pan. Sprinkle the fish with salt and pepper and pour over the lemon juice. Serve immediately

Ancileddi cu Pumaruoru

FISH WITH TOMATO SAUCE

Here's a very quick recipe that was given to me by my friend Giovanni Iapichino in Palermo, Sicily. He loves it with *tonno*, fresh tuna, which is plentiful in Sicilian waters, but swordfish or halibut can be used.

SERVES 4

2   *pounds tuna steaks, cut ½ inch thick*

2   *tablespoons olive oil*

1   *clove garlic, finely minced*

4   *cups Fresh Tomato Basil Sauce (page 87)*

1   *tablespoon chopped fresh parsley*

Salt and freshly ground black pepper to taste

Preheat the oven to 450°F.

Oil a baking dish large enough to hold the fish steaks and place them in a single layer in the dish. Brush the fish lightly with the olive oil and sprinkle with the garlic. Spoon the tomato sauce over the fish, then sprinkle with the chopped parsley and salt and pepper.

Cover the dish with foil and bake for 20 minutes, or until the fish flakes easily. Serve immediately.

Frutta di Mare con Capperi

SEAFOOD WITH CAPERS

Sometimes I take my inspiration for recipes from places where I have eaten. Once in Riva di Garda I was intrigued with a seafood dish that was pungent with capers. Capers are the tiny unopened flower buds of a bush that grows in the Mediterranean between the crags of mountains and in desert areas. They are preserved in a brine solution or packed in salt. Either way, a jar lasts a long time and just a few added to a dish can make all the difference.

SERVES 4 TO 6

2 tablespoons butter	Salt and freshly ground black pepper to taste
1 large clove garlic, minced	
1 teaspoon crushed red pepper flakes	3 tablespoons capers in brine, drained
1/8 teaspoon white pepper	2 tablespoons chopped fresh parsley
1 pound fresh or canned plum tomatoes, pureed	1 pound sea scallops
2/3 cup heavy cream	1/2 pound skinless salmon fillet, cut into 1-inch pieces
1 tablespoon chopped fresh thyme or 1 teaspoon dried	1 pound fettucine

In a large skillet, melt the butter. Add the garlic and sauté until soft. Add the pepper flakes and white pepper and cook for 1 minute. Add the pureed tomatoes and mix well. Lower the heat to medium low and slowly stir in the cream. Simmer for 6 to 7 minutes to reduce slightly. Add the thyme, salt and black pepper, capers, and parsley, mix well, and set aside.

In a 2-quart saucepan, bring 4 cups of water to a boil. Add the scallops and salmon, reduce the heat, and simmer for 3 minutes, or until the scallops turn milky-white and the salmon is a light pink. Carefully remove the seafood, using a slotted spoon, and add to the sauce.

In a large pot of boiling water, cook the fettucine until *al dente*. Drain well and add to the sauce.

Reheat the mixture over medium-high heat, carefully tossing to mix. Transfer to a serving platter and serve immediately.

Note: I often use fettucine made from Pasta al Pepe Nero (page 50) in this dish.

Calamari al Forno

BAKED SQUID

We always had a meatless meal on Christmas Eve. My mother and grandmother prepared the endless fish dishes that we would eat before going to midnight Mass. There were eels in tomato sauce, fried smelts, sardines in olive oil, deep-fried squid, and baccalà served in a fish stew. I had all I could do to face this meal: The thought of eating squid or eels was worse than almost anything I could imagine. My aversion to squid has passed and I now make stuffed squid on Christmas Eve. The squid body becomes a little pouch for holding a savory filling. For this dish, you want squid that are about 6 to 7 inches long.

SERVES 4

8 medium squid	1/4 cup olive oil
1 1/2 cups fresh bread crumbs	2 cloves garlic, chopped
1/2 cup grated Pecorino Romano cheese	1 medium onion, minced
3 tablespoons chopped fresh parsley	4 cups crushed fresh (about 8 medium tomatoes) or canned plum tomatoes
1 large egg, slightly beaten	1/2 cup dry red wine
Salt and freshly ground black pepper to taste	

Clean the squid as for Frutta di Mare (page 172), but do not slice up the bodies. Chop the tentacles fine.

In a bowl, mix the bread crumbs, cheese, parsley, egg, and salt and pepper. Add the tentacles and mix well. Stuff about 1/4 cup of the mixture into the cavity of each squid. Sew the openings shut with kitchen string or use toothpicks to close them. Set aside.

Preheat the oven to 350°F.

In a large skillet, heat the oil. Add the garlic and onion and sauté until soft. Add the tomatoes and red wine and simmer the sauce, uncovered, for about 15 minutes, or until slightly thickened. Season with salt and pepper.

Spread a thin layer of the sauce over the bottom of a 9- × -12-inch baking dish. Add the squid in a single layer. Pour over enough sauce to almost cover the squid. Cover the dish with foil and bake for 30 to 35 minutes, or until the squid is tender when pierced with a fork. Serve immediately.

Calamari della Mamma

MAMA'S SQUID

This colorful squid dish, served on every Christmas Eve, will always stay etched in my memory. My mother brought it to the table on a huge platter, the steam from the hot spaghetti clouding her like dense fog. All the grown-ups sat ready for this earthy delicacy, while the children squirmed and covered their faces with their hands. How our tastes change.

SERVES 8 TO 10 AS AN APPETIZER

3 pounds squid	1 bunch broccoli
1¼ cups plus 1 tablespoon virgin olive oil	1 pound spaghetti
2 cloves garlic, peeled	⅔ cup grated Pecorino Romano cheese
1½ teaspoons crushed red pepper flakes	Freshly cracked black pepper to taste

Clean the squid and cut it up as directed for Frutta di Mare (page 172). In a large pot of boiling salted water, cook the squid rings until tender, 15 to 20 minutes. About 5 minutes before the rings are cooked, add the diced tentacles. Drain the squid and set aside.

In a frying pan, heat the 1¼ cups oil over medium heat. Add the garlic cloves and cook for 2 to 3 minutes, just to flavor the oil; as soon as the garlic turns golden, remove and discard it. Add the pepper flakes and sauté for 1 minute, being careful not to burn them. Add the cooked squid, remove from the heat, and cover to keep warm.

Cut the woody stems from the broccoli and cut the florets and tender stems into 1-inch pieces. In a large pot of boiling water, cook the broccoli until crisp-tender, about 5 minutes. Scoop the broccoli out of the water with a strainer and add to the cooked squid; cover to keep warm.

Add the spaghetti to the boiling water and boil until *al dente*. Drain the spaghetti, reserving ½ cup of the cooking water. Add the cooking water to the squid and broccoli mixture and reheat over low heat if necessary.

Oil a large platter with the 1 tablespoon olive oil and put the spaghetti on the platter. Pour over the warm squid mixture and toss to mix well. Sprinkle with the cheese and add a good grinding of black pepper. Serve at once.

Cappesante alla Griglia

GRILLED SCALLOPS

Italian *cappesante*, scallops, are very sweet. The best ones I ever had were in landlocked Umbria! I was amazed at the amount of seafood available there. One day, while staying in Perugia, I drove to a nearby fishmarket that had the most beautiful display of succulent-looking scallops, still in their colorful tortoiseshell-patterned shells. I asked one of the fish vendors the secret to cooking scallops: He looked at me amusedly, while he quickly opened a scallop shell, scooped out the pearl-colored scallop, and popped it into his mouth! This recipe for Italian-style scallops grills the scallops first.

SERVES 4 TO 6

1	tablespoon grated lemon zest	1/3	cup fresh basil leaves, torn in pieces
	Juice of 2 medium lemons		Salt and freshly ground black pepper to taste
1/2	cup olive oil		
1	teaspoon minced garlic	2	pounds sea scallops

In a shallow dish large enough to hold the scallops in a single layer, combine all the ingredients, in the order given. Toss the scallops to coat them well with the marinade. Cover the dish and refrigerate for 1 hour.

Heat the grill and brush the rack lightly with oil. Thread 5 or 6 scallops each on individual skewers and place them on the hot grill. Grill, basting occasionally with the marinade and turning the skewers, until just cooked through, about 5 minutes. Serve immediately.

Note: I serve this with Pomodori al Forno (page 186).

Cappesante con Asiago

SCALLOPS WITH ASIAGO CHEESE

I developed this seafood and pasta dish one day when I had Asiago cheese on hand. This cow's milk cheese from northern Italy is available here, but it is not well known. A semihard cheese with a wonderful nutty flavor, it is good as an eating cheese, grated over pasta, or melted in a cream sauce for scallops and fettucine. This delicious dish can be put together very quickly. You can use store-bought fettucine if you wish.

SERVES 4 TO 6

1 1/2 pounds fresh sea scallops

ASIAGO CREAM SAUCE

8   tablespoons (1 stick) unsalted butter

2   cloves garlic, minced

1 1/2 cups heavy cream

3/4 cup grated Asiago cheese

Salt and freshly ground black pepper to taste

1   teaspoon grated nutmeg

1   pound homemade or store-bought fettucine

1/4 cup chopped fresh parsley

In a 2-quart saucepan, bring 4 cups water to a boil. Add the scallops, reduce the heat, and simmer until they turn milky-white, about 3 to 4 minutes. Drain in a colander and set aside.

To make the sauce, in a large frying pan, melt the butter over medium heat. Add the garlic and sauté until soft. Lower the heat and add the cream, Asiago cheese, salt and pepper, and nutmeg. Stir until smooth, set aside, and cover to keep warm.

In a large pot of boiling water, cook the fettucine until *al dente*. Drain well. Add the fettucine and scallops to the warm sauce. Gently stir to mix and coat the fettucine and scallops with the sauce, and reheat over low heat if necessary. Transfer to a serving platter, sprinkle with the parsley, and serve immediately. Delicious!

Variation: Use a combination of fresh shrimp and scallops.

Gamberi alla Griglia

SHRIMP ON THE GRILL

Some of the best fish dishes I have eaten have been in little out-of-the-way places in Italy. Italian cooks understand that simple treatment of fish is best. That is why you often find grilled fish on the menu. In the summer, when I serve shrimp, I often prepare them this popular Italian way, first grilling them and then marinating them.

SERVES 6 AS AN APPETIZER

MARINADE

⅔ cup extra-virgin olive oil

2 cloves garlic, finely minced

3 tablespoons red wine vinegar

2 sprigs fresh rosemary or 1 teaspoon dried

Salt and freshly ground black pepper to taste

1 pound (about 35) medium shrimp, peeled and deveined

In a shallow nonmetal dish, mix all the marinade ingredients. Set aside.

Thread 5 or 6 shrimp each on individual skewers. Set aside.

Heat the grill and brush the grate with a little olive oil. Grill the shrimp until just cooked through, about 5 minutes on each side.

Remove the shrimp from the skewers and add them to the marinade; toss to coat. Cover and refrigerate for several hours, turning them frequently in the marinade.

Let the shrimp come to room temperature, in the marinade, before serving. Serve with some of the marinade poured over them and accompany with crusty Italian bread.

Note: I like to throw a couple of fresh rosemary sprigs on the coals before grilling. They impart a wonderful rosemary-smoked taste to the shrimp.

Gamberi con Salsa d'Arugola

SHRIMP WITH ARUGULA SAUCE

Arugula, also called "rocket," is a member of the chicory family, and its peppery, sharp flavor lends itself to many uses in Italian cooking. I use it sparingly in fresh green salads, but in Italy I had it pureed as a sauce over cooked shrimp. I expected that the flavor would be too strong, but I was pleasantly surprised. It made an interesting color contrast too, the vibrant green sauce against the pink shrimp. I serve this in the summer as an antipasto, but it could also make a nice lunch, accompanied by a good loaf of Italian bread and a dry white wine.

SERVES 8

2 tablespoons white vinegar	2 cups extra-virgin olive oil
2 pounds (about 40) large shrimp in the shell	1 soft-boiled egg, yolk only
1½ cups packed arugula leaves, stems removed, washed, and dried	1 red bell pepper, cored, seeded, and diced
1 teaspoon sea salt	Lemon wedges, optional

In a large pot, bring 6 cups of water to a boil. Add the vinegar and shrimp, cover, and bring back to the boil. Cook until the shrimp shells turn red, about 3 to 4 minutes. Drain the shrimp and let cool. Peel and devein.

Place the arugula and salt in a food processor or blender and pulse to puree. Then, with the motor running, slowly add the olive oil. Add the egg yolk and pulse until smooth.

Arrange 5 or 6 shrimp each on individual salad plates. Drizzle over the sauce and sprinkle the shrimp with the diced red peppers. If you wish, garnish each plate with a lemon wedge, serve with good crusty bread.

Vongole con Vermicelli

CLAMS WITH VERMICELLI

When I was in Venice a few years ago, I got lost in the confusing maze of narrow streets. I happened upon a display of seafood that vendors were arranging for sale. The variety was spectacular: everything from orange-red spiny lobsters to tiny glistening clams. That night my husband and I ate at *La Barcaiola*, where we both ordered little clams, or *vongole*, with vermicelli. They were delicate and sweet. I have substituted littleneck clams in my version of this memorable dish.

SERVES 6

3	dozen littleneck clams in the shell	7	fresh plum tomatoes, peeled, seeded, and diced
¼	cup water		
2	tablespoons chopped fresh parsley	½	cup dry white wine
½	cup olive oil		Salt and freshly ground black pepper to taste
3	cloves garlic, chopped	1	pound vermicelli

Wash the clams well and discard any with cracked shells. Soak the clams in a bowl of cold water for about 45 minutes, changing the water frequently.

Rinse the clams, put them in a large frying pan, and add the ¼ cup water. Cover the pan and cook over medium-high heat until the clams open, about 5 minutes. Remove the clams from the pan, discarding any that have not opened, and strain the cooking liquid into a bowl. Set aside. Remove the clams from their shells and place in a small bowl. Add the chopped parsley and toss to mix.

In a frying pan, heat the olive oil. Add the garlic and sauté until soft. Add the tomatoes and cook for 5 minutes. Add the wine and reserved clam liquid and cook for about 5 minutes, until the sauce has reduced a bit. Add the clams and salt and pepper. Remove from the heat; cover to keep warm.

Meanwhile, in a large pot of boiling water, cook the vermicelli until *al dente*. Drain the vermicelli and place on a large platter. Pour the warm clam sauce over the pasta and toss well. Serve immediately.

Frutta di Mare

SEAFOOD SALAD

Squid are very delicate if prepared right and can be stuffed and baked, fried, or used in combination with other fish for a light marinated fish salad. A successful squid salad depends on two things: the size of the squid (they should be small for this dish) and the cooking time (do not overcook them).

SERVES 8

MARINADE

Juice of 2 to 3 lemons (to taste)

1/2 cup extra-virgin olive oil

3 cloves garlic, peeled and crushed

1/4 cup chopped fresh parsley

1/3 cup chopped fennel leaves

1/2 cup diced red bell pepper

2 tablespoons red wine vinegar

1 teaspoon coarse salt, or to taste

Coarsely ground black pepper to taste

2 pounds small squid

1 teaspoon coarse salt

1/2 pound medium shrimp, peeled and deveined

1 pound bay scallops

In a shallow nonmetal dish, combine all the marinade ingredients. Mix well and set aside.

Remove the head of each squid by pulling it away from the body. Cut off the tentacles below the eyes and discard the heads. Pull out the membranes from the interior cavity of each squid body, and remove the plasticlike spine bone from the inside of the squid. Pull off the tough outer skin. Wash the squid bodies and tentacles thoroughly in cold water. Cut the bodies into 1/4-inch rings and dice the tentacles. Set aside.

In a 2-quart saucepan, bring 4 cups of water to a boil. Add the coarse salt and shrimp, and boil until the shrimp turn pink, about 3 minutes. With a slotted spoon, remove the shrimp and let cool. Add the scallops to the boiling water and boil for 3 minutes. Remove the scallops with a slotted spoon and let cool. Add the squid rings to the boiling water and boil until tender, about 15 to 20 minutes. About 5 minutes before the rings are cooked, add the diced tentacles. The squid should be firm but not chewy; drain well.

Add the squid, shrimp, and scallops to the marinade and toss well. Adjust the seasoning if necessary. Cover and let marinate for to 2 to 3 hours in the refrigerator, turning the mixture frequently.

Transfer the salad to a serving platter and let come to room temperature before serving.

Verdure

VEGETABLES

IF SOMEONE asked me what is the singular outstanding characteristic of Italian food, I would have to say freshness. Nowhere is this more apparent to me than in Italy's local street markets and home gardens, where the variety, color, and porcelainlike luster of its vegetables seem to be the work of an artist's palette.

Since ancient times, vegetables have played a major role in the Italian diet. Centuries ago, leeks, fennel, and broccoli were even revered for their healing abilities.

Vegetables are always in season somewhere in Italy. The tender spring peas of the Veneto are essential to the classic *risi e bisi,* rice and peas. The wonderful, almost sculpted-looking artichokes of Umbria, available from May to November, are tender enough to eat raw. In the summer, the noble eggplant and ruby red tomatoes of Campania show their inexhaustible versatility.

When I travel through the countryside of Italy, I marvel at not only the amount of commercial farmland under cultivation, but also the endless number of little home gardens with vegetables and fruits growing in front as well as back yards; some are tucked beside railroad tracks, others ring the *autostrada,* and still others are hedged next to bridges and factories. Land is precious in Italy and every inch that can be cultivated is coveted.

Vegetables are treated and cooked in as many ways as there are regions of Italy: raw for salads, and boiled, baked, fried, stuffed, grilled, or sautéed. No matter how they are prepared, they are never overdone. Italian cooks retain all the vibrancy of vegetables, the texture, color, and taste. Many vegetables are cooked *al dente,* like pasta. This is especially true of green beans, broccoli, and cauliflower.

In many regions of Italy, vegetables are either boiled or steamed and then served with a simple dressing of olive oil or lemon juice. Some regions serve cooked vegetables at room temperature, rather than hot. On the way to Viterbo, I stopped at a small bar for lunch and ordered a plump and juicy *pomodoro al forno,* a baked tomato stuffed with rice and basil. It was served cold, and it was delicious. In Torgiano, at ristorante Tre Vaselle, the chef had a particular fondness for cooked spinach, shredded and served at room temperature with a dressing of olive oil. In Perugia, wild thistles, or cardoons, are dipped in a batter and then fried.

The variety of Italian vegetables is vast, but the rules for cooking them are few: Use what is in season and keep the treatment simple.

Cavolfiore Fritto

FRIED CAULIFLOWER

The fried cauliflower dish that we always had on Christmas Eve was probably my favorite vegetable. A big platter of snowy white florets, nestled under a generous coat of freshly toasted bread crumbs, was a specialty of the house.

SERVES 4 TO 6

1 head cauliflower	¼ to ½ cup olive oil
Flour for dredging	Salt and freshly ground black
2 large eggs	pepper to taste
1½ cups toasted fresh bread crumbs	

Remove the outer leaves and core of the cauliflower. Cut the head into florets, leaving the stems about 1 inch long. Wash the cauliflower well in cold water. In a large pot of well-salted boiling water, cook the cauliflower until *al dente*, about 5 minutes. Drain, let cool, and then pat dry with a towel.

Spread the flour on a plate. Break the eggs into a shallow bowl and mix well with a fork. Spread the bread crumbs on another plate. Dredge the florets in the flour, shaking off the excess. Dip in the beaten eggs and then the bread crumbs to coat. Set the florets on a plate to dry slightly and to set the bread crumbs.

In a large skillet, heat ¼ cup of the olive oil. Sauté the cauliflower florets a few at a time, turning occasionally, until the bread crumbs are browned; add additional oil as needed. Drain the cauliflower on brown paper. Arrange the florets on a serving platter, sprinkle with salt and pepper, and serve immediately.

Broccoli Casalinghi

HOMESTYLE BROCCOLI

Broccoli is one of those vegetables with a negative image. We had it many ways when I was a kid, and I admit it was not my favorite. Many people think that steamed or boiled broccoli is just bland; I agree. I cook it the way it was done at home, in a frying pan with olive oil, garlic, and very little water. The result is tender broccoli, still verdant green and very tasty.

SERVES 4 TO 6

1   bunch broccoli

¼   cup olive oil

2   cloves garlic, chopped

1½ teaspoons crushed red pepper flakes

Salt and freshly ground black pepper to taste

¼   cup grated Pecorino Romano cheese

Trim off the thick woody stems from the broccoli and cut the broccoli into 1½-inch florets, separating the florets. Set aside.

In a large skillet, heat the olive oil over medium heat. Add the garlic and sauté until the garlic begins to soften. Add the pepper flakes and cook for 1 minute. Add the broccoli and stir to coat with the oil. Cook for 2 minutes, stirring, then reduce the heat to medium low, cover, and cook for 3 minutes, stirring occasionally.

Add ¼ cup of water to the pan, cover, and cook until the broccoli is crisp-tender, about 6 minutes; add additional water if needed to keep the broccoli from burning.

Transfer the broccoli to a serving dish and sprinkle with salt and pepper and the cheese. Serve immediately.

Note: I always add a little olive oil to vegetables that are boiled be-cause it helps to retain their color. In this dish, the broccoli remains vibrant because of the olive oil. At home, bread crumbs fried in olive oil were sometimes sprinkled over the broccoli.

Carciofi con Fettucine e Menta

ARTICHOKES WITH FETTUCINE AND MINT

Italian artichokes are much smaller than our globe artichoke. At home, artichokes were marinated in olive oil and vinegar and served as an antipasto, or they were boiled, stuffed, and baked. Grandma Galasso liked to make them the Roman way, stuffed with lots of garlic and mint. I go a little further and add fettucine.

SERVES 6

6   medium artichokes
    Juice of 1 large lemon
½   cup olive oil
½   pound fettucine
4   cloves garlic, finely minced

¾   cup grated Pecorino Romano cheese
¼   cup minced fresh mint
    Coarsely ground black pepper

Roll the artichokes back and forth across a countertop to loosen the leaves a bit. Cut the stems off the bottoms and remove the tough outer leaves. Cut off about ¼ inch of the tops. Spread the center leaves of each artichoke to expose the fuzzy interior choke and remove the fuzzy choke; I use a small melon baller for this. Rinse the artichokes well.

Place the artichokes upright in a pot just large enough to hold them and add water to cover them by 1 inch. Add the lemon juice and 1 tablespoon of the olive oil. Cover and bring to a boil. Reduce the heat to medium and boil gently for 30 to 35 minutes, or until you can easily pull a leaf from one of the artichokes. Drain them immediately and refresh under cold water. Place them upside down on a towel.

Meanwhile, in a large pot of boiling water, cook the fettucine until *al dente;* drain well and toss with 1 tablespoon of the olive oil.

Preheat the oven to 350°F.

In a skillet, heat ¼ cup of the olive oil. Add the garlic and sauté until soft. Add the fettucine and cook, stirring, over medium-high heat for 2 to 3 minutes. Remove from the heat and stir in the Pecorino Romano cheese and mint.

Place the artichokes upright in an oiled baking dish. Divide the fettucine mixture evenly among the artichokes, filling the center cavity of each one to the top. Give each artichoke a grinding of black pepper and drizzle the remaining 2 tablespoons olive oil over the tops.

Cover the dish tightly with foil and bake until heated through, about 20 minutes. Serve at once.

Cavolo Ripieno di Carne

STUFFED CABBAGE

Cabbage was another one of those dreaded vegetables that we children seemed to get plenty of. My mother made stuffed cabbage, boiled cabbage, baked cabbage, and a meatball and cabbage soup. For stuffed cabbage, she carefully parboiled the cabbage first, just to loosen the leaves from the core. This made the leaves pliable and easy to roll.

SERVES 6

1 head green cabbage	1 tablespoon fresh rosemary or 1 teaspoon crushed dried
2 slices stale Italian bread, cut into chunks	
	¼ cup chopped fresh parsley
½ cup Homemade Beef Broth (page 32) or water	Salt and freshly ground black pepper to taste
8 tablespoons (1 stick) butter	¼ teaspoon allspice
¼ cup minced onion	½ teaspoon cinnamon
1½ pounds ground veal or beef or a combination	

In a large pot of boiling salted water, parboil the cabbage for about 8 minutes, or until the leaves are wilted. Drain and let cool.

Meanwhile, soak the bread in the beef broth or water for 2 to 3 minutes, or until softened. Squeeze dry with your hands and set aside.

In a heavy skillet, melt 4 tablespoons of the butter and sauté the onion very slowly over low heat until deep brown and almost caramelized. Remove the onion to a large bowl. Add the ground meat to the skillet and brown over medium-high heat. Add the meat to the onion, along with the herbs, spices, and bread. Mix well with your hands, but do not overmix.

Using about 3 tablespoons of the meat mixture, form an elongated roll about 3 inches long. Set on a plate and continue to form rolls with the remaining meat mixture. Set aside.

Preheat the oven to 350°F.

Remove the core from the cabbage with a knife and carefully peel off the leaves, one at a time, keeping them whole if possible.

Place a meat roll on the bottom of a cabbage leaf, fold over the sides, and roll up like an egg roll; secure with toothpicks. Repeat with the remaining meat rolls. Place the cabbage rolls seam side down in a baking dish in a single layer. Melt the remaining 4 tablespoons butter and pour over the cabbage rolls. Add ½ cup water. Cover the casserole with foil and bake for 45 minutes. Serve immediately.

Note: These were always served with boiled potatoes. They can be frozen for future use after baking, or they can be baked a day ahead and reheated.

Melanzane alla Griglia

GRILLED EGGPLANT

The Umbrians are fond of grilling fresh vegetables. When I was in cooking school in Perugia, Chef Mario Ragni showed us how to prepare eggplant on the grill. At first I was skeptical because eggplant by itself is rather dull. It was what Chef Mario did after he grilled the eggplant that gave it new life. Make the marinade and slice the eggplant several hours before you are ready to grill.

SERVES 4 TO 6

3 *cloves garlic, peeled and crushed*	*Salt and freshly ground black pepper to taste*
¾ *cup finely minced fresh parsley*	
½ *cup extra-virgin olive oil*	2 *medium eggplants*

In a bowl, mix the garlic with the parsley and slowly whisk in the olive oil. Season with salt and pepper and let sit at room temperature for several hours.

Trim the eggplant and slice lengthwise into ¼-inch slices. Salt each slice and place in a colander set in a bowl. Fill another bowl with water and set it on top of the eggplant to act as a weight. Let stand for 2 to 3 hours, to remove excess moisture from the eggplant.

Heat the grill. Wipe the eggplant slices dry with paper towels. Oil the grill rack and place the eggplant slices on the grill. Grill until browned and soft, about 5 minutes on each side.

Arrange the eggplant in a shallow serving dish and pour the olive oil mixture over it. Serve at room temperature.

Note: For a different presentation, cut Tuscan bread (page 106) or other good hearty bread into large chunks and toast for a few minutes on the grill. Serve the eggplant on top of the bread with some of the dressing spooned over.

Timballo di Melanzane e Bucatini

MOLDED EGGPLANT AND BUCATINI CASSEROLE

The rich volcanic soil and the warm climate of the Campania region in southern Italy produces some wonderful vegetables, especially eggplant and tomatoes. Herbs, such as basil, grow thick and lush, their addicting smell wafting gently over the farmlands. Southern Italians use more vegetables and herbs than meat in their diet, and they prepare them in many interesting ways, like this *timballo* (drum) of eggplant. Essentially a high-class casserole, it is actually based on an idea borrowed from the Renaissance, when a law was passed forbidding the serving of more than three courses at a meal. By combining several courses in one, the clever cooks of the Renaissance created the timballo. You can prepare this recipe in steps, making the sauce and meatballs on one day and forming the timballo the next. (Bucatini is a thick tubular spaghetti.)

SERVES 10 TO 12

3	large eggplants (at least 11 inches long)		Salt and freshly ground black pepper to taste
	Salt		
½	cup toasted fresh bread crumbs	2	cups bucatini broken into thirds
		1	pound ground veal
	SAUCE	1	large egg, beaten
2	tablespoons olive oil	2	tablespoons dry white wine
¼	cup finely chopped onion	2	tablespoons plus ¼ cup grated Pecorino Romano cheese
1	rib celery, finely chopped		
1	large carrot, finely chopped	½	cup toasted fresh bread crumbs
2	cloves garlic, minced	1	teaspoon salt
5	cups chopped fresh or canned plum tomatoes (about 10 medium tomatoes)	2	tablespoons butter
		1½	cups cubed mozzarella cheese (about 6 ounces)
¼	cup dry red wine	¼	cup chopped fresh parsley
1	bay leaf		Peanut oil for frying

Cut off the stems of the eggplants and cut the eggplants lengthwise into ¼-inch-thick slices. Layer the slices in a colander set in a bowl, salting each layer. Put a large bowl of water on top of the eggplant to act as a weight. Let sit for at least 1 hour to remove the excess water from the eggplant.

Generously butter a 3½-inch-deep 9-inch round mold or cake pan and thoroughly coat the inside with the toasted bread crumbs. Shake out the excess crumbs. Refrigerate the mold until needed.

To make the sauce, in a large saucepan, heat the olive oil. Add the onion, celery, and carrot and sauté until soft. Add the garlic and sauté until soft. Add the tomatoes, red wine, and bay leaf, stir well, and bring to a simmer. Cover, reduce the heat, and simmer gently for 30 minutes. Season with salt and pepper and set aside.

In a large pot of boiling water, cook the bucatini until *al dente*. Drain and set aside.

In a bowl, combine the veal, beaten egg, white wine, the 2 tablespoons grated cheese, the bread crumbs, and salt. Mix well. With your hands, form the mixture into small meatballs the size of large grapes.

In a frying pan, heat the butter and fry the meatballs until browned. Transfer the meatballs to a large bowl and add the bucatini, mozzarella cheese, and parsley. Add 2 cups of the tomato sauce, mix well, and set aside.

Wipe the eggplant slices free of salt. In a large frying pan, heat ½ cup of the peanut oil. Fry the eggplant slices a few at a time, adding more oil as necessary, until slightly softened, about 2 minutes on each side. Drain them on brown paper.

Preheat the oven to 325°F.

Line the prepared mold with slices of eggplant, draping the slices lengthwise over the bottom and up the sides of the mold. Overlap the slices a little and make sure that the eggplant completely covers the bottom of the mold; it should overhang the outside of the mold by at least 3 inches. Carefully add the meatball and bucatini mixture to the mold, packing it in and smoothing the top. Turn the overhanging edges of the eggplant over the top of the mold; the meatball mixture should be completely covered by the eggplant.

Spread ½ cup of the tomato sauce over the top of the mold and sprinkle with the ¼ cup grated cheese. Bake, uncovered, for 30 minutes. Remove the mold from the oven and let it cool slightly.

In a small pan, heat the remaining tomato sauce. Run a knife around the edges of the mold to loosen it and then invert the mold carefully onto a serving dish. Cut the mold into wedges and serve with the warm sauce.

Note: This impressive "casserole" requires only a salad and crusty bread to make a meal.

Finocchio con Prosciutto

FENNEL AND PROSCIUTTO

Fennel is not a familiar vegetable in this country. Every time it appears towering over everything else in my grocery cart, I am asked, "What is that?" But Italians are well acquainted with this ancient vegetable, *finocchio*, which is a member of the celery family. The feathery leaves are eaten in salads and cooked in soup. The bulbous white part is eaten raw or braised. Fennel has a pronounced taste of licorice—and you either love it or hate it.

SERVES 4

1 medium bulb fennel	Freshly ground black pepper to taste
Salt	
1 tablespoon olive oil	4 slices prosciutto
1 tablespoon butter	6 dried tomatoes packed in olive oil, homemade (page 218) or store-bought, chopped
2 cloves garlic, chopped	
¼ cup diced white onion	¼ cup dry white wine
	Grated Parmigiano-Reggiano cheese

Remove the feathery tops of the fennel and set aside. Cut off the long stalks and save for another use, such as soup. Remove the tough outer layer of the fennel bulb if necessary and trim the core. Cut the bulb into quarters.

In a large pot, bring 2 quarts of water to a boil. Add 2 teaspoons salt, the fennel quarters, and reserved fennel tops, cover, and boil until a knife easily pierces the fennel quarters. Do not overcook; they should hold their shape. Drain, and discard the fennel tops.

Preheat the oven to 350°F.

In an ovenproof frying pan, heat the olive oil and butter. Add the garlic and sauté until soft. Remove and discard the garlic and add the onion to the pan. Sauté until soft and add the fennel quarters. Sprinkle with salt and pepper, cover, and cook for 3 minutes. Remove the fennel to a dish to cool; set the frying pan aside.

Wrap each fennel quarter in a slice of prosciutto. Return the fennel quarters to the ovenproof frying pan. Sprinkle the dried tomatoes over the fennel quarters. Add the wine. Cover the pan with foil and bake for 20 minutes, or until heated through. Serve immediately, and pass grated Parmigiano-Reggiano cheese at the table to sprinkle over the top.

Note: This recipe can easily be doubled. It also can be baked a day ahead and reheated.

Finocchio e Fichi Secchi al Forno

BAKED FENNEL AND FIGS

I made this recipe for very important dinner guests who are in the flour business. I know the old rule about not trying anything new on guests, but I decided to be daring and came up with a new way to treat fennel. I must say I did worry a bit, but everyone loved it. The fennel and fig flavors are a natural for one another. You can put the whole dish together a day ahead and it will wait happily in the refrigerator until baking time.

SERVES 8

2	large bulbs fennel	1	cup dried figlets, coarsely chopped
4	tablespoons butter	¼	cup pine nuts
½	cup finely minced white onion		Salt and freshly ground black pepper to taste
1	cup dried figs, coarsely chopped		

Trim the feathery leaves and the stalks from the fennel. Remove any tough outer layers from the bulbs and discard. Put the fennel in a large pot, add water to cover, and bring to a boil. Reduce the heat and simmer gently for 30 minutes, or until a knife easily pierces the fennel. Drain the bulbs upside down in a colander.

Preheat the oven to 350°F.

In a large skillet, melt 2 tablespoons of the butter. Add the onion and sauté for 5 minutes, or until very soft. Add the figs, figlets, pine nuts, and salt and pepper. Cook for 5 minutes. Remove from the heat and set aside.

Cut the cooled fennel bulbs lengthwise into quarters. Carefully remove and discard the tough inner cores. Place the fennel wedges in a buttered baking dish and fill the fennel cavities with the fig mixture.

Melt the remaining 2 tablespoons butter and drizzle over the fennel. Cover the dish with foil and bake for 20 minutes, or until heated through. Serve immediately.

Note: Serve this as the vegetable accompaniment to Vitello alla Marsala (page 143).

Peperoni al Forno

BAKED PEPPERS

Colorful sweet peppers abound in Italian markets and they are inexpensive. Peppers are prepared in numerous ways: marinated for antipasti, stuffed and baked, made into filling for pasta, pureed for sauces, and sliced raw for salads. I love to make stuffed sweet red peppers the Neapolitan way. Make this in the summer when red peppers are less expensive.

SERVES 8

8 large red bell peppers	¼ to ½ cup plus 2 tablespoons olive oil
¼ to ½ cup peanut oil	10 ½-inch slices Italian bread
2 small eggplants, peeled and diced	1 cup diced mozzarella cheese (about ¼ pound)
½ cup finely chopped pitted Gaeta olives	6 fresh plum tomatoes, chopped
1 tablespoon capers, rinsed and drained	1 cup toasted fresh bread crumbs
¼ cup finely chopped fresh basil	½ cup grated Parmigiano-Reggiano cheese

Place the peppers on an oiled grill or broiler pan and grill or broil them, turning them occasionally, until they are blackened all over. Place them in a paper bag, close the bag, and let them cool. Peel off the skins. Remove the core, cut down one side of each pepper, and open them out flat. Carefully remove the seeds and set the peppers aside.

In a skillet, heat ¼ cup of the peanut oil and fry the eggplant in batches, until browned, adding more oil as necessary. Remove the eggplant to a large bowl. Add the olives, capers, and basil, and mix well.

Wipe out the skillet and add ¼ cup of the olive oil. Heat the oil and fry the bread slices a few at a time, adding more oil as necessary, until browned on both sides. Drain on brown paper. Tear the bread into small chunks and add to the eggplant mixture. Add the cheese and plum tomatoes, and mix well.

Preheat the oven to 350°F. Combine the bread crumbs and Parmigiano-Reggiano.

Place about ½ cup of the eggplant mixture on one end of each pepper and roll each pepper up like a jelly roll. Place the peppers in an oiled baking dish and drizzle them with the 2 tablespoons olive oil. Sprinkle the bread crumb mixture over the top. Bake for 15 minutes or until heated through. Serve immediately.

Peperoni e Porcini

PEPPERS AND PORCINI

Porcini are those wonderful Italian mushrooms with the woodsy flavor. Some of them grow to enormous size, and they are excellent grilled over a wood fire. Unfortunately, they have limited availability when fresh and are generally prohibitive in price. Fresh shiitake mushrooms can be substituted, but to me, the flavor pales in comparison. I use dried porcini, which are still costly, but a little goes a long way. Dried porcini tend to be very sandy, so be sure to soak them well and strain the soaking water several times before using it in cooking.

SERVES 4

½ cup dried porcini mushrooms
   (about ½ ounce)

2 tablespoons olive oil

1 tablespoon chopped garlic

1 cup thinly sliced red bell peppers

1 cup thinly sliced yellow bell peppers

1 cup thinly sliced fennel bulb

Salt and freshly ground black
   pepper to taste

Put the porcini in a bowl and add just enough water to cover them. Set aside to soak until they are soft, about 30 minutes.

Drain the porcini in a strainer lined with cheesecloth set over a bowl. Reserve ¼ cup of the porcini water. Dice the porcini.

In a large skillet, heat the olive oil and sauté the garlic until soft. Add the sliced peppers and fennel and sauté for 5 minutes. Add the porcini and reserved porcini soaking water, cover the skillet, and simmer for 5 minutes. Season with salt and pepper and serve immediately.

Pomodori al Forno

OVEN-BAKED TOMATOES

In late summer, when I am inundated with plum tomatoes, I make this stuffed tomato dish, which was frequently on the dinner table at home. Use plump, fully ripe tomatoes. The stuffing can vary according to the whim of the cook, but I think the added touch of anchovy is very nice.

SERVES 6

6	medium fresh plum tomatoes	1½	teaspoons anchovy paste
1	cup chopped cooked broccoli	½	cup toasted fresh bread crumbs
¾	cup diced Provolone cheese (about 3 ounces)	2	teaspoons minced fresh parsley
2	tablespoons olive oil		Freshly ground black pepper to taste
1	teaspoon minced garlic		

Core the tomatoes and cut them in half lengthwise. Gently squeeze out some of the juice and pulp. (Reserve for another use such as stock, or discard.) Trim a small piece off the bottom of each tomato so it will sit without tilting. Place the cut halves in a buttered baking dish large enough to hold them in a single layer. Set aside.

Preheat the oven to 350°F.

In a bowl, combine the broccoli and cheese. Set aside.

In a frying pan, heat the olive oil. Add the garlic and sauté until soft. Stir in the anchovy paste, add the bread crumbs, and mix well. Add the bread crumb mixture to the broccoli and cheese. Add the parsley and pepper and mix well.

Divide the broccoli mixture evenly among the tomato halves. Bake the tomatoes until the cheese is bubbly and the crumbs are beginning to brown, about 25 minutes. Serve immediately.

Torta di Pomodori Secchi

DRIED TOMATO TART

My Grandmother Saporito always used plum tomatoes in her cooking. Roma is a variety of plum tomato that is meaty and has far fewer seeds than other types. I did my fair share of scalding and skinning these tomatoes for sauce, which we then canned for the long winter months ahead. As for me, well, I make sauce with fresh Roma tomatoes, but I don't can them . . . I dry them to use in many other ways. I use a dehydrator and then pack the tomatoes in olive oil. Or I freeze them to use on pizza, in soups, and appetizers, and in this scrumptious tart. The minced basil in the tart shell dough is refreshing.

SERVES 8

PASTRY

2   cups unbleached all-purpose flour

¼   teaspoon salt

8   tablespoons (1 stick) butter, chilled and cut into small pieces

¼   cup finely minced fresh basil

2   large eggs, beaten

¼   cup sesame seeds

4   large eggs

¼   cup finely diced mozzarella cheese

¼   cup finely diced Provolone cheese

1   cup ricotta cheese, well drained

1   cup heavy cream

1   cup dried tomatoes packed in oil, homemade (page 218) or store-bought, drained and diced

In a bowl, mix the flour and salt together. Cut in the butter with a fork or use your hands until the mixture is coarse. Add the basil and mix to blend.

Beat the 2 large eggs in a bowl with a fork, add to the flour mixture, and mix until a ball of dough is formed. Wrap the dough in wax paper and chill it at least 1 hour.

Preheat the oven to 350°F.

Spread the sesame seeds in a small baking dish and toast them in the oven until lightly browned, about 5 minutes. Remove from the oven and let cool. Turn the oven temperature up to 400°F.

Roll out the dough on a floured surface to fit a 10-inch tart pan. Pat the dough into the pan, cover, and refrigerate while you make the filling.

In a large bowl, beat the 4 large eggs well with a whisk. Add the cheeses and stir to mix well. Add the heavy cream and dried tomatoes; mix well. Pour the mixture into the prepared crust and bake for 35 to 40 minutes, or until a knife inserted in the center comes out clean. Five minutes before the tart is done, sprinkle the sesame seeds over the top.

Let the tart cool on a wire rack for about 10 minutes before cutting into wedges. Serve warm.

Zucchini con Anice

LITTLE SQUASH WITH ANISE

For some reason still unexplained, the Italians have always had a love affair with zucchini—maybe because it just won't quit growing once it's planted. I remember club-size zucchini harvested in old bushel baskets and then carefully brought to the kitchen sink, where the forest green skin was washed and dried until it shined. From there they were given full treatment: pickled, canned, fried, stuffed, boiled, sautéed, or pureed. By the end of the summer, I longed for the first frost to kill off this prolific plant, and when it finally did, I smiled—but only until the canned version surfaced from the root cellar in the dead of November. Over the years, I've refined my taste for zucchini. The following recipe is a creation I came up with when I was faced with what to do with my own abundance of zucchini.

SERVES 4

2 tablespoons olive oil

2 cloves garlic, finely minced

1 teaspoon crushed red pepper flakes

2 medium zucchini, cut in 2-inch-long matchsticks

1 teaspoon anise seeds

3 tablespoons minced fresh summer savory or thyme

1 tablespoon minced fresh basil

Salt and freshly ground black pepper to taste

1/4 cup grated Pecorino Romano cheese

In a large frying pan, heat the olive oil. Add the garlic and sauté until soft but not browned. Add the red pepper flakes and zucchini and stir well. Cover and simmer over low heat for 10 minutes, stirring occasionally. Sprinkle over the anise seeds and cook for 1 minute. Remove from the heat and add the summer savory or thyme, basil, and salt and pepper. Toss well.

Transfer the zucchini to a serving dish and sprinkle with the cheese. Serve immediately.

Sformato di Spinaci

MOLDED SPINACH SOUFFLÉ

The Italians have their own version of a soufflé. In contrast to the French soufflé, the Italian *sformato* has fewer eggs and therefore does not rise to impressive heights. I particularly like the molded spinach soufflé that is a specialty of Umbria. It is dense with spinach and topped with tomato sauce.

SERVES 6 TO 8

3¼ pounds (or 5 10-ounce packages) fresh spinach	¾ cup grated Parmigiano-Reggiano cheese
5 tablespoons butter	2 eggs, separated, at room temperature
1½ cups Fresh Tomato Basil Sauce (page 87)	¼ cup heavy cream
¼ cup toasted fresh bread crumbs	1½ teaspoons grated nutmeg

Stem and wash the spinach. Put it in a large pot and cook, without adding any water, until it is wilted, about 5 minutes. Drain the spinach and squeeze out as much excess liquid as possible. (You should have about 5 cups of cooked spinach.)

In a saucepan, melt 4 tablespoons of the butter over medium-high heat. Add the spinach and ½ cup of the tomato sauce and cook, stirring, until very thick, about 5 to 6 minutes. Set aside.

Preheat the oven to 325°F.

Mix the bread crumbs and ¼ cup of the Parmigiano-Reggiano cheese together. Grease a 6-cup mold with the remaining 1 tablespoon butter and thoroughly coat the inside of the mold with the breadcrumb-cheese mixture. Refrigerate the mold until ready to use.

In a bowl, beat together the egg yolks and heavy cream. Add the spinach mixture and ¼ cup of the cheese. Mix well.

In another bowl, beat the egg whites until they hold stiff peaks. Fold them into the spinach mixture with a spatula. Pour the mixture into the prepared mold and sprinkle the top with the remaining ¼ cup cheese. Tap the mold gently on the countertop to settle the ingredients. Bake for 35 to 40 minutes, or until a skewer inserted in the center comes out clean. Let cool.

In a small pan, heat the remaining 1 cup tomato sauce. Run a knife around the sides of the mold and invert it onto a serving dish. Cut the *sformato* into slices and serve with the warm sauce on the side.

Patate della Nonna

GRANDMA'S POTATOES

Grandma Galasso could cook anything . . . but there were no written recipes, just her make-do attitude that came out of her recollections of a hard life in Avellino, Italy. I suppose that's why most of her cooking was a collage of what was already in the pantry or refrigerator. One of my favorite memories is the way she could take leftover mashed potatoes and turn them into a meal. The fillings for this dish usually varied, from bits of ham and cheese to leftover spinach and carrots. Use your imagination!

SERVES 6 TO 8

4 large eggs

4 cups mashed potatoes

2 tablespoons butter, softened

¼ cup grated Pecorino Romano cheese

2 tablespoons minced fresh parsley

1 cup cooked spinach or broccoli, well drained and chopped

½ cup diced ham

½ teaspoon grated nutmeg

Flour for dreding

2 cups toasted fresh bread crumbs

Vegetable oil for deep-frying

In a large bowl, beat 2 of the eggs. Add the mashed potatoes, butter, cheese, and parsley and mix well. Set aside.

In a bowl, mix the spinach or broccoli with the ham and season with the nutmeg. Set aside.

Flour a work surface and, with floured hands, roll quarter cupfuls of the potato mixture into balls. Make a small trench in the center of each ball and insert about 1½ tablespoons of the spinach or broccoli mixture. Reshape and smooth the potato ball so that the filling is enclosed.

In a shallow dish, beat the remaining 2 eggs with a fork. Spread the bread crumbs on a plate. Roll each potato ball in the flour, dip in beaten eggs, and roll in the bread crumbs. Set on a plate to dry slightly.

In a deep fryer or deep heavy pan, heat the vegetable oil to 375°F. Fry the balls in batches until they are browned on all sides. Drain on brown paper. Serve at once.

Note: Sometimes my grandmother formed the potatoes into cylinders. At holiday time they were shaped into "oranges" or "pears," with a piece of cinnamon stick at the top for a stem.

Patate e Porri al Forno

BAKED POTATOES AND LEEKS

Leeks, or *porri*, have been part of the Italian diet since ancient times. Many old cooking manuscripts are full of recipes for leeks. I like to combine them with potatoes for an interesting side dish that can be served with any kind of roasted meat or chicken. Make sure to wash the leeks several times before cooking to remove the stubborn dirt.

SERVES 6 TO 8

¹/₂ cup toasted fresh bread crumbs	¹/₄ pound prosciutto, diced
4 large baking potatoes	8 tablespoons (1 stick) butter, cut in small pieces
2 medium leeks, white part only, washed and sliced paper-thin	Salt and freshly ground black pepper to taste

Preheat the oven to 350°F. Butter a 9-inch round baking dish or springform pan and coat the inside of the pan with the bread crumbs.

Peel the potatoes and cut them into thin rounds.

Arrange a layer of potatoes in the bottom of the buttered dish, overlapping the slices. Sprinkle over some of the leeks, prosciutto, butter, and salt and pepper. Make another layer of potatoes and continue layering until you reach the top of the dish. Finish with a layer of potatoes. Dot the potatoes with butter and sprinkle with salt and pepper. Cover the pan tightly with foil and bake for 1 hour, or until the potatoes are fork-tender.

Serve directly from the baking dish or, if using a springform pan, remove the sides and invert the potatoes onto a serving dish.

Patate Paesane

COUNTRY POTATOES

We always had Italian-style potato dishes at home but little did I realize then that Italian cooking did not embrace the potato until well into the nineteenth century. Like tomatoes, potatoes were brought to Europe from the New World, and like tomatoes, they were regarded as poisonous by the Europeans. Historically, the potato has been poor man's food but Italian cooks have made potatoes fashionable and they are cooked in a myriad of ways, especially in southern Italy. I had this country potato dish in Sorrento.

SERVES 6

4 large baking potatoes, peeled and thinly sliced

1 large red onion, thinly sliced

1 teaspoon salt

2 cloves garlic, minced

1 tablespoon chopped hot Italian green pepper

¼ cup chopped fresh parsley

1 teaspoon dried oregano

1 cup diced fresh or canned plum tomatoes (about 2 medium tomatoes)

½ cup olive oil

Preheat the oven to 350°F.

Generously grease a 9-×-12-inch baking dish with olive oil.

Toss the potatoes and onions together, sprinkle with the salt, and put them in the prepared dish. Combine all the remaining ingredients and pour over the potatoes and onions. Cover the dish with foil and bake for 15 minutes. Remove the foil and bake for 25 minutes longer, or until the potatoes are tender. Serve immediately.

Fiori di Zucca Ripieni

STUFFED SQUASH BLOSSOMS

Nobody hated *zagoots*, zucchini, more than I did when I was a kid. *Zagoots* was a dialect word for zucchini, and Grandma Galasso made sure we ate not only zucchini but its flower blossoms as well! Every summer we could count on this showing up on the table, because Grandma always picked the male blossoms of the zucchini plant, which would not bear fruit. You can buy the blossoms in the market. Or use hollowed-out zucchini and fill it with this stuffing.

SERVES 4

8	*zucchini blossoms*	2	*cups diced zucchini*
1	*tablespoon butter*	1	*large egg, beaten*
	¼ *cup toasted fresh bread crumbs*		¼ *cup toasted fresh bread crumbs*
			½ *cup diced Provolone cheese (about 2 ounces)*
	STUFFING		
2	*tablespoons olive oil*		
2	*teaspoons minced garlic*	8	*tablespoons (1 stick) butter, melted*
	¼ *cup diced red onion*		

Open up each zucchini blossom and carefully remove the stamens and pistils. Rinse very gently in cold water, drain, and set aside.

In a frying pan, melt the 1 tablespoon butter and fry the bread crumbs until golden brown. Set aside.

To make the stuffing, in a large frying pan, heat the olive oil. Add the garlic and sauté until soft. Add the onion and zucchini and sauté until barely tender, about 3 minutes. Remove the mixture to a bowl, add the remaining stuffing ingredients, and mix well.

Preheat the oven to 350°F.

Fill the cavity of each zucchini blossom with about 3 tablespoons of the stuffing mixture. Fold the tips of the blossom over and secure them with a toothpick. Place the blossoms in a buttered baking dish, and drizzle them with the melted butter. Cover the dish with foil and bake for 15 minutes. Remove the foil, sprinkle over the buttered crumbs, and bake for 5 minutes more. Serve immediately.

Note: This is a wonderful and colorful dish to serve with Pollo con Vino alla Pierrette (page 150).

Piccoli Zucchini Ripieni

SMALL STUFFED SQUASH

My husband, Guy, has always liked to grow vegetables and flowers. Every year in early January, colorful seed catalogues from all over the fifty states are strewn across the kitchen table and the delicate process of planning the garden begins. We always lean toward a mostly Italian-style garden, some of the seeds even coming from Italy. One year we planted a non-Italian variety of squash called Jersey Golden. They are like little golden pumpkins and are perfect for stuffing. Small zucchini can also be used in this recipe.

SERVES 6

6 *small Jersey Golden squash (about the size of small oranges) or 2 zucchini, about 10 inches long*

4 *tablespoons butter*

1 *cup toasted fresh bread crumbs*

2 *tablespoons minced fresh thyme*

Salt and freshly ground black pepper to taste

Preheat the oven to 350°F. Grease a baking dish.

If using the Jersey Golden squash, cut off the tops; if using zucchini, cut them into 3-inch lengths. Gently scoop out the insides of each squash, making sure to leave a shell about ¼ inch thick; reserve 1½ cups of the pulp. If using zucchini, scoop out and discard the seeds; then scoop out the pulp, leaving ¼-inch-thick walls. Reserve 1½ cups of the zucchini pulp. Set aside the hollowed-out squash.

In a skillet, melt 1 tablespoon of the butter. Add the bread crumbs and stir to coat well. Remove the crumbs to a bowl. Add the remaining 3 tablespoons butter to the skillet and cook the reserved squash pulp until soft but not mushy. Stir in the thyme and salt and pepper.

Fill the squash with the cooked squash pulp, packing it in tightly. Place the filled squash in the baking dish. Cover and bake until tender, about 25 minutes. Sprinkle the bread crumbs over the squash and bake, uncovered, for 5 minutes more. Serve immediately.

Note: This dish is great served alongside grilled chicken, lamb, or pork.

Insalate

SALADS

SALAD WAS always served at the end of every meal in our house. My grandmothers thought of a green salad as a *digestivo*, the best way to settle one's stomach after a main dish. There are also antipasto salads of vegetables, fish, and rice that begin a meal and there are hearty salads, like bread or bean salad, that are the meal.

Thick creamy salad dressings are unheard of in Italy; good extra-virgin olive oil and red wine vinegar is the standard dressing, although fresh lemon juice is sometime used in place of vinegar. The closest thing to croutons on an Italian salad is a bread salad called *panzanella*, which uses moistened stale bread mixed in with the other ingredients.

There are many types of greens used in Italian salads, like arugula, a type of chicory with a slightly bitter, peppery taste; the regal maroon-and-white-striped radicchio; and even humble dandelion greens, which my Grandmother Galasso picked wherever she spotted them. Fresh herbs also play a role in Italian salads, basil and parsley being the most popular, but mint, thyme, and oregano are also used.

When making a green salad, make sure you have washed the lettuce well, drained it, and thoroughly dried it so that the olive oil adheres to the leaves. Good red wine vinegar or balsamic vinegar enhances the flavor of salads. The ratio of oil to vinegar I use is 3 to 1. I always add the oil first, then salt and pepper, and last the vinegar. I have never seen anyone in Italy rub a salad bowl with garlic before adding the ingredients. For green salad, garlic may be pressed or minced very fine and added to the ingredients, but it is more often omitted.

Condimento di Gorgonzola

GORGONZOLA DRESSING

A lot of people do not like Gorgonzola cheese, and I suspect it's because they have not tasted it when it is fresh. It is a buttery, soft, green-mold cow's milk cheese that comes from the town of Gorgonzola in Lombardy. The cheese has been in existence for over one thousand years. Its distinctive blue veining comes from penicillin mold and its taste becomes sharper with age. I use it in cream-based sauces for pasta (see Rotolo di Pasta, page 60) and in this dressing on a green salad.

MAKES ¾ CUP

¼ cup crumbled Italian Gorgonzola

1½ teaspoons Dijon mustard

6 tablespoons extra-virgin olive oil

⅛ teaspoon salt

⅛ teaspoon freshly ground black pepper

Put the cheese and mustard in a food processor or blender and blend until smooth. With the motor running, slowly add the olive oil through the feed tube in a thin steady stream and process until well blended. (Or mash the cheese and mustard together in a bowl with a fork. Slowly whisk in the oil, drop by drop, and whisk until smooth.) Add the salt and pepper and mix well.

Transfer the dressing to a bottle and refrigerate. It will keep for up to 2 weeks.

Insalata d'Arugola, Radicchio, e Romana

ARUGULA, RADICCHIO, AND ROMAINE SALAD

Arugula is a member of the chicory family. It is a very easy plant to grow and lasts well after the first frost. It is also now available in most grocery stores. Its pungent, peppery leaves are best as part of an *insalata verde*, mixed with other greens, rather than served alone.

SERVES 4

6 leaves radicchio

8 leaves arugula

6 large leaves romaine

DRESSING

1 clove garlic, finely minced

¹/₄ cup extra-virgin olive oil

2   to 3 tablespoons red wine vinegar
     (to taste)

     Salt and freshly ground black
     pepper to taste

Wash all the lettuces and drain well. Dry thoroughly, tear into small pieces and place in a salad bowl.

In a small bowl, whisk together all the dressing ingredients. Drizzle the dressing over the salad and toss gently. Serve at once.

Insalata di Cavolfiore

CAULIFLOWER SALAD

Caltanissetta, Sicily, was home to Nonna Saporito. When she was a girl, the family grew most of their own food. Vegetables, not meat, made up the bulk of the family diet. One of the salads she often made was a spicy cauliflower salad. Big chunks of Grandma's homemade bread were used to sop up the juices.

SERVES 6

1   medium head cauliflower, outer
     leaves and core removed

¹/₂ cup olive oil

2   teaspoons minced garlic

3   tablespoons red wine vinegar

¹/₂ cup pitted and diced cured black
     olives

¹/₂ cup diced red onion

¹/₂ cup diced red bell pepper

3   tablespoons capers in brine,
     drained

3   tablespoons chopped fresh parsley

     Salt and freshly ground black
     pepper to taste

Separate the cauliflower into small florets. Rinse well in cold water and drain. In a large pot of boiling salted water, cook the floretes until *al dente*, about 5 minutes. Drain and place them in a bowl.

Pour the olive oil over the cauliflower, and toss to coat well. Add all the remaining ingredients and toss to mix well. Let the salad marinate for several hours at room temperature, stirring occasionally, before serving.

Insalata Rinforzata

REINFORCED SALAD

In Sicily, a special salad is made at Christmastime called *insalata rinfor-zata* (reinforced salad). At home, it was always made in large quantities; whatever remained was saved in the refrigerator and fresh ingredients, or reinforcements, were added to the leftovers. Grandma said this salad was meant to give everyone who ate it *forza*, or strength.

SERVES 6

1 large head cauliflower, outer leaves and core removed

Salt

1 cup cured black oilves, pitted

3 tablespoons capers packed in salt, rinsed and drained

6 to 8 anchovy fillets (to taste), coarsely chopped

½ cup pickles, sliced

DRESSING

½ cup extra-virgin olive oil

¼ cup red wine vinegar

Salt and coarsely ground black pepper to taste

Cut the cauliflower into small, uniform florets. Rinse well in cold water and drain. Put the florets in a large pot and add cold water to cover. Add 1 teaspoon salt and bring to a boil. Boil the cauliflower until *al dente*, about 5 to 6 minutes; drain.

Meanwhile, in a salad bowl, combine the olives, capers, anchovies, and pickles.

Add the hot drained cauliflower to the salad bowl. In a small bowl, whisk together all the dressing ingredients. Add to the vegetables and toss well. Cover the bowl with plastic wrap and let the salad marinate in a cool place for about 1 hour before serving.

Piselli, Pomodori, e Peperoni

PEAS, TOMATO, AND PEPPER SALAD

Just about all the Italian families we knew had a vegetable garden. Every spring the trade-off would begin, as a bag of beans, a basket of tomatoes, or loads of spring peas would pass between families. My mother did not waste her time or anyone else's. Whoever was around shelled the peas, skinned the tomatoes, or did whatever else she needed to make her job easier. I hated shelling peas and when I was done, one huge bushel was reduced to just one medium-size bowl of peas to be mixed with other vegetables for a colorful raw salad.

1 pound fresh plum tomatoes, diced	2 cloves garlic, minced
1 large green bell pepper, diced	1 tablespoon diced red onion
1½ cups shelled fresh peas	2 tablespoons minced fresh parsley
	2 tablespoons minced fresh thyme
DRESSING	Salt and freshly ground black
3 tablespoons red wine vinegar	pepper to taste
⅔ cup olive oil	

In a salad bowl, combine the diced vegetables and peas.

In a small bowl, combine all the dressing ingredients and whisk together. Pour over the vegetables and toss to coat well. Cover the salad with plastic wrap and let stand in a cool place for 1 hour before serving.

Insalata di Mozzarella e Pomodori Secchi

MOZZARELLA AND DRIED TOMATO SALAD

This refreshing simple salad can be made even in the dead of winter. Follow the recipe for Pomodori Secchi (page 218) and use the fresh whole-milk mozzarella cheese called fiore di latte, available in Italian markets; it has a very delicate flavor.

2 cups thinly sliced fresh mozzarella cheese (about ½ pound)	Salt and freshly ground black pepper to taste
¾ cup dried tomatoes packed in olive oil (page 218), coarsely chopped (reserve the oil)	2 tablespoons red wine vinegar
¼ cup fresh basil leaves, torn in pieces	

Arrange the mozzarella in a shallow serving dish, overlapping the slices. Sprinkle over the dried tomatoes and about ½ cup of their oil, the basil, and salt and pepper. Then sprinkle with the wine vinegar.

Cover with plastic wrap and let sit at room temperature for at least 3 hours. Tilt and turn the dish now and then so that the juices flow over and around the cheese.

Gently toss the salad and serve.

Insalata di Zucchini

ZUCCHINI SALAD

The word *zucchini* means small squash, and this vegetable should not be allowed to grow into *zucchone*, or big squash. At the height of the season, my Grandmother Galasso would bring just-picked bushels of variously sized zucchini into the kitchen. There she stood, in black dress and white apron, determined and ready to pickle, fry, boil, and bake what seemed to her a treasure from heaven. The most memorable dish she concocted was zucchini salad, for which she picked out the smallest and most tender ones. I have added colorful yellow zucchini to her dish.

SERVES 4 TO 6

2 medium green zucchini	3 tablespoons balsamic vinegar
2 medium yellow zucchini	3 tablespoons minced fresh basil
	2 tablespoons minced fresh thyme or
DRESSING	marjoram
½ cup extra-virgin olive oil	Salt and coarsely ground black
2 cloves garlic, minced	pepper

Preheat the oven to 350°F.

Cut the zucchini into thin slices. Spread them in a single layer on an oiled baking sheet and bake, turning them once, until soft but not mushy, about 20 minutes. (You can also brush the slices lightly with olive oil and grill them until soft.)

In a bowl, combine all the dressing ingredients and whisk until well blended. Pour about 2 tablespoons of the dressing into a shallow serving dish. Arrange the zucchini in the dish, slightly overlapping the slices and alternating the colors for a nice visual effect. Pour the remaining dressing over the zucchini. Cover the dish and let marinate at room temperature for several hours, or overnight, before serving, tilting the dish occasionally to move the dressing up and over the zucchini.

Note: Served over grilled slices of Italian bread, this makes a delicious appetizer.

Fagioli in Peperoni

BEANS IN PEPPERS

Cannellini are small white beans that in Tuscany are ready for harvest in June. Picked fresh, they require just a little cooking time and the simplest adornment, like extra-virgin olive oil and a good grinding of black pepper. When they are dried, they need to soak overnight before cooking. This helps to plump up the beans and cut down on the cooking time. Some cooks claim that the soaking procedure is not necessary. The cooking time, however, will be much longer, possibly several hours.

SERVES 8

1½ cups dried cannellini beans

1   6-ounce can tuna packed in olive oil (undrained), flaked

¼ cup thinly sliced red onion

¼ cup thinly sliced white onion

2   teaspoons minced garlic

¼ cup extra-virgin olive oil

Juice of ½ lemon

Salt and freshly ground black pepper to taste

8   bell peppers (an assortment of red, yellow, and green)

¼ cup chopped fresh parsley

Extra-virgin olive oil

Soak the beans overnight in water to cover.

Drain, put the beans in a pot, and add cold water to cover. Bring to a boil and cook until tender, about 30 to 35 minutes.

Drain the beans well and put them in a large bowl. Add the tuna, onions, garlic, olive oil, lemon juice, and salt and pepper and mix well. Set aside.

Slice off the tops of the peppers and reserve. Trim the bottoms of the peppers if necessary so they will stand upright. Remove the seeds, and rinse and dry the peppers.

Divide the bean mixture evenly among the peppers, filling them to the top. Sprinkle with the chopped parsley and drizzle a little extra-virgin olive oil over each pepper. Replace the reserved tops. Serve at room temperature.

Note: This is a novel way to take a salad to a picnic, and there is no serving dish to wash, since the peppers become edible containers.

OLD RECORDS show that balsamic vinegar, *aceto balsamico*, was being made as early as the seventh century by the Romans. The word *balsamic* means "aromatic," according to Signorina Bona Tirelli, an expert on the production of balsamic vinegar, and a native of Modena, where the famed vinegar is made. She stressed that making it is even today a closely guarded secret among Modenese families, as it has been for centuries, each family passing on its particular method to the next generation.

Balsamic vinegar is made from the Trebbiano grape, grown on the middle hills of Modena and the border areas of Bologna. Modenese families believe that only these areas have the right *misti* (mixture) of air temperature, humidity, and soil to produce the grapes for the vinegar. They must be picked at just the right moment and left to dry for a week on mesh screens. They are then squeezed by foot to extract the juice, because a machine crushing would be too brutal a process. As the grapes are crushed, the juices run through square openings in the casks to waiting tubes.

The *barili*, or casks, used for holding, fermenting, maturing, and aging the vinegar must be made by hand. They are constructed from a combination of fruit woods, including cherry, apple, and pear. The wood for the casks must be cut at certain hours of the day and certain times of the year, usually from October to March, when the trees are dormant. The casks must conform to a certain size and thickness to allow for enough evaporation to occur.

The grape juice is cooked in special copper pots for twelve to twenty-four hours—this is the most critical step. Then active vinegar bacteria

Balsamic Vinegar

is added with wine vinegar. The mixture is put into the first cask and left to rest for one year. After a year, half of the contents of the cask is put into a second cask and left to rest for another year. What is left behind in the first cask is the "mother" for the production of balsamic vinegar. The vinegar in the second cask gets put into a third one for four years. Finally, after six years, the first bottle of *aceto balsamico giovane,* or young vinegar, can be tapped. At this point, the color is transparent, and the acidity count varies from 6 to 18 percent. Vinegars allowed to age for twelve to twenty-five years develop a deep mahogany color and a flavor that is extremely concentrated. The classification of this vinegar is set by law and it is judged for its acidity, cleanness, and taste by experts like Tirelli.

Very few bottles of this prized flavor enhancer are produced in any given year. Since 1956, the Friends of Aceto Balsamico have presented an award for the best vinegar. Bona Tirelli let me sample her prized vinegar, which was kept in an etched glass bottle. Reverently, she poured a few precious drops onto a silver spoon; the flavor is indescribable.

Tirelli explained that the Modenese use the vinegar in their everyday food preparation. It is never exposed to cooking heat, as this would destroy its unique flavor and burn off the alcohol content. The oldest vinegars are used very sparingly, often sprinkled over slivers of the Parmigiano-Reggiano cheese served after the meal. Scant drops are sprinkled over boiled meats and it is used as an accompaniment to steak. One teaspoon of a younger vinegar is enough to dress a green salad or perk up fresh fruits like strawberries or peaches.

Insalata di Fagioli

BEAN SALAD

Beans and bread are the basis of many classic Tuscan dishes including salads. Some bean salads are simply dressed with extra-virgin olive oil and a bit of salt, but I like this marinated bean dish made with soppressata, a cooked and aged salame. This is a hearty salad, suitable for a luncheon or served with grilled meat. If you can't find soppressata, use Genoa salame.

SERVES 8

1½ cups dried cannellini beans

¼ pound soppressata, cut into thin strips

DRESSING

⅓ cup red wine vinegar

1½ teaspoons Dijon mustard

½ teaspoon crushed red pepper flakes

2 tablespoons chopped fresh herbs (a combination of parsley, thyme, and oregano)

Salt and freshly ground black pepper to taste

⅔ cup extra-virgin olive oil

Soak the beans overnight in water to cover.

Drain the beans and place in a pot. Add fresh water to cover and bring to a boil. Cook the beans until tender but not mushy, about 30 minutes. Drain and place them in a bowl. Add the soppressata strips, toss to mix, and set aside.

Place all the dressing ingredients except the olive oil in the bowl of a food processor. With the motor running, slowly add the oil through the feed tube and process until smooth. Or put all the ingredients in a jar, cover tightly, and shake well.

Pour the dressing over the beans and soppressata and mix well. Let the salad marinate for several hours at room temperature before serving.

Note: You can make this salad several days ahead; just be sure to bring the salad to room temperature a few hours before you plan to serve it. Good crusty Tuscan bread is the perfect accompaniment.

Fagiolini alla Menta

BEANS WITH MINT

My Grandmother Galasso loved to make salads of tender young green beans and mint. She put mint in just about everything, mainly because it grew so profusely in a little patch of dirt near the kitchen door. The trick to this salad is to use very young green beans and to put the beans into the dressing while they are still hot so they will absorb the mint-infused oil.

SERVES 8

DRESSING

1/3 cup extra-virgin olive oil

3 tablespoons red wine vinegar

2 cloves garlic, minced

1/2 cup minced fresh mint

1 teaspoon chopped fresh oregano or 1/2 teaspoon dried

Salt and freshly ground black pepper to taste

1 pound tender green beans

1 tablespoon olive oil

In a 9- × -12-inch nonmetal dish, whisk all the dressing ingredients together. Set aside.

Trim the beans. Put them in a large pot and add cold water to cover. Add the olive oil, bring to a boil, and boil until *al dente*, about 10 minutes. The beans should still have a little bite to them.

Drain, and immediately add the beans to the dressing, turning and coating them well. Cover the dish and let the beans marinate for several hours at room temperature before serving.

Insalata di Finocchio ed Arancia

FENNEL AND ORANGE SALAD

This Sicilian salad is colorful and unusual. My grandmother used to tell us that when there was nothing to eat in Sicily, there were always *tarocchi*, or blood oranges, so called because of their deep red color. Blood oranges are available in late June and early July, but when I can't get them, I use navel oranges.

SERVES 4 TO 6

6 *medium blood or navel oranges*

1 *medium bulb fennel, trimmed and cut into thin strips*

2 *tablespoons finely minced fennel leaves*

3 *tablespoons finely chopped walnuts*

½ *cup extra-virgin olive oil*

Salt and freshly cracked black pepper to taste

Romaine lettuce leaves

Peel the oranges and remove as much of the pith (white membrane) as possible. Slice the oranges into thin rounds and place them in a shallow dish, slightly overlapping them. Sprinkle over the fennel strips, fennel leaves, and walnuts. Drizzle the olive oil over, and sprinkle with salt and cracked pepper. Cover tightly with plastic wrap and let the salad stand at room temperature for several hours. Every so often, tilt and turn the dish so that the oil and juices that have collected flow over and around the oranges.

To serve, arrange the salad on a bed of Romaine lettuce and pour the juices over.

Insalata di Spinaci

SPINACH SALAD

Spinach is used in many ways in Italian cooking: in rustic pies, in bread, as a filling for stuffed pasta, in gnocchi, and in soup. In Torgiano, it seemed to be part of every meal. Simply steamed and dressed with olive oil, it was served as a vegetable accompaniment. But when combined with paper-thin slices of cheese and mushrooms, it was outstanding as a salad.

SERVES 8

1   pound fresh spinach, rinsed, dried well, and cut crosswise into thin strips

1½ cups sliced mushrooms (sliced paper-thin)

Salt and freshly ground black pepper to taste

½   cup extra-virgin olive oil

¼   cup balsamic vinegar

1   cup paper-thin shavings Parmigiano-Reggiano cheese

Place the spinach and mushrooms in a salad bowl. Sprinkle with salt and pepper.

In a small bowl, whisk the olive oil and balsamic vinegar together. Pour over the salad and toss. Sprinkle over the cheese shavings and toss again. Serve immediately.

Insalata di Patata alla Menta

MINT POTATO SALAD

I loved to eat my Grandmother Galasso's potato salad on a hot and steamy August day. The most important ingredient was fresh mint that, picked early in the morning, scented the entire kitchen. It was generously combined with the hot potatoes and the other ingredients to marinate for several hours before serving. Sometimes, tender young peas were added raw to this dish.

SERVES 8

DRESSING

⅔ cup extra-virgin olive oil

¼ cup red wine vinegar

3 cloves garlic, minced

1 cup fresh mint leaves, torn in small pieces

6 large all-purpose potatoes or 12 small red-skinned potatoes

1 cup fresh young peas, optional

Salt and freshly cracked black pepper to taste

In a large shallow serving dish, combine all the dressing ingredients. Stir to blend, and set aside.

Wash the potatoes but do not peel. Put the potatoes in a large pot, add water to cover, and bring to a boil. Boil until tender, but not overly soft. If using all-purpose potatoes, cut them into ¼-inch slices; cut red potatoes in half. Place the hot potatoes cut sides down in the dressing. Add the peas, if desired.

Cover the salad and let sit at room temperature for several hours before serving, turning the potatoes occasionally in the dressing. Season with salt and pepper and serve.

Insalata di Carote

CARROT SALAD

This carrot salad is colorful as well as fun to prepare. The carrots are marinated for several hours, then tied in small bundles and arranged attractively on a serving platter. They are a perfect picnic accompaniment to Pitta (page 124).

SERVES 8

MARINADE

1/2 cup extra-virgin olive oil

Juice of 1/2 lemon

3 tablespoons red wine vinegar

1 tablespoon minced fresh parsley

1 teaspoon chopped fresh oregano or 1/2 teaspoon dried

1 teaspoon sugar

1 1/2 teaspoons minced garlic

Salt and freshly ground black pepper to taste

1 pound carrots

1 bunch scallion tops (8 pieces)

In a shallow dish, whisk together all the marinade ingredients. Set aside.

Scrape the carrots with a vegetable peeler and trim off the tops. Cut the carrots into pieces 3 inches long and 1/4 inch thick. Put the carrots in a saucepan, add water to cover, and bring to a boil. Boil until *al dente*, about 5 minutes. Drain and immediately add them to the marinade. Mix well and set aside to marinate for 3 hours.

In a skillet, bring 2 cups water to a boil, add the scallion tops, and boil for 1 to 2 minutes, or until wilted. Drain and refresh under cold running water. Dry on paper towels.

Divide the carrots into 8 bundles. Tie each bundle with a scallion top and place them on a decorative platter. Pour the remaining marinade over the carrots. Serve at room temperature.

Insalata di Sedano, Funghi, e Formaggio

CELERY, MUSHROOM, AND CHEESE SALAD

When I'm in Italy, I always take a notebook to the places where I eat to write down recipes or ideas. Recently, in Bologna, I wandered into a restaurant on Via de Carbonesi called Cesari. The menu looked inviting and reminded me of why Bologna is called "Bologna the Fat"—the cooking is very rich. After indulging in tortelli, an oval-shaped pasta filled with ricotta cheese and sweet red peppers, I decided on a simple celery salad, which included mushrooms and exquisite Parmigiano-Reggiano cheese. The cheese is critical to this salad, so be sure to use only the real thing.

SERVES 6

2 cups thinly sliced celery

1 cup thinly sliced mushrooms

1/4 cup thin slivers Parmigiano-Reggiano cheese

DRESSING

1/4 extra-virgin olive oil

2 tablespoons red wine vinegar

1 teaspoon salt

Freshly ground black pepper to taste

In a salad bowl, combine the celery, mushrooms, and cheese.

In a small bowl, whisk together all the dressing ingredients. Pour the dressing over the salad, toss, and serve at once.

Note: I'm always open to suggestions for recipes. My husband, Guy, thinks a handful of peppery arugula is a good addition to this salad.

Panzanella

BREAD SALAD

Panzanella is made all over Italy. My grandmothers referred to it as "bread in a swamp," because this is a salad of vegetables and stale bread that is first soaked in vinegar or water. Be sure to use a good firm peasant-style bread. This is a great summer salad and is best served at room temperature.

SERVES 6

4   slices stale bread

1   cup coarsely chopped fresh plum tomatoes (2 medium tomatoes)

¼   cup thinly sliced white or red onion

1   cup chopped green bell pepper

1   cup seeded and chopped cucumber

2   tablespoons capers

¼   cup minced fresh parsley

2   tablespoons minced fresh basil

DRESSING

6   tablespoons olive oil

2   tablespoons red wine vinegar

2   cloves garlic, minced

   Salt and freshly ground black pepper to taste

Soak the bread slices in water for 1 to 2 minutes, or just until you can crumble them easily into pieces. Squeeze dry and put into a salad bowl. Add the tomatoes, onion, green pepper, cucumber, capers, and herbs and toss to mix.

In a small bowl, whisk together all the dressing ingredients. Pour the dressing over the salad and toss well. Cover with plastic wrap and let the salad sit in a cool place for 2 to 3 hours before serving.

Condimenti

CONDIMENTS

I N THE OLD brown two-story house where I grew up, there was a coliseum-size basement with an enormous coal-burning furnace. Beyond it was a still, dark area leading to an old wooden door, and behind that door was my mother's and Grandma Galasso's fruit cellar. I always felt uneasy when I was sent there; my heart pounded as I opened the door and groped in the darkness to find the overhead string that turned on the light, and all the while I was thinking that someone was in there. It was a cool and musty little room with crudely constructed wooden shelves that held colorful canning jars filled with fresh pears in mint syrup, peaches with cinnamon sticks and cloves, pink applesauce, and mahogany-colored Bing cherries. One shelf was devoted to jars of tomato sauce and ketchup. There was grape juice pressed from Concord grapes, all kinds of relishes, and pickled zucchini. I shuddered at the jars of preserved pig's feet, which I never ate, nestled next to the row of green and yellow beans preserved in vinegar.

I don't have my own fruit cellar, but I do have my pantry filled with wine bottles of homemade herb-infused vinegars and olive oil and jars of eggplant and oven-dried tomatoes packed in olive oil. And in my refrigerator are fresh herbs I've packed in salt and my homemade velvety-smooth basil mayonnaise.

Aceto Basilico

BASIL VINEGAR

In our basement, there was a collection of empty gallon-size wine bottles that my grandmother had saved. In the summer, the cumbersome bottles were brought upstairs, given a good scrubbing and scalding, and then stuffed with fresh herbs, such as basil and parsley. A funnel was placed over the mouth of the bottle and wine vinegar was added, filling the bottles to the brim. Then they were left to steep for weeks so the herbs would flavor the vinegar. Almost any fresh herbs can be used this way. I like combining herbs too, for thyme-mint vinegar, or parsley-chive vinegar. I use these vinegars on salads, in marinades, and to deglaze chicken dishes. You don't need gallon wine bottles to do this. I save interesting bottles of different sizes, fill and label them, and often give them as Christmas presents with a favorite recipe for using the vinegar.

3 or 4 sprigs basil per bottle

1 clove garlic, peeled, per bottle

Apple cider or red wine vinegar

Sterilized glass bottles and caps or corks

Wash and dry the basil sprigs. Place 3 or 4 sprigs in each bottle. With a knife, make a small slit in the garlic cloves. Add 1 clove to each bottle and fill the bottles with vinegar. Cap or cork the bottles and place them outside in the sun or in a sunny place indoors to "ripen" for 4 or 5 days.

Let the vinegar sit for at least 6 weeks before using; the vinegar will keep for up to 6 months.

Olio di Basilico

BASIL OIL

When it's high garden season, I head for the patch on the hill where my husband, Guy, has planted our Italian garden. The four rows of basil plants swing happily in the breeze, the unmistakable peppery scent lingering in the hot summer air. I pinch off the tops of the plants to make them bushy and prevent them from going to flower. Soon I realize I have a fearful amount of basil to deal with. Some will be made into pesto, some leaves will be packed in salt and stored in the refrigerator, and what is left over will go into my basil-flavored vinegars and oils. Other herbs such as fennel, rosemary, thyme, oregano, and chives can also be preserved this way.

3 or 4 sprigs basil per bottle

1 clove garlic, peeled, per bottle

Extra-virgin olive oil

Sterilized clear wine bottles and new corks

Wash and dry the basil carefully. Put 3 or 4 basil sprigs into each bottle. With a small knife, make a slit in the garlic cloves. Add 1 clove to each bottle. Fill the bottles with olive oil and cork the bottles.

Store the oil in the refrigerator and use within 3 weeks. Bring the oil to room temperature before using. You will have oil with a beautiful basil flavor, and the leaves stay perfectly preserved.

Note: Use Basil Oil as you would any other oil in salads. It also is wonderful for browning chicken, pork, and veal, and it is equally good tossed with fresh pasta.

Melanzane sott'Olio

EGGPLANT UNDER OIL

Eggplant was prepared in every way imaginable in our house. I used to loathe the stuff, finding every excuse not to eat it. Now, when my own garden is overrun with regal-looking purple eggplants, I preserve them for antipasto, using the same method my grandmothers used. A loaf of crusty Italian bread, a glass of robust red wine, some Pecorino Romano cheese, and these eggplant slices make a great lunch.

3   medium eggplants

Red wine vinegar

Coarse salt

4   or 5 cloves garlic, finely minced

3   to 4 tablespoons diced red bell peppers

3   to 4 tablespoons diced green bell peppers

3   to 4 tablespoons diced yellow bell peppers

Fresh basil leaves

Freshly ground black pepper to taste

Extra-virgin olive oil

3   to 4 sterilized pint jars

Wash and dry the eggplants, remove the stems, and cut the eggplants crosswise into ¼-inch slices. Place them in a deep nonmetal bowl and add vinegar to cover. Place a double layer of wax paper over the eggplant and set a bowl filled with water on top of the eggplant to keep it submerged in the vinegar. Let the eggplant marinate for 2 days at room temperature.

Squeeze the vinegar out of the eggplant slices with your hands and place a layer of 2 or 3 slices in each jar, sprinkling it with ½ teaspoon salt. Continue adding eggplant, sprinkling each layer with salt; when the jars are half full add ¼ teaspoon minced garlic, 1 tablespoon each of the peppers, 1 or 2 basil leaves, and pepper to each jar. When the jars are three-quarters full of eggplant, add olive oil to cover the eggplant, pushing down on the eggplant with a wooden spoon to submerge it under the oil. Top off each jar with more oil before capping it. Let the jars sit overnight at room temperature.

If the eggplant has absorbed some of the oil and the slices are poking through the oil, add more oil to completely cover the eggplant. Cap again and let sit overnight.

Add more oil if necessary so that the eggplant is fully submerged under the oil, cap the jars, and put them in a very cool place. Let them ripen for at least 6 weeks before using them. Refrigerate after opening; bring the eggplant to room temperature before using. The eggplant will keep for up to 6 months.

Note: Do not cut corners with this recipe. Clean, sterilized jars and caps are a must, as are the freshest ingredients.

Conserva di Erbe

PRESERVED HERBS

To make the fresh herbs from my garden last all year, I preserve them in sea salt. This is a very old method used by the ancient Egyptians, Greeks, and Romans. I usually use it for fresh basil and sage leaves, picked early in the day from the garden.

Fresh basil, oregano, sage, and/or   Sterilized pint jars
rosemary
Coarse sea salt

Gently wash the herbs and dry them well. Remove and discard the stems (or leave short stems if desired).

Cover the bottom of each jar with a ¼-inch layer of salt. Add a few herb leaves, then a layer of salt, and continue making alternate layers of herbs and salt until the jar is three-quarters full. Seal the jars with their lids and place in the refrigerator.

To use, remove the desired amount of herbs and rinse and dry them well. (Make sure the remaining herbs are covered with salt.) The herbs will have lost some of their color, but the flavor will be as fresh as the day you picked them.

Salsa Maionese al Basilico

BASIL MAYONNAISE

Very rarely did my mother or grandmothers make *maionese*, but from my travels through the kitchens of Italy, I have found it is made and used frequently. In the summer, when I am up to my elbows in fresh basil leaves, I make a flavored mayonnaise that is great on fresh grilled salmon, scallops, or shrimp. It can also be used as a spread on crostini, or as a dressing for a cold rice salad. I put it in small jars and refrigerate it until needed; I also like giving it as a little hostess gift. If you don't have a garden, you can always buy a bunch of fresh basil.

MAKES ABOUT 3 CUPS

2	large egg yolks	¼	cup fresh lemon juice
1	large egg	1	cup fresh basil leaves, washed and thoroughly dried
	½ teaspoon salt		About 2 cups extra-virgin olive oil
	⅛ teaspoon white pepper		

Put all the ingredients except the olive oil in a food processor or blender, and pulse until the basil is coarsely chopped. With the motor runnning, add the olive oil in a thin continuous stream until a smooth consistency is obtained; you may not need all the oil.

Transfer the mayonnaise to small jars, cap, and store in the refrigerator. Use within 1 week.

Pomodori Secchi

DRIED TOMATOES

I'm very lucky to have a husband whose interests complement my love of cooking. Every January he eagerly awaits the mailman's delivery of seed catalogs. Cold winter nights are spent planning and laying out on paper the garden that will yield its bounty in July and August. I use the same methods my mother and grandmothers used to preserve the tomatoes, eggplant, and other vegetables that my husband so lovingly raises.

Tomatoes can be dried in the oven or in a dehydrator. If using a dehydrator, follow the manufacturer's instructions.

Unblemished, meaty fresh plum tomatoes	Extra-virgin olive oil
Fresh basil leaves, optional	Sterilized pint jars

Wash and dry the tomatoes. Cut them in half lengthwise and place them cut sides down on wire racks set on baking sheets. Place the racks in a 225°F. oven and let the tomatoes dry until they are the consistency of dried apricots. This may take up to 2 days, depending on the size of the tomatoes.

Layer the tomatoes into sterilized jars, adding a few basil leaves if you wish. Add extra-virgin olive oil to cover. It is absolutely critical that the tomatoes be completely submerged under the olive oil at all times. Don't pack too many tomatoes in a jar. Cap the jars and place them in a cool spot overnight.

If the tomatoes have absorbed some of the oil and are poking through it, add more oil so that the tomatoes are submerged. Check the jars 2 or 3 more times, adding more oil if necessary, before capping them for the final time.

Store in a cool place for at least 6 weeks before using the tomatoes. Refrigerate after opening; bring the tomatoes to room temperature before serving.

Dolci e Frutte

DESSERTS AND FRUITS

D*OLCI,* OR SWEETS, have traditionally been reserved for special occasions, although my recent observations in Italy tell me this is no longer the case. Pastry shops seem to abound in every town and city. My favorites are Sandri's in Perugia and Nannini's in Siena, although I have indulged in pastries from many more. From morning to late afternoon, Italians wander into these sweet paradises to select a delectable treat to have with espresso or cappuccino. From the dense fruitcake called *panforte* to smooth and light *zabaglione*, Marsala-laced custard, the choices can be agonizing for a dessert lover.

My mother did most of the baking of traditional Italian desserts like Sicilian *cassata*, cannoli, *pastiera di Pasqua*, (Easter pie with ricotta cheese and cinnamon), and *torta di frutta*. For holidays, feast days, and birthdays, we could always count on a lavish spread of sweet delights. Homemade *torrone* took hours to make, but was very special. Made with egg whites, whole almonds, and sugar, it is more a candy than a dessert.

As tempting as Italian desserts are, and as rapidly as old traditions are changing, it is still customary to have fresh fruit to end a meal, or sometimes to begin it, as with the classic *prosciutto e melone*.

Every region of Italy grows several types of fruit. Sweet apples, as well as grapes and pears, tumble down from the Aosta Valley in the north to the rest of Italy. Smooth, juicy apricots and golden tart lemons grow in terraced rows on the hillsides ringing Lake Garda; black currants come from the Friuli-Venezia Giulia region; and rich, red cherries as shiny as glass marbles thrive in Liguria. The most wonderful peaches I have ever eaten come from Reggio-Emilia. There are also scarlet strawberries and plump melons from Rome, purple plums and exotic pomegranates from Naples, prickly pears and delicate figs from Basilicata, and sugar-sweet blood oranges, tangerines, and citron from Sicily. Italians have a wonderful way of presenting fresh fruit at the table—it is served standing in a bowl of cool water. You pick and choose your fancy and eat it (even a banana) with a fork and knife. Of course, fruit is also used in many desserts, from fresh fruit tarts glistening under a transparent sugar glaze to *semifreddi*, chilled fruit and cream combinations. Stuffed and baked fruits, especially pears and peaches, with *amaretti*, almond cookies, are popular too, as well as fruits macerated in wine or liqueur. Fruit, particularly pears, and cheese, are often a final statement to a meal.

Italian ice cream, or *gelato*, is the best in the world and that made from fresh fruit juices is superb. Just walk around any piazza in Italy and you will see people enjoying luscious fruits and *gelati* of all types. And you will be hard-pressed to pass by any *pasticceria* window without a startled stop to marvel at the display of glorious fresh fruit pastries.

Panettone con Gelato

PANETTONE WITH ICE CREAM

When I make panettone for the holidays, I make a lot of them to give as gifts. People always love receiving this beautiful bread and I usually include the recipe, as well as some other suggestions about how to serve it—like panettone stuffed with ice cream!

SERVES 8 TO 10

1 *large Panettone (page 126)*
1 *quart chocolate ice cream, softened*
1 *pint pistachio ice cream, softened*

5 *or 6 candied cherries, cut in half*
Whipped cream, optional

Cut a 1-inch-thick slice off the top of the bread; reserve this top. Using a long thin knife, neatly hollow out the bread, leaving a ½-inch-thick base and wall. (Reserve the bread from the inside for Torta di Panettone, page 225, or another use.)

Line the sides of the hollowed-out bread with a ½-inch-thick wall of softened chocolate ice cream. Place the panettone in the freezer to let the ice cream harden, about 10 minutes. When the chocolate ice cream is hard, make a second wall of pistachio ice cream inside it. Return to the freezer to let harden. When hard, fill completely with chocolate ice cream, and smooth the top. Press the cherry halves around the edge of the ice cream. Replace the top of the bread, wrap it carefully in foil, and return to the freezer to harden.

To serve, let the panettone thaw slightly. Then cut it in wedges or in rounds and serve with a little whipped cream on the side, if you wish.

Torta di Whisky alla Mamma

MAMA'S WHISKEY CAKE

My mother's whiskey cake was served at every holiday meal. This dense cake, soaked liberally with whiskey, filled with a delicious vanilla custard, and covered all over in a cloud of fluffy meringue, won the acclaim of all who were privileged to sample it. Make the filling a day ahead, so you won't have so many steps when you assemble the cake.

SERVES 24

CUSTARD FILLING

1	cup sugar
1/4	cup cornstarch
4	cups milk
4	large egg yolks
1	tablespoon vanilla

CAKE

1 1/2	cups cake flour
1 1/2	cups sugar
6	large eggs, separated, at room temperature

1/2	cup cold water
1	teaspoon vanilla
3/4	teaspoon cream of tartar
6	tablespoons bourbon whiskey

MERINGUE TOPPING

1 1/2	teaspoons cornstarch
1/4	cup water
6	large egg whites, at room temperature
1	tablespoon bourbon whiskey
1/2	cup sugar

To make the filling, in a small bowl, mix the sugar and cornstarch.

In the top of a double boiler, bring the milk to just under a boil. Reduce the heat to low. Add 1/4 cup of the hot milk to the sugar and cornstarch mixture, and stir to make a paste. Stir the paste into the milk in the double boiler, raise the heat to medium high, and cook, stirring constantly with a wooden spoon, until the mixture thickens enough to coat the back of the spoon. Remove from the heat and let cool slightly.

In a bowl, beat the egg yolks until pale and thick. Beat in 1/4 cup of the warm milk mixture and return to the double boiler, cook, stirring over medium-high heat for 5 minutes, or until thickened. Transfer to a bowl and stir in the vanilla. Cover the bowl with a sheet of buttered wax paper and refrigerate until ready to use.

Preheat the oven to 325°F.

To make the cake, sift the flour 3 times and set aside.

In a large bowl, beat the sugar and egg yolks with an electric mixer until thick and pale yellow in color. Gradually beat in the water, then the vanilla. With a spatula, fold in the sifted flour 2 tablespoons at a time. Set aside.

In another bowl, beat the egg whites with the cream of tartar until stiff peaks form. Fold the whites into the egg yolk mixture and pour the batter into an ungreased 10-inch tube pan. Bake for 40 minutes, or until a wooden skewer inserted in the middle of the cake comes out clean. Invert the cake pan over the neck of a wine or soft drink bottle and let the cake cool completely.

Run a knife around the sides of the pan to release the cake and turn it out onto a plate. With a serrated knife, cut the cake into ¼-inch slices.

Line a 9- × -12-inch ovenproof platter or baking sheet with a layer of cake slices. Fill in any spaces with pieces of cake. Sprinkle 2 tablespoons of the whiskey evenly over the cake slices. Spread the cake slices with half of the custard filling. Place a second layer of cake on top of the custard filling, filling in any gaps with pieces of cake. Sprinkle with another 2 tablespoons of the whiskey. Make a second custard layer and top with a third layer of cake. Sprinkle the top of the cake with the remaining 2 tablespoons whiskey. Refrigerate the cake while you make the meringue.

Preheat the oven to 325°F.

To make the meringue, in a small saucepan, dissolve the cornstarch in the water. Cook over medium-high heat, stirring, until well blended, but still liquid. Set aside to cool.

In a large bowl, beat the egg whites with an electric mixer until foamy. Add the whiskey and beat for 1 minute. Beat in the sugar 1 tablespoon at a time, and beat until the whites form stiff peaks. Slowly beat in the cornstarch mixture and beat for 3 minutes more.

Frost the cake with the meringue, making sure to spread the meringue all around the bottom of the cake to seal the edges. Bake until the meringue is golden brown, about 6 to 8 minutes; be careful, as it will brown quickly. Let the cake cool for 5 minutes, then refrigerate it for at least 2 hours before serving.

To serve, cut into small squares.

Note: This cake will keep for up to a week in the refrigerator.

Panforte di Siena

One of the most famous cakes of Siena is its *panforte*, which means "strong bread." It is chewy, dense, and perfumed with cinnamon and pepper. It is sold in flat rounds, brightly wrapped in paper, or by the piece. Sadly, this cake is rarely made in homes nowadays, and most panforte is commercially produced.

SERVES 10 TO 12

²/₃ cup hazelnuts

½ cup slivered almonds

½ cup chopped candied orange peel

½ cup chopped candied lemon peel

¼ cup Dutch-process cocoa

½ cup unbleached all-purpose flour

1   teaspoon cinnamon

½ teaspoon grated nutmeg

½ teaspoon ground cloves

1   teaspoon white pepper

½ cup sugar

½ cup honey

Confectioner's sugar

Parchment paper

Preheat the oven to 350°F. Butter an 8-inch cake pan, line it with parchment paper, and butter the paper.

Spread the hazelnuts on a baking sheet and toast for 10 minutes, or until lightly browned. Let cool. Lower the oven temperature to 325°F.

Chop the hazelnuts coarsely with the almonds. Put the nuts in a bowl and add the candied peels, cocoa, flour, and spices; mix well. Set aside.

In a saucepan, combine the sugar and honey and cook, stirring with a wooden spoon, until the sugar dissolves. Bring the mixture to a boil and cook, stirring, for 3 to 4 minutes, or until a bit of the mixture forms a soft ball when dropped in cold water. Add to the dry ingredients and mix well.

Pour the mixture into the prepared cake pan. Spread the batter evenly in the pan; the cake will be no more than about ½ inch thick.

Bake for 25 minutes, or until firm to the touch. While still warm, invert the cake onto a wire rack. Carefully peel off the parchment and let cool completely.

Sprinkle the top of the cake generously with confectioner's sugar. Serve cut in thin wedges.

Note: I find using a well-greased ceramic pie dish eliminates the need for parchment. This cake will keep for at least 2 weeks if well wrapped in foil.

Torta di Panettone

PANETTONE CAKE

It's rare when panettone is left over, but when that does occur, I make bread pudding. My grandmothers never wasted a crumb of bread, be it humble peasant bread or a rich holiday panettone.

SERVES 8 TO 10

5 cups 1-inch pieces stale panettone	4 large eggs, separated
½ cup sweet Marsala wine	⅓ cup sugar
4 cups milk	½ cup almonds or hazelnuts, chopped
½ cup light cream or half-and-half	
½ teaspoon cinnamon	Confectioner's sugar
½ teaspoon grated nutmeg	Candied cherries
1 tablespoon grated orange zest	Fresh mint leaves
1 tablespoon grated lemon zest	

In a large bowl, moisten the bread with the Marsala wine. Set aside. Preheat the oven to 325°F. Butter a 9- × 12-inch baking dish.

In a saucepan, bring the milk and cream to a boil; boil for 1 minute. Remove from the heat and stir in the cinnamon, nutmeg, and lemon and orange zests.

In a large bowl, beat the egg yolks and sugar until smooth. Stir in the milk mixture. Add the milk mixture to the soaked bread, then add the nuts. Mix gently.

In a clean bowl, beat the egg whites until they hold stiff peaks. Fold into the bread mixture. Pour the mixture into the buttered dish. Place the dish in a large baking pan and add hot water to come halfway up the sides of the baking dish. Bake until set, about 2 hours. Turn off the oven and let the cake cool completely in the oven.

To serve, dust the top of the cake with confectioner's sugar. Garnish with candied cherries and mint leaves.

Anguille di Trasimeno

EELS OF TRASIMENO

When I was in Perugia, the capital city of the landlocked region of Umbria, I took a baking class from Signorina Carla Sandri, owner of Sandri's Pasticceria. First on the day's schedule was the making of the "eels of Trasimeno," Trasimeno being the largest lake in central Italy, and a favorite vacation spot for Perugians. I didn't dare ask how eels could fit into the category of pastry. I soon found out that these eels were made from almonds, candied fruit, and egg whites, shaped to look like the real thing. This is a very old recipe traditionally served at Christmas.

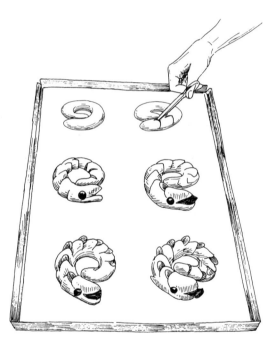

1   *pound blanched whole almonds,*
    plus 16 for decoration

1²/₃ *cups sugar*

  ¹/₂ *cup candied citron, finely*
     chopped

  ¹/₂ *cup candied orange peel, finely*
     chopped

4   *large egg whites*

2   *candied cherries, cut in quarters*

  ¹/₂ *cup apricot jam*

Chop the 1 pound almonds very fine by hand (or use a food processor, but it will cause the oils in the almonds to break down somewhat). Put them in a bowl, add the sugar, citron, and orange peel, and mix well. In a bowl, lightly beat the egg whites with a fork. Gradually add enough of the egg whites to the almond mixture to form a dough; all of the whites may not be needed. With floured hands, work the dough until it holds together.

Preheat the oven to 300°F. Grease and flour a baking sheet.

Divide the dough in half. Using the palms of your hands, roll out each half to form an eel or serpent shape about 13 inches long, with one end wider for the head and the other one narrower for the tail. Place them on the baking sheet.

Cut 7 Vs on the top of each eel with scissors, working toward the tail. Place a whole almond in each V to simulate scales. Use the cherries for the eyes and almonds for tongues.

Bake for 35 to 40 minutes, or until nicely browned. Carefully remove to a rack and let cool.

In a small saucepan, heat the apricot jam until melted and smooth. Brush the warm glaze over the eels. Cut in pieces and serve.

Cannoli

The queen of all southern Italian desserts is cannoli. These crisp, flaky cylinders are filled with sweetened ricotta cheese, nuts, citron, and bits of chocolate. Sicily lays claim to cannoli, which probably originally came from the Arabs, who influenced so much of Sicily's cooking.

I use an old recipe my mother gave me that was given to her by her mother, and her mother before that. Originally, sheep's milk ricotta was used. I still use my grandmother's old wooden forms, fashioned from a broom handle, to make the cylinders, but you can buy stainless steel ones in kitchenware stores.

MAKES 14 TO 18

FILLING

1½ cups whole-milk ricotta cheese, well drained

3 tablespoons sugar

1½ teaspoons cinnamon

1½ cups coarsely chopped milk chocolate (4 to 5 small bars)

¼ cup pistachio nuts, coarsely chopped

DOUGH

1 cup unbleached all-purpose flour

1 tablespoon sugar

1 tablespoon butter or lard

4 to 5 tablespoons dry white wine or sweet Marsala wine

2 cups vegetable oil

Colored sprinkles

Confectioner's sugar

In a bowl, combine all the filling ingredients and mix well. Refrigerate, covered, until ready to fill the cannoli shells.

To make the dough, place the flour in a bowl or food processor. Add the butter or lard and sugar and mix with a fork, or pulse, until the mixture resembles coarse meal. Slowly add the ¼ cup of wine and shape the mixture into a ball; add a little more wine if the dough appears too dry. It should be soft but not sticky. Knead the dough on a floured surface until smooth, about 10 minutes. Wrap the dough and refrigerate for 45 minutes.

Place the chilled dough on a floured work surface. Divide the dough in half. Work with 1 piece of dough at a time; keep the remaining dough refrigerated. Roll the dough out to a very thin long rectangle about 14 inches long and 3 inches wide, either by hand or using a pasta machine set to the finest setting. Cut the dough into 3-inch squares. Place a cannoli form diagonally across 1 square. Roll the dough up around the form so the points meet in the center. Seal the points with a little water. Continue making cylinders until all the dough is used.

In an electric skillet, heat the vegetable oil to 375°F. Fry the cannoli 3 or 4 at a time, turning them as they brown and blister, until golden brown on all sides. Drain them on brown paper. When they are cool enough to handle, carefully slide the cannoli off the forms.

To serve, use a long iced tea spoon or a pastry bag without a tip to fill the cannoli with the ricotta cheese mixture. Dip the ends into colored sprinkles, arrange them on a tray, and sprinkle confectioner's sugar over the tops. Serve at once.

Note: If you prefer, you can fry the cannoli in a deep fryer. Be sure to fill the cannoli just before serving—any sooner will make the shells soggy.

Pasta Frolla

PASTRY DOUGH

This is a basic pastry dough that can be used to make various fruit tarts and small pastries. The name comes from the word *frollare*, to make tender. Be careful not to overwork the dough, or it will be tough. Use this dough to make filled fruit tarts.

MAKES 1 POUND 6 OUNCES, ENOUGH FOR 2 10-INCH PASTRY SHELLS

2 cups unbleached all-purpose flour	8 tablespoons (1 stick) butter, at room temperature, cut into small pieces
1 cup pastry flour	
1½ teaspoons salt	1 large egg, beaten
2 tablespoons sugar	5 to 6 tablespoons cold water

In a bowl, mix the flours, salt, and sugar together. Add the butter and work it in until the mixture is the texture of coarse corn meal. Add the beaten egg and just enough water to make a pliable dough. Do not overmix. Form the dough into a ball, wrap in plastic wrap, and refrigerate for 1 hour before using.

Note: In Sandri's Pasticceria in Perugia, Signorina Sandri uses lard instead of butter to give the dough extra flakiness. You might want to try using half butter and half shortening.

Sfogliatelle della Nobilità

PASTRY OF THE NOBLES

When I was in Sorrento, I went to the *pasticceria* to do what most Italians do everyday—pick out a tempting pastry to have as a little snack. There were so many kinds that it was blind luck that I should choose *sfogliatelle*. These are flaky pastries that look like seashells when baked. They are filled with a mixture of sweetened ricotta cheese, semolina, and cinnamon. Sometimes citron pieces are also added. In talking with the owners of the shop, I learned that these regal gems were originally made only for the noble families of the Renaissance and that is the reason why they are called *sfogliatelle della nobilità*, pastry of the nobles. *Sfogliatelle* means many folds or leaves, similar to the many layers created by puff pastry dough. I have experimented with frozen puff pastry, and I like the results better.

MAKES ABOUT 16

FILLING

1   cup milk

¼   cup semolina flour

1   cup whole-milk ricotta cheese, well drained

1   large egg, beaten

¼   cup sugar

1   tablespoon grated lemon zest

1   1-pound package frozen puff pastry (2 sheets), thawed, or 1 recipe Puff Patry for Sfogliatelle (recipe follows)

4   tablespoons lard or butter, melted

Confectioner's sugar

Cinnamon

Parchment paper, optional

To make the filling, in a saucepan, bring the milk to a boil over medium-high heat. Add the semolina flour in a thin steady stream, stirring constantly with a wooden spoon, and cook, stirring, until the mixture is thickened and smooth, about 3 to 4 minutes. Transfer to a bowl and let cool for 5 minutes.

Add the cheese, egg, sugar, and lemon zest to the semolina mixture and beat well. Set aside.

Preheat the oven to 425°F. Line 2 cookie sheets with parchment paper, if available.

Roll 1 sheet of the puff pastry out to a 16-×-22-inch rectangle on a floured, and preferably cold, surface (I use a marble slab). Starting at a short edge, brush one third of the sheet with some of the melted lard or butter and begin rolling the pastry sheet up tightly like a jelly roll; brush the remaining two thirds of the sheet with lard or butter and roll up.

Cut the roll into 2-inch-thick slices. Form each piece into a small sea-shell shape by pushing your thumbs against the center of the piece and spreading it out to a small cup shape.

Fill each shell with about 2 tablespoons of the semolina filling and place them 1 inch apart on the parchment-lined sheets or on ungreased cookie sheets. Repeat with the remaining pastry and filling. Bake for 15 minutes or until nicely browned. Let cool slightly on the cookie sheets and then transfer to racks to cool completely.

To serve, sprinkle the sfogliatelle with confectioner's sugar and then sprinkle a line of cinnamon down the center of each one.

Note: These can be assembled ahead of time, placed on cookie sheets, wrapped in foil, and frozen for later baking. Bake them frozen, allowing about 10 to 12 minutes more baking time.

PUFF PASTRY DOUGH FOR SFOGLIATELLE

1 POUND 6 OUNCES PASTRY DOUGH

2	cups unbleached all-purpose flour	¾ cup (1½ sticks) butter
1	cup fine semolina or pastry flour	½ cup water
⅛	teaspoon salt	½ cup lard, melted

In a bowl or food processor, combine the flours and salt and mix or process well to blend. Cut the butter into small pieces and work into the dough with a pastry blender or pulse in the food processor. Add the water gradually and mix or process until a ball of soft dough forms. Wrap the dough in plastic wrap and refrigerate several hours before continuing with the recipe.

When ready to roll, divide the dough in half and work with one piece at a time. Roll each piece into a 16- × 22-inch rectangle on a floured and cold marble slab. Starting at the short end of each piece, brush one third of the sheet with some of the melted lard and roll up the pastry tightly, jelly-roll fashion. Brush the remaining two thirds of the sheet with lard and roll up.

Cut the roll into 2-inch-thick slices and proceed as for the recipe using the prepared puff pastry (above).

Torta di Frutta Fresca

FRESH FRUIT TART

Italians have never been heavy dessert eaters, and such treats were traditionally reserved for special occasions. I recall the fancy spreads my grandmothers and mother put out for religious feast days and family parties, but we never had dessert after everyday meals. Today this is all changing in Italy. In the middle of the morning, afternoon, or early evening, you see people flocking to the *pasticerria* or to *il bar* to have biscotti, gelati, and glistening slices of fresh fruit tarts with luscious cream or almond fillings. All these and more are washed down with copious cups of cappuccino, espresso, or *aqua minerale*. When I want a fancy Italian dessert, a fresh fruit tart is what I crave. You can use any combination of fresh fruits here, or you can choose just one type of fruit.

SERVES 8 TO 10

PASTRY

2   cups unbleached all-purpose flour

½   cup sugar

5   tablespoons butter, chilled and cut in pieces

1   large egg

     Pinch of salt

¼   teaspoon grated nutmeg (see Note)

1   teaspoon almond extract

2   tablespoons ice water

2   tablespoons apricot jam

4   cups hulled strawberries or an assortment of blackberries, raspberries, melon balls, and/or seeded green and black grapes

½   cup water

¾   cup sugar

3   tablespoons cornstarch

1   teaspoon almond extract

     Mascarpone cheese, optional

To make the pastry, in a food processor, combine the flour, sugar, and butter and pulse until the mixture resembles coarse corn meal. Add the egg, salt, nutmeg, and almond extract. Pulse just to blend. With the motor running, add the water gradually through the feed tube and process until the mixture begins to form a ball; you may not need all of the water. (If you prefer, combine the flour, salt, and sugar in a bowl and use a pastry blender to work the mixture until it resembles coarse corn meal. Mix in the egg, salt, nutmeg, and almond extract. Add the water gradually, adding just enough to form the mixture into a ball of dough.) Wrap the dough in waxed paper and chill for at least 2 hours, or overnight.

Preheat the oven to 400°F.

Place the dough between 2 clean sheets of waxed paper and roll it out to fit a 10-inch tart pan with a removable bottom. Fit the dough into the pan and trim off the excess dough. Prick the dough in several places with a fork. Put a sheet of foil or waxed paper over the dough and weigh it down with dried beans or rice. Bake for 12 minutes, remove the foil and beans, and bake for about 3 to 5 minutes more, or until light golden brown. Let cool on a rack.

In a small saucepan, heat the apricot jam until smooth and melted. Brush the crust with the jam to seal it. Reserve ½ cup of fruit for the glaze, and arrange the remaining fruit in a decorative pattern in the tart shell. Set aside while you make the glaze.

Cut the reserved fruit into coarse pieces and place in a saucepan. Add the ½ cup water and bring to a boil. Boil until the fruit is soft, about 3 minutes. Transfer to a strainer set over a bowl. Mash the fruit with a wooden spoon and press against the solids to extract as much of the juices as possible. Discard the solids. Add enough water to the strained juices to make 1 cup.

In a saucepan mix the sugar and cornstarch together. Slowly add the strained juice and mix well. Place the saucepan over medium-high heat and cook, stirring constantly with a wooden spoon, until the mixture begins to thicken and becomes clear, about 4 to 5 minutes. Remove from the heat and stir in the almond extract. Let cool for 5 minutes.

Using a pastry brush, coat the fruit in the tart shell with the glaze, letting some of the glaze run down between the fruit. Chill the tart for at least 2 hours.

To serve, slice the tart and place a dollop of mascarpone on the side of each serving, if you wish.

Note: Nutmeg is optional in the tart shell; some Italian chefs use grated lemon rind.

Variation: A thin layer of mascarpone can be spread over the crust before the fresh fruit is added.

P REPARING Easter dinner was more important in our house than any Easter finery, although we all had new hats or shoes for the occasion. Holy Saturday was spent cooking . . . and reflecting. No music or television was allowed the whole day. My job was to deliver honey balls, or *struffoli,* Easter breads, homemade sausage, and pasta, already dressed in sauce, to our pastor, Monsignor Bernardo. I arrived at the rectory balancing the honey balls gaily wrapped in purple cellophane in one hand and the breads snuggled together in a big Easter basket in the other. The monsignor's eyes always lit up, but he was expecting this, as he did for every holiday. He pinched me on the cheek so hard that it smarted and stayed red for a long time. I hurriedly wished him *Buona Pasqua,* then it was back home to help ready the table for our own celebration.

Everything was hustle and bustle. My mother worked furiously to finish the *pasta grattata* for the soup; Grandma Galasso was cleaning broccoli; and my job was to decorate the lamb cakes, all twelve of them, with coconut and jelly beans.

On Easter Sunday we went to mass and then all of Grandma's children and their children came to our house for coffee and sweets. When they went home, each took a lamb cake. Late in the day we sat down to our meal, which most of the children didn't eat, since they were so stuffed with chocolate rabbits and colored eggs.

Easter Dinner

Zuppa di Pasta Grattata (page 33)
GRATED PASTA SOUP

Pasta con Salsa Fresca di Pomodori e Basilica (page 87)
PASTA WITH FRESH TOMATO BASIL SAUCE

Salsiccia Fresca (page 140)
FRESH SAUSAGE

Abbacchio al Forno (page 137)
ROAST LAMB

Broccoli Casalinghi (page 176)
HOMESTYLE BROCCOLI

Insalata Mista
MIXED SALAD

Struffoli (page 266)
HONEY BALLS

Zabaglione (page 240)

Torta di Agnello
LAMB CAKE

Torta di Mele d'Edgardo

EDGARDO'S APPLE CAKE

I travel to Italy every year, first to renew my connection to my family roots and second to learn more about the cooking of traditional Italian food. Sometimes I cook with professional chefs and we have a good time comparing notes about how things should be done. Recently I spent some time in Montalcino, a quiet little town in Tuscany that is home to the famous Brunello wines. There I cooked with Edgardo San-doli, a dynamic television chef and authority on Italian rice. Together we taught cooking classes for Americans who were hungry to learn about the variety of the food of Italy. This recipe is one that Edgardo shared in his classes. The ingredients are simple enough; it was how he measured them that caught everyone's attention. Cooks in Italy usually do not use measuring spoons, though Edgardo claims that an Italian soup spoon is equal to our tablespoon. They do, however, weigh out their flour, sugar, and butter in grams.

SERVES 8

4	large eggs		Grated zest of 1 small lemon
½	cup sugar	¼	cup heavy cream or sour cream
½	cup unbleached all-purpose flour	6	cups sliced peeled apples (4 to 5 medium apples), or a combination of apples and fresh pineapple chunks
1	teaspoon baking powder		
1	tablespoon vanilla		
		2	tablespoons apricot jam

Preheat the oven to 350°F. Butter and flour a 9-inch springform pan.

In a large bowl, beat the eggs until foamy. Add the sugar and beat until smooth. Mix the flour with the baking powder and beat in until well blended. Add the vanilla, lemon zest, and heavy cream or sour cream, and beat until smooth. Add the apples and mix gently with a spoon to coat well. Pour the mixture into the springform pan and bake for 30 minutes, or until nicely browned on top. Transfer the cake to a rack to cool.

In a small saucepan, heat the jam until it is melted and smooth. Using a pastry brush, brush the top of the cake carefully with the warmed jam. Cut in wedges to serve.

Note: Italian cream, panna doppia, is much richer and heavier than our heavy cream. Thick sour cream has somewhat the same consistency as Italian heavy cream.

Sfinci

LITTLE SWEET PIZZE

Of all the saints' feast days, none was more sacred in our home than St. Joseph's Day, observed on March 19. The affection that Italians, especially Sicilians, have for this saint, reaches cult proportions. Both of my grandmothers took this day very seriously. Sometimes the observance occurred during Lent, which meant that it was the only time I could expect a sweet treat until Easter. After attending mass, my grandmothers would get to work making the food for the table to honor San Giuseppe. There were breads in many shapes and sizes, but what I really looked forward to were the *sfinci*, fried puffs of dough. They were mounded on large decorative trays and brought to the dining room. A solemn statue of Saint Joseph stood on the best lace tablecloth in the center of the table. Around him were plates of food, flowers, and candles. I would reach for the sfinci, only to get a tap on the wrist from Grandma to remind me that we would pray first, then eat.

MAKES 2 TO 2½ DOZEN

2	cups water	6	large eggs
2	tablespoons sugar	1	tablespoon bourbon whiskey
½	teaspoon salt	2	teaspoons baking powder
2	tablespoons butter		Vegetable oil for deep-frying
2	cups unbleached all-purpose flour		Confectioner's sugar

In a saucepan, bring the water to a boil. Add the sugar, salt, and butter, stirring constantly with a wooden spoon. Lower the heat and stir in the flour a tablespoon at a time. Remove the pan from the heat and let cool slightly.

When the mixture has cooled to warm, add the eggs one at a time, beating well after each addition. Add the whiskey and baking powder and mix well.

In a deep fryer or deep heavy pan, heat the vegetable oil to 375°F. Drop the dough about 6 to 8 large teaspoonfuls at a time into the hot oil and fry until golden. Drain on brown paper and let cool.

Dust with confectioner's sugar and serve.

Tiramisù alla Patrizia

PATRIZIA'S "PICK-ME-UP"

Patrizia Auricchio, the wife of the president of the Auricchio Cheese Company, is an excellent cook. Her family lives in Cremona, Italy, and she makes frequent trips from Wisconsin, where she now lives, to her homeland. Patrizia makes the best tiramisù I have ever eaten. This could have something to do with the fact that Errico, her husband, is partial to the wonderful and creamy mascarpone dessert cheese that his company painstakingly produces. You can find Italian ladyfingers in the gourmet section of your grocery store.

SERVES 8

3 large eggs, separated

½ cup plus ⅛ teaspoon sugar

1 tablespoon plus 1 cup espresso or strong coffee

2 tablespoons cognac

1 cup (10 ounces) mascarpone cheese

2 tablespoons Dutch-process cocoa

About 20 Italian ladyfingers, toasted

In a bowl, combine the egg yolks, the ½ cup sugar, the 1 tablespoon espresso, and the cognac. Beat the mixture with a rotary beater until foamy, 2 to 3 minutes. Add the mascarpone cheese and beat for 3 to 5 minutes, or until the mixture is very smooth.

In a large bowl, combine the egg whites and the ⅛ teaspoon sugar and beat until the egg whites are stiff. Gently fold the mascarpone mixture into the whites. Set aside.

Pour the 1 cup espresso into a shallow bowl. Dip both sides of each ladyfinger quickly in the espresso. Arrange a layer of 6 or 7 ladyfingers in the bottom of a decorative serving bowl. Spread about one third of the mascarpone mixture over the ladyfingers. Continue layering the ladyfingers and mascarpone mixture, finishing with a mascarpone layer. Sift the cocoa over the top and refrigerate for 1 hour before serving.

To serve, spoon into individual dessert dishes.

Semifreddo con la Frutta

The term *semifreddo* is used to refer to one of various partially frozen desserts; often it is composed of cake and a filling. In this recipe, however, a frozen custard is prepared first and then given a glistening cover of caramelized fresh fruit. It is a refreshing ending to any meal. Make the custard the day before you plan to serve this.

SERVES 6 TO 8

SEMIFREDDO

4   large egg yolks

7   tablespoons sugar

1   tablespoon sweet Marsala wine

2   cups heavy cream

²/₃   cup sugar

3   cups mixed cut-up fresh fruit, such as cubed peeled peaches, plums, and apples and/or halved grapes

To make the semifreddo, put the egg yolks and sugar in the top of a double boiler. Add the Marsala wine, and whisk over medium-high heat until the custard thickens and increases in volume. Immediately remove the custard from the heat, transfer it to a large bowl, and set it in a bowl of ice. Beat until the mixture is cool, about 10 minutes. Cover and refrigerate until well chilled, about 1 hour.

In a large bowl, whip the cream until it holds stiff peaks. Fold it into the cold custard. Pour the mixture into a 6- or 8-cup mold. Refrigerate overnight, then put it in the freezer for 1½ hours before serving.

In a heavy saucepan, cook the sugar over high heat, stirring constantly, until it dissolves. Add all the fruits except grapes, if using, and cook for 5 minutes, or until they have begun to release their juices and the liquid has thickened to a syrupy consistency. Add the grapes, if using. Remove from the heat and let cool.

To unmold the semifreddo, wrap a hot damp towel around the mold. Invert onto a serving platter and lift off the mold. Spoon the caramelized fruit over the top of the semifreddo and serve immediately.

Zabaglione

The last thing to be eaten on Easter and many other holidays was a custard dessert called *zabaglione*. It was rich and smooth and made you feel warm all over because of the sweet Marsala wine used in the recipe. My Grandmother Galasso said that this was a dessert for all those people who had problems of one sort or another, because once you ate it, all your troubles would disappear. You'll know what she meant when you try it.

SERVES 4

4 *large egg yolks*	7 *tablespoons sweet Marsala wine*
¼ *cup sugar*	4 *whole coffee beans*

In the top of a double boiler, combine the egg yolks and sugar and whisk until the mixture is thick and pale. Set the double boiler over medium heat, and whisk in the Marsala wine, a little at a time; the mixture will become foamy and double in volume. Do not let the mixture get too hot or the eggs will scramble; reduce the heat if necessary. Cook, whisking constantly, until the custard coats the back of a spoon. Immediately remove it from the heat.

Place a coffee bean in each of 4 wineglasses and spoon the custard into the glasses. Serve immediately.

Fragole in Aceto Balsamico

STRAWBERRIES IN BALSAMIC VINEGAR

Fragole, strawberries, are seen in all the outdoor markets in Italy starting in June. They are used in fresh fruit tarts and often dressed up in red wine for a simple but satisfying dessert. In Modena, strawberries are marinated in balsamic vinegar, made from the must of the Trebbiano grape and aged in special fruit-wood barrels. The beauty of this dessert lies in the fact that even if the berries are slightly underripe, their flavor will be magically transformed by the vinegar.

SERVES 4 TO 6

1 *quart fresh strawberries*   2¹/₂ *tablespoons balsamic vinegar*
6 *tablespoons sugar*

Hull the berries. Because rinsing strawberries tends to bruise their tender flesh, a better way is to put a clean damp sponge on a plate or cutting board and gently roll each berry over the sponge. Rinse the sponge occasionally as you work. Cut the berries in half and place them in a glass bowl. Sprinkle with the sugar and let stand for 5 minutes. Add the balsamic vinegar and gently toss.

Refrigerate for at least 1 hour, or up to 4 hours, before serving.

Mele con Salsa di Lampone

APPLES WITH RASPBERRY SAUCE

Traditionally this dessert is made with *aspretto di lampone*, fermented raspberries that have been aged in fruit wood for at least six months. A good raspberry vinegar works just as well.

SERVES 8 TO 10

2 *cups raspberries (fresh or unsweetened frozen)*

3 *tablespoons raspberry jam*

2 *tablespoons sugar*

¹/₄ *cup white dessert wine (such as Moscato)*

1 *to 2 tablespoons raspberry vinegar (to taste)*

8 *to 10 medium Golden Delicious apples, peeled, cored, and thinly sliced*

Mascarpone cheese or sweetened whipped cream

In a food processor or blender, puree the raspberries. Add the jam and sugar and pulse to blend. Add the wine and vinegar, and blend well.

Put the apples slices in a large bowl, pour the sauce over, and mix gently to coat the apple slices. Cover the bowl and refrigerate for 1 hour.

Spoon the fruit with its sauce into individual dessert bowls and top with a dollop of mascarpone cheese or whipped cream. Serve immediately.

Macedonia di Frutta

FRUIT SALAD

Grandma Galasso loved Christmas and Easter, because all her sons and daughters and their families came to our house to see her and to eat. Her birthday, on January 10th, was another special event. It started with Grandma's annual appearance as a contestant on a radio show called "The Breakfast Club." She would have to choose a category; her favorite topic was food and she always managed to win a prize. The grandchildren sat on the floor of the parlor at home, listening to the radio, cheering Grandma on. Then in the evening, we always took her out to a fancy restaurant. When she returned home from her whirlwind day, there was a huge *torta di whisky* and fresh fruit salad. The fruit salad was my grandmother's favorite dessert. Whenever I make it, I use whatever fruits are in season. This dessert is a common item on Italian menus. Some fruit salads are served simply, others have ice cream or whipped cream as an accompaniment.

SERVES 4

1½ cups strawberries, hulled

2 large grapefruit, halved, fruit removed in sections, shells reserved

1 Cortland apple, cored and diced

1 pear, cored and diced

1 banana, peeled and sliced

2 tablespoons fresh lemon juice

½ cup confectioner's sugar

¼ cup kirsch

Fresh mint leaves

Combine all the fruit in a serving bowl. Add the lemon juice and toss gently. Add the confectioner's sugar and kirsch and toss gently again. Cover and refrigerate for 2 to 3 hours before serving.

Remove any pulp or membrane from the grapefruit shells and place a half shell on each of 4 individual plates. Divide the fruit salad evenly among the shells. Garnish with mint leaves and serve immediately.

Pere e Cioccolata

PEARS AND CHOCOLATE

A few years ago I visited the famous Perugina chocolate factory in Umbria. Mountains of cocoa beans are used to make the world-famous candies this company is known for; my favorites are the *baci*, or chocolate kisses. While I was there I bought some Perugina cocoa and chocolate to cook with. One of the desserts now in my file is pears with chocolate, a great combination and a truly eye-catching dessert for company. For a dramatic effect use half dark and half white chocolate.

SERVES 6

6 *Anjou pears*
9 *tablespoons butter*
¹/₃ *cup sugar*
¹/₂ *teaspoon cinnamon*
¹/₂ *teaspoon ground cloves*
1 *cup dry white wine*

1 *10-ounce package frozen raspberries in syrup or 1¹/₄ cups fresh raspberries plus ¹/₄ cup sugar*
1 *cup semisweet chocolate bits or coarsely chopped chocolate (or ¹/₂ cup dark and ¹/₂ cup white chocolate)*
Fresh mint leaves

Peel the pears but leave the stems on. Cut a small piece off the bottom of each pear to make it stand up. In a large saucepan, melt 4 tablespoons of the butter. Add the pears and gently cook them for about 5 minutes, turning them frequently and basting with the butter. Mix the sugar with the cinnamon and cloves and sprinkle over the pears. Add the wine and simmer the pears, covered, until they are fork-tender but not mushy, about 20 to 25 minutes. Baste them occasionally with the cooking liquid. Remove the pears with a slotted spoon and let drain; discard the cooking liquid.

Meanwhile, in a food processor or blender, process the raspberries (with the sugar) until smooth. Strain the sauce through a sieve into a bowl, discard the seeds, and set aside.

In the top of a double boiler set over simmering water, melt the chocolate with the remaining 5 tablespoons butter. If using half white and half dark chocolate, melt each separately, using 2¹/₂ tablespoons of butter for each. Keep warm.

Place the pears on individual serving dishes and carefully drizzle some of the warm chocolate over each pear. If using white and dark chocolate, drizzle the dark chocolate on first, let it set for 5 minutes, then drizzle on the white chocolate for a marbled effect. Spoon the raspberry sauce around the base of the pears and garnish with mint leaves. Put any remaining raspberry sauce in a dish and pass at the table.

Pere al Cardinale

PEARS CARDINAL STYLE

Fruit always tastes to me better in Italy. The apples have a unique aroma; fragrant blackberries are as large as walnuts; grapes are intoxicating and addictive; and the peaches look green but have a sweet-tart flavor and a moist firm flesh. It must be the rich soil and climate that account for this. Italians do some especially delicious things with pears, the most prized of all Italian fruits. A spectacular way to have them is in a ruby-red wine sauce.

Alkermes is a liqueur made from cinnamon, vanilla, and cochineal. It has a vivid red color that stains very easily. In this recipe, it gives the pears a deep, rich red color like that of the robes worn by the cardinals of Florence. You can buy it in specialty shops or by mail order through food catalogs.

SERVES 6

6   slightly underripe Anjou or Bartlett pears

6   tablespoons plus 1/2 cup sugar

1/2 cup Alkermes or raspberry or cranberry juice

About 3 cups dry red wine

Confectioner's sugar

Fresh mint leaves

Preheat the oven to 350°F.

Remove a small slice from the bottom of each pear to make it stand upright. Using a vegetable peeler, remove 4 or 5 long narrow strips of skin from each pear to create a striped effect. Place the pears upright in a 3-inch-deep baking dish just large enough to hold the pears snugly.

Sprinkle each pear with 1 tablespoon of the sugar. Drizzle the Alkermes or juice over them and add enough wine to almost cover the pears. Bake them, uncovered, for about 35 minutes, or until they are soft and easily pierced with a knife. Do not overcook them or they will collapse and be mushy. Transfer the pears to a serving dish and pour the cooking liquid into a saucepan.

You should have about 2 cups of liquid; if necessary, add wine to equal 2 cups. Add the ½ cup sugar, stir, and bring to a boil. Reduce the heat to medium and cook until the liquid is reduced by half. Pour this sauce over the pears.

Baste the pears frequently with the sauce as it cools; the sauce will thicken and glaze the pears. Refrigerate the pears for 1 hour before serving.

Place the pears on individual serving dishes, spoon some sauce around the bottom of each pear, and sprinkle the pears with confectioner's sugar. Garnish each plate with a mint leaf and serve.

Pesche Ripiene

STUFFED PEACHES

A few years ago my husband and I visited "his side" of the family in Benevento. We had been staying at the Bellevue Syrene in Sorrento, so the Esposito family sent their oldest son, Michele, to make the three-hour drive to pick us up. As we returned to Benevento, I tried to make polite conversation . . . in Italian. It was an exhausting mental exercise, to think first of all of what to say and then how to say it in grammatically correct Italian. Guy, my husband, sat in the back seat, smiling and nodding his approval. It seemed the whole town knew we were coming. After a rousing greeting of *benvenuti*, we were ushered into the summer kitchen where "mangia, mangia" was the phrase of the day. The dinner was just what I expected, from *antipasto* to *biscotti*, but I particularly remember the fresh peaches with amaretti cookies for dessert: what a simple idea, yet what an unusual taste.

SERVES 6

6 *large ripe peaches*	¼ *cup sugar*
14 *amaretti cookies*	¾ *cup Vin Santo or sweet Marsala wine*
2 *tablespoons pine nuts*	2 *to 3 tablespoons butter*

Preheat the oven to 400°F.

Cut the peaches in half and remove the pits. Scoop out most of the flesh from each half but leave a firm shell about ¼ inch thick. Put the flesh into a bowl and mash well; set the peach halves aside.

Coarsely crumble the amaretti into a small bowl, add the pine nuts, and mix well. Reserve ½ cup of the crushed amaretti mixture and add the rest to the peach flesh. Add the sugar and enough of the wine just to moisten the mixture and mix just to blend.

Place the peach halves cut sides up in a buttered ovenproof dish. Divide the peach mixture evenly among the peaches. Sprinkle with the reserved amaretti mixture and dot each half with butter. Pour the remaining wine around the peaches and bake for 25 to 30 minutes, or until the peach shells are easily pierced with a knife.

Arrange 2 peach halves on each plate and spoon the cooking juices over.

Castagne al Forno

ROASTED CHESTNUTS

No Christmas would have been complete for me without roasted chestnuts. A long-handled iron pan, like an old-fashioned bedwarmer, was originally used to roast them in the fireplace, but the pan has long since disappeared. The aroma of roasted chestnuts drew us to the table to sit and talk as we gingerly removed the tender nuts from the crackling shells, which seemed to fly all over the place as we split them open. Chestnuts are used in many ways in Italian cooking. Chestnut flour produces a delicious pasta; the classic *Monte Bianco* is made with pureed chestnuts; and ground-up chestnuts are combined with herbs and spices for stuffings.

SERVES 10 TO 12

4 *pounds chestnuts*

Preheat the oven to 450°F.

With a small sharp knife, cut an X in the top of each chestnut, to prevent it from exploding in the oven. (Once in a while this fails to work.) Spread the chestnuts on a baking sheet and roast them for 15 to 20 minutes or until the shells are puffed and split. Transfer the chestnuts to a bowl and let sit until cool enough to handle.

Crack the shells with your hands or use nutcrackers and picks to remove the nutmeats.

Biscotti

COOKIES

COOKIES COME in fanciful shapes and sizes, many with symbolic meaning, in every region of Italy. Some have very forbidding names, like my favorite, *osse dei morte*, bones of the dead. But there are also gentler names like *baci di dame*, ladies' kisses, and *biscotti di regina*, queen's cookies. It may surprise you to know that cookies, especially the harder versions, are eaten in the morning in Italy. Breakfast as we know it does not exist. On their way to work or school, Italians stop into the neighborhood bar or pastry shop to have a quick *biscotto* or *cornetto* to see them through the morning.

The most popular cookies in our house were anise biscuits, the licorice flavoring permeating not only the cookies, but the whole house as well for days. We ate them dipped in red wine or dunked into coffee, which softened them up a bit.

When my grandmothers and mother made cookies, they dealt in large numbers. Very often they were called upon to make wedding cookies for relatives and friends. No Italian wedding would ever be complete without huge pyramided centerpieces of seed cookies, almond paste cookies, fruit-filled cookies, meringues, chocolate raisin cookies, pine nut cookies, and a host of others. The baking would start well in advance of the wedding and clean bushel baskets, each holding a single type of cookie, were covered with dishtowels and kept in the cold "back room" until the big day.

Many of the old Italian cookie recipes are lost today, no longer made at home. At one time, religious orders were responsible for baking certain types of cookies, and most of these have now disappeared. Many of the recipes in this chapter have never been written down, but are part of my family's collective memory, with numerous individual interpretations. Every relative I talk with makes the traditional cookies a little differently. I have included my favorites from home and from my travels in Italy.

Biscotti di Anice

ANISE COOKIES

Biscotti is a catchall word that can be used for any cookie. The literal translation is "twice cooked," because some Italian cookies such as these anise cookies are baked first as long, flat loaves, then sliced and baked again. They are a family favorite, traditionally dunked in a glass of Vin Santo, a dessert wine, or in coffee. They were the most requested breakfast food of an Italian student from Reggio Emilia who lived with us one summer.

MAKES ABOUT 3 DOZEN

1 cup unblanched whole almonds	5¹/₃ tablespoons butter or shortening
3¹/₄ cups unbleached all-purpose flour, sifted	6 large eggs
2¹/₂ tablespoons baking powder	1 cup sugar
¹/₂ teaspoon salt	2 tablespoons anise extract

Preheat the oven to 350°F. Lightly grease 2 cookie sheets.

Spread the almonds on an ungreased cookie sheet and toast them for 10 minutes, stirring once or twice. Transfer the nuts to a bowl and set aside.

In a large bowl, combine the flour, baking powder and salt. Add the butter and rub the mixture with your hands until it has the texture of coarse corn meal.

In a large bowl, beat the eggs well with a whisk or electric mixer. Beat in the sugar, then the anise extract. Stir in the flour mixture and mix until a firm dough is formed. Add the almonds and knead into the dough.

Turn the dough out onto a floured surface. With floured hands, divide the dough in half and shape each half into a 12- × -3-inch rectangular loaf. Place the loaves on the greased cookie sheets and bake for 25 minutes, or until firm to the touch and puffed and light golden. Remove from the oven and let cool for 5 minutes.

Cut each loaf on the diagonal into 1-inch slices. Place the slices on their sides on the cookie sheets and bake them for about 7 minutes on each side, or until toasted and golden brown. Transfer to wire racks to cool.

The cookies will keep in an airtight container for several weeks.

Biscotti di Noce

NUT COOKIES

My relatives each had a special recipe for biscotti that made their cookies a little different from the others. Some added different kinds of nuts or extracts, and some used lard as opposed to butter. The one thing that remained the same was the way the cookies were eaten. They were always dunked into wine to soften them a bit. My biscotti are not too sweet, and the combination of nuts and orange zest gives the cookies their excellent texture and taste.

MAKES ABOUT 3 TO 3½ DOZEN

3 *large eggs*	2 *cups plus 1 tablespoon unbleached all-purpose flour*
¾ *cup sugar*	1 *teaspoon baking soda*
2½ *tablespoons butter, melted*	⅔ *cup whole hazelnuts*
1 *tablespoon grated orange zest*	⅓ *cup unblanched whole almonds*
1 *tablespoon vanilla*	

Preheat the oven to 350°F. Lightly grease 2 cookie sheets.

In a large bowl, beat the eggs and sugar with a wire whisk until thick and pale yellow. Whisk in the butter, orange zest, and vanilla and mix well. Sift the flour and baking soda together and stir into the egg mixture, mixing well. Stir in the nuts. The dough will be sticky.

Using 2 spoons, divide the dough in half and place half the dough on a greased cookie sheet. Shape it into a flat loaf 10 inches long and 4 inches wide, tapering it slightly at the ends. Repeat with the remaining dough. Bake for 20 minutes, or until firm to the touch. Remove from the oven and let cool for 3 to 4 minutes.

Transfer the loaves carefully to a cutting board and cut the loaves on the diagonal into ½-inch slices. Place the slices on their sides on the cookie sheets and bake for about 7 minutes on each side, or until well toasted and hard. Transfer the cookies to a rack to cool.

They will keep in an airtight container for up to a month.

Quaresimali

LENTEN COOKIES

Sometimes the names of Italian sweets seem almost more intriguing and
fascinating than the sweet itself. Such is the case with the names of
many cookies. There are references in old cooking manuscripts to special cookies that were made only during the Lenten season, called *quar-
esimali*. The name comes from the word for Lent, *quaresima*. These
cookies will last almost as long as the Lenten season.

MAKES ABOUT 3½ DOZEN

3 cups unblanched whole almonds	1½ teaspoons cinnamon
¼ cup honey	1¼ teaspoons baking powder
½ cup sugar	4 tablespoons butter, softened
2 cups unbleached all-purpose flour	2 large eggs
¾ cup brown sugar	1 large egg beaten with 1 tablespoon water for egg wash
¼ teaspoon ground cloves	

Preheat the oven to 375°F. Lightly grease 2 cookie sheets.

Spread the almonds on a cookie sheet and toast them for about 8 minutes. Transfer the almonds to a bowl and let cool. Lower the oven
temperature to 350°F.

Reserve 2¼ cups of the almonds. With a sharp knife, chop the remaining ¾ cup of almonds fine. Transfer to a bowl, add the honey,
and blend well.

In a large bowl, combine all the remaining dry ingredients and mix
well.

In a small bowl, beat the eggs with the softened butter until well
blended. Add to the honey and almond mixture and mix well. Add to
the dry ingredients, along with the reserved almonds, and mix with
your hands until the dough is well blended. The dough will be stiff.

Divide the dough in half and, with floured hands, form each piece into
a loaf 12 inches long by 3 to 4 inches wide. Place the loaves on the
greased cookie sheets and brush the tops of each loaf with the egg wash.
Bake for 20 to 25 minutes, or until lightly browned.

Transfer the loaves to a cutting board and carefully cut each loaf on
the diagonal into slices about ½ inch thick. Place the pieces on their
sides on the cookie sheets and bake for 7 minutes on each side, or until
well toasted and hard.

Transfer to wire racks to cool completely. Store in an airtight container.

Biscotti di Nodo

ITALIAN KNOT COOKIES

Whenever anyone in our family got married, my Grandmother Saporito did three things: She made a bedspread for the happy couple, said the rosary, and baked these orange-scented knot cookies because two people's lives were about to become entwined.

MAKES 3 TO 3½ DOZEN

3 cups unbleached all-purpose flour	FROSTING
2¼ teaspoons baking powder	1½ cups confectioner's sugar, sifted
½ teaspoon baking soda	4 to 5 tablespoons evaporated milk or half-and-half
½ teaspoon salt	1 teaspoon almond extract
4 tablespoons unsalted butter, softened	Green or red food coloring, optional
½ cup sugar	
3 large eggs	Colored sprinkles
1 tablespoon orange zest	
1 tablespoon orange juice, freshly squeezed	

Sift the flour, baking powder, baking soda, and salt together. Set aside.

In a large bowl, cream the butter and sugar until light and fluffy. Add the eggs one at a time, beating well after each addition. Beat in the orange zest and juice. Beat in the dry ingredients gradually, and beat well to mix. The dough will be soft; wrap it in waxed paper and refrigerate it for 1 hour to make it easier to handle.

Preheat the oven to 350°F. Lightly grease 2 cookie sheets.

Place the dough on a well-floured surface. Pinch off small egg-size pieces of dough and roll each piece into a rope about 7 inches long and the width of your middle finger. Tie into a loose knot and place 1 inch apart on the greased cookie sheets. Bake for 12 to 15 minutes, or until lightly browned. Transfer the cookies to wire racks to cool slightly. Frost when still slightly warm.

To make the frosting, in a bowl, combine the sugar and ¼ cup of the milk and beat until smooth. Add more milk if necessary to make a thin frosting. Beat in the almond extract. Add food coloring if desired.

Dip the top of each cookie into the frosting, shaking off the excess. Place them on racks and sprinkle with colored sprinkles. Let the frosting dry before storing. These will keep in an airtight container for up to a week; or freeze them for up to 3 months.

Biscotti di Margherita Ricci

RITA RICCI'S COOKIES

Rita Ricci was a friend of my Grandmother Galasso and my mother. I remember her as a roly-poly woman with rosy cheeks, who could have passed for Mrs. Santa Claus. She was always cooking and then giving away what she cooked. Over endless cups of dark brewed espresso, and these cookies, she and my grandmother would talk in Italian about how things used to be in the old country. Her original recipe calls for 4 dozen eggs, a 3-pound can of shortening, 8 cups sugar, 20 teaspoons baking powder, 4 tablespoons vanilla, rind and juice of 4 lemons, and 20 cups of flour. I've reworked her instructions and made the quantities much easier to manage. (Mrs. Ricci's recipe says it will make one half bushel of cookies.)

MAKES 4½ DOZEN

4	large eggs		1	tablespoon fresh lemon juice
1½	cups sugar		2	tablespoons grated lemon zest
2	teaspoons vanilla			
1	cup vegetable shortening, melted			FROSTING
½	cup milk		1½	cups confectioner's sugar, sifted
6	cups unbleached all-purpose flour		¼	cup milk
2	tablespoons baking powder		2	teaspoons vanilla
				Red or green food coloring, optional

In a bowl, beat the eggs until pale yellow. Add the sugar and vanilla and beat until thick and light colored. Add the melted shortening and milk, beating well. Sift the flour and baking powder together and stir into the egg mixture. Stir in the lemon juice and zest, mixing well. The dough will be soft; wrap it in wax paper and refrigerate for 1 hour to make it easier to handle.

Preheat the oven to 350°F. Lightly grease 2 cookie sheets.

Place the dough on a well-floured surface. Break off egg-size pieces of dough and roll each piece into an 8-inch rope. Bring the ends together, pinch to seal, and twist to form a figure 8. Place the twists 1 inch apart on the greased cookie sheets. Bake for 20 minutes, or until lightly colored and firm to the touch.

Transfer the cookies to wire racks to cool slightly before frosting.

To make the frosting, in a bowl, combine the sugar, milk, and vanilla and beat until smooth. Add food coloring if desired.

While the cookies are still warm, dip the top of each twist in the frosting. Place the cookies on racks to let the frosting dry before storing. The cookies will keep in an airtight container for up to 1 week or can be frozen for up to 3 months.

Note: These cookies can also be shaped into knots instead of figure 8s.

Viscotta ca Giuggiulena

SESAME COOKIES

Giovanni Iapichino came from Palermo, Sicily, to study plant science at the University of New Hampshire, where I met him. One night I invited him to dinner and made a Sicilian meal, which only made him homesick for the food of his native land. When Giovanni's grant ran out, he returned to Palermo, but a few months later, he sent me his mother's recipe for *viscotta ca giuggiulena*, sesame seed cookies, as well as a cookbook from Palermo, with this inscription: *Grazie infinito per il tuo regalo, spero che questo libro sia d'aiuto nel tuo lavoro.* (Many thanks for your gift, I hope that this book will help you in your work.)

MAKES ABOUT 2 DOZEN

2½ cups unbleached all-purpose flour

1¼ cups finely ground semolina flour or pastry flour

1 tablespoon baking powder

⅔ cup sugar

½ cup lard or ¼ cup lard and ¼ cup margarine (see Note)

2 large eggs, beaten

Grated zest of 1 lemon

⅔ cup milk

1 egg beaten with 1 tablespoon water for egg wash

2 cups sesame seeds

Preheat the oven to 350°F. Lightly grease 2 cookie sheets.

In a bowl, mix the flours and baking powder together, then add the sugar and mix. Add the lard (and margarine) and work it into the flour mixture until it resembles coarse corn meal. Add the eggs and lemon zest, then add the milk a little at a time and work the mixture until a ball of dough is formed.

Divide the dough into 4 pieces. Roll each piece on a floured surface into a rope about 18 inches long and the thickness of your middle finger. Cut the ropes into 2-inch pieces. Dip each piece into the egg wash, roll in the sesame seeds to coat on all sides, and place 1 inch apart on the cookie sheets. Bake for 20 to 25 minutes, or until nicely browned. Transfer to wire racks to cool.

Note: Lard gives these cookies the proper texture and flavor.

Biscotti Sposalizi

MARRIAGE COOKIES

When I got married, my mother made not only my wedding cake but also a huge assortment of the traditional Italian cookies. A few weeks before the wedding, my aunts were pressed into service to bake chocolate bride's cookies, vanilla- and anise-flavored cookies, seed cookies, wedding knot cookies, "S" cookies, and a host of others: There were literally bushels of cookies. Samples of each type were wrapped in colorful netting, tied with silver ribbons, and given to each guest to take home.

MAKES 3 TO 4 DOZEN

1¾ cups unbleached all-purpose flour, sifted

8 tablespoons (1 stick) butter or shortening

¾ cup sugar

½ teaspoon grated nutmeg

1 teaspoon cinnamon

½ teaspoon baking powder

¾ teaspoon baking soda

¼ cup Dutch-process cocoa

¼ cup walnuts, coarsely ground

1 cup raisins, coarsely chopped

½ cup milk

FROSTING

1½ cups confectioner's sugar, sifted

2½ tablespoons heavy cream

1 teaspoon butter or margarine, softened

1 teaspoon rum extract

Colored sprinkles

Preheat the oven to 350°F. Lightly grease 2 cookie sheets.

In a bowl, beat the flour and butter or shortening until well blended. Beat in the sugar, spices, baking powder, baking soda, cocoa, nuts, and raisins. Stir in the milk and mix well to make a soft dough.

Drop teaspoonfuls of the dough about 1 inch apart onto the greased cookie sheets. Bake for 10 minutes, or until firm. Transfer to wire racks to cool.

In a bowl, combine all the frosting ingredients and beat until smooth. Dip the tops of each cookie into the frosting. Place the cookies on racks and sprinkle the tops with colored sprinkles. Let the frosting dry before storing. These will keep in an airtight container for up to 2 weeks or they can be frozen for 3 to 4 months.

Biscotti di Signora Tigani

MRS. TIGANI'S COOKIES

Like so many other Italian women in our neighborhood, Mrs. Tigani had come to America in the 1890s with her husband. Left with only fading memories of the Italy she loved, she often visited my Grandmother Galasso. They would sit on the back porch, dressed in black, and talk in their native dialect. Their voices would rise and fall as they spoke about *i figli* or *le donne* or even *morte*, death. Whenever I had to go to Mrs. Tigani's house to take her something from my grandmother, like just-picked cardoons or dandelions, I was usually rewarded with a cookie. The ones I liked best were her spicy chocolate drops.

MAKES 3½ DOZEN

3¼ cups unbleached all-purpose flour

1½ cups sugar

1 tablespoon baking powder

¼ cup spicy cocoa (see Note)

1 teaspoon freshly ground black pepper

1 teaspoon ground cloves

1½ teaspoons cinnamon

¾ cup vegetable shortening

½ teaspoon salt

½ cup milk

½ cup chopped walnuts

FROSTING

1½ cups confectioner's sugar, sifted

3 to 3½ tablespoons milk

1 teaspoon rum extract

Colored sprinkles

Preheat the oven to 350°F. Lightly grease 2 cookie sheets.

Sift all the dry ingredients together into a large bowl. Work in the shortening with your hands until the mixture resembles coarse corn meal. Add the milk and nuts and mix well with your hands until well blended.

Pinch off 1-inch pieces of the dough and roll them into balls. Place them 1 inch apart on the cookie sheets and bake for 15 to 20 minutes or until firm.

While the cookies are baking, make the frosting.

In a bowl, combine the confectioner's sugar, 3 tablespoons of the milk, and the rum and beat until smooth. Add additional milk if necessary to make a thin frosting.

Remove the cookies from the oven and dip the tops of the warm cookies into the icing. Place on wire racks and sprinkle with colored sprinkles. Let the frosting dry before storing. These will keep in an airtight container for up to 1 week, or can be frozen for up to 2 months.

Note: Spicy cocoa is used for baking and for hot drinks. It is flavored with allspice and nutmeg. If you cannot find spicy cocoa, use regular baking cocoa mixed with ½ teaspoon each allspice and nutmeg.

Ricciarelli

ALMOND COOKIES

One of the best things to come out of Tuscany, besides Dante's *Divine Comedy*, are the almond cookies called *ricciarelli*. Almonds have been used generously in Italian cooking for centuries, for everything from sauces for meats to elaborate almond paste desserts. The Sienese and the Sicilians seem to have a particular passion for almonds; even the shells are put to good use in Sicily, where they are thrown on the fire to give a special flavor to grilled meats. The Sienese almond paste cookies are a signature item in all of the pastry shops in Siena.

MAKES 4 TO 5 DOZEN

4 large egg whites, at room temperature	¼ cup plus 1 tablespoon fresh orange juice
3¼ cups sugar	Confectioner's sugar
3½ cups unblanched whole almonds, finely ground	Parchment paper
1 tablespoon grated orange zest	

Preheat the oven to 300°F. Line 2 cookie sheets with buttered parchment paper.

In a large clean bowl, beat the egg whites until foamy. Beat in the sugar 1 tablespoon at a time, then beat until the egg whites form stiff peaks. Gently but thoroughly fold in the ground almonds, orange zest, and orange juice.

Using 2 teaspoons, spoon a teaspoonful of batter onto a cookie sheet and shape into a 1-inch-long oval. Repeat with the remaining batter, spacing the cookies about 2 inches apart. Bake for about 20 minutes, or until firm to the touch.

Let the cookies cool on the sheets before removing them with a spatula. Dust with confectioner's sugar.

Note: These can be made ahead and frozen for up to 2 months in plastic bags.

Brigidini

WAFFLE COOKIES

Brigidini are wafflelike cookies that are also called *pizzelle* in this country. They also go by many other names, like *ferratelle* or *cialde*, in different regions of Italy. They are made in a special *ferratella*, a long-handled waffle iron. My Grandmother Saporito made them one at a time, holding the iron over a gas flame. The old irons have wonderful raised designs, like shafts of wheat, Roman heads, or tiny figures of people, that become imprinted into the cookie. Some even had the coat of arms of wealthy families of the Renaissance. Today you can find electric waffle irons for brigidini in any good cookware store; some make 4 to 6 cookies at a time, so they can be done very quickly. In Italy, these treats are sold at many of the street fairs.

MAKES 3 TO 4 DOZEN

3½ cups unbleached all-purpose flour

1¼ cups sugar

½ pound (2 sticks) butter or margarine, melted

6 large eggs

1 tablespoon anise oil (see Note)

4 teaspoons baking powder

1 tablespoon anise seeds

Preheat the waffle iron or pizzelle maker according to the manufacturer's instructions.

In a large bowl, combine all the ingredients except the anise seeds, and beat well. Stir in the anise seeds. Place 1 tablespoon of batter in the center of each section of the waffle iron or pizzelle maker. Close the lid, hold down the handle, and count to 35. Lift the lid: The cookies should be light golden in color. Remove them carefully, using a fork, and place on a rack to cool. Repeat with the remaining batter.

These will keep in an airtight container for 2 to 3 weeks or can be frozen for up to 3 months.

Note: If you can't find anise oil, use anise extract, which contains less alcohol and more water. When I use the extract, I use an entire 1-ounce bottle for the right flavor, but this is a matter of personal taste.

These can be made ahead and frozen.

Cucidati

SICILIAN FIG COOKIES

Fig-filled cookies are an absolute must on any Sicilian table. I remember my mother making this heavy fruit-laden cookie that reminded me of Fig Newtons. It seems she gave them to just about everyone at holiday time, including the milkman.

MAKES 4 DOZEN

4 cups unbleached all-purpose flour	1½ cups raisins
1½ tablespoons baking powder	½ cup honey
¼ teaspoon salt	1 teaspoon cinnamon
½ cup sugar	½ cup orange marmalade
1 cup vegetable shortening	1¼ cups walnuts or almonds, coarsely chopped
1 large egg	
1 tablespoon vanilla	1 large egg white beaten with 1 tablespoon water for egg wash
½ cup milk	Colored sprinkles
FILLING	
2 cups dried figs	
2 cups dried dates, pitted	

Sift the flour, baking powder, and salt together into a large bowl. Add the sugar and stir well. Cut in the shortening with a fork and work the mixture until it looks like corn meal. In a bowl, beat the egg, vanilla, and milk together. Add to the flour mixture and work the mixture with your hands into a rough dough.

Turn the dough out onto a floured work surface and knead for 5 minutes, or until smooth. The dough will be soft. Cut the dough into 4 pieces, wrap each piece in plastic wrap, and chill for 45 minutes.

To make the filling, grind the figs, dates, and raisins in a meat grinder or in a food processor until coarse; or coarsely chop. Place the mixture in a bowl, add all the remaining filling ingredients, and mix well. The mixture will be thick. Set aside.

Preheat the oven to 375°F. Lightly grease 2 cookie sheets.

Work with 1 piece of dough at a time, keeping the remaining dough covered. On a floured surface, roll out each piece of dough to a 12-inch square. Cut the dough into 4- × -3-inch rectangles, and spoon 2 tablespoons of the filling mixture down the center of each rectangle. Carefully fold over the long edges of each rectangle to meet in the center, then pinch the seam to close it securely, and turn the cookie seam side down. Pinch the ends closed and fold the ends under. Shape the cookies into crescents and place seam side down on the cookie sheets. Make 2 or 3 diagonal slits in the top of each crescent with scissors. Brush with the egg wash and sprinkle with colored sprinkles.

Bake for 25 minutes, or until golden brown. Transfer to wire racks to cool.

Note: I wrap the crescents individually in plastic wrap, twist the ends, and tie them with ribbons. They make wonderful Christmas presents. They can be made ahead and frozen.

Cenci

FRIED PASTRIES FROM MONTALCINO

There are many regional versions of these sweet fried confections, called *cenci*, or rags, because originally they were made from tattered bits and pieces of leftover dough. My Grandmother Saporito cut hers with a pastry wheel into narrow strips, loosely tied them into knots, and dropped them into hot oil. The crispy sweets were piled high on a plate and covered with a blanket of confectioner's sugar. This version, which comes from Montalcino, makes a dough that is a little softer than the southern type.

MAKES 5 TO 5½ DOZEN

5   large eggs
½ cup sugar
   Grated zest of 1 large lemon
1   tablespoon vanilla

4 to 4½ cups unbleached all-purpose flour
1 teaspoon baking powder

Peanut oil for deep-frying
Confectioner's sugar

In a large bowl, beat the eggs and sugar with a whisk until well blended. Whisk in the lemon zest and vanilla. Sift 4 cups of the flour and the baking powder together and add to the egg mixture. Mix with your hands to form a ball of dough. Turn the dough out onto a floured surface and knead it until it is soft, but no longer sticky; add more flour if necessary.

Cut the dough into 4 pieces. Roll each piece out on a floured surface with a rolling pin to a thickness of ¼ inch. With a pastry wheel or a sharp knife, cut into strips 5½ inches long and 2½ inches wide. Make two 2-inch-long slits side by side in the center of each strip. Place the strips on a kitchen towel, and roll out and cut the remaining pieces of dough. A pasta machine, set to the finest setting, can also be used for thinning the dough.

In a deep fryer, heat the peanut oil to 375°F. Fry the strips a few at a time until golden brown. Drain on brown paper and let cool.

Sprinkle with confectioner's sugar and serve.

Note: This recipe makes a lot, but you can freeze the fried dough. Freeze, unsugared, in plastic bags. To serve, let defrost completely, then sprinkle with confectioner's sugar.

Struffoli

HONEY BALLS

It just wasn't Easter in our house without *struffoli*, little fried puffs coated with honey. What was so memorable about them was not so much their sticky exterior but their special pyramid shape on the serving platter.

MAKES 3½ TO 4 DOZEN

3   large eggs

1   tablespoon butter, softened

1   teaspoon plus ½ cup sugar

2   cups unbleached all-purpose flour, sifted

½   teaspoon baking powder

1   cup honey

Flour for dusting

Vegetable oil for deep-frying

Colored sprinkles

In a bowl, whisk together the eggs, butter, and the 1 teaspoon sugar until foamy. Sift the flour with the baking powder and stir into the egg mixture. With your hands, work the mixture into a soft dough.

Divide the dough into 4 pieces. On a floured surface, roll each piece into a rope about the width of your index finger and 12 inches long. Cut the ropes into 1-inch pieces. Toss the pieces with enough flour to dust them lightly, and shake off the excess flour.

In a deep fryer, heat the oil to 375°F. Fry the struffoli a few handfuls at a time, until puffed up and golden brown. Transfer with a slotted spoon to brown paper to drain.

In a large saucepan, combine the honey and the ½ cup sugar and heat over low heat, stirring, until the sugar has dissolved; keep warm over low heat. Add the fried balls a few at a time, and turn them with a wooden spoon to coat on all sides. Transfer the balls to a large plate and mound them into a pyramid, shaping it with wet hands.

Sprinkle with the colored sprinkles and let stand for 1 to 2 hours. Then just break off pieces with your hands to eat.

Taralli

RING-SHAPED BISCUITS

The first time my husband and I visited Milan, we had no idea where to eat dinner. We knew we wanted to taste northern specialties like risotto, veal chop Milanese-style, and polenta, but since we were so tired, we chose a restaurant near the train station. It was called La Porta Rossa (The Red Door). One look at the menu told me that seafood, southern style, was the specialty, and that the establishment was owned by Pugliese. Puglia is the region at the heel of the Italian boot, and Esposito is a very common name there. When the *cameriere* saw our last name on my credit card, it was as if we were long-lost relatives of the owners. They gave us ceramic pitchers to take home and newspapers about Puglia as well as a bagful of *taralli*, honey-and-anise-flavored cookies that look like miniature bagels. When we went back the following evening, we were welcomed as family and given another bag of taralli; I asked how they were made and this is what I came away with.

MAKES 2½ DOZEN

6 large eggs	2 tablespoons anise extract
½ cup honey	2 tablespoons anise seeds
½ cup vegetable oil	6 cups unbleached all-purpose flour

In a large bowl, beat the eggs with a whisk. Slowly add the honey, whisking constantly. Gradually whisk in the oil and whisk for 2 to 3 minutes longer. Then add the anise extract and anise seeds and mix well. Add the flour 1 cup at a time, and mix until a ball of dough is formed. The dough will be sticky.

Turn the dough out onto a floured surface and knead for 10 minutes. With floured hands, pinch off pieces of dough the size of golf balls and roll them into ropes 6 inches long and the width of your middle finger. Pinch the ends of each roll together to form a ring. Place the taralli on kitchen towels as you form them.

In a large pot of boiling water, cook the taralli in batches: Drop the rings a few at a time into the water and boil for 5 minutes after they have returned to the surface. (They will look a little wrinkled at this point, but will smooth out as they bake.) Remove the taralli with a slotted spoon and place them on clean towels. Let stand for 30 minutes.

Preheat the oven to 425°F. Lightly grease 2 cookie sheets.

Place the rings ½ inch apart on the baking sheets and bake for 20 minutes, or until lightly browned. Transfer to wire racks to cool.

MAIL-ORDER SOURCES

The following companies have mail-order services and catalogs. If you cannot get ingredients or equipment in your area, write or call them.

A & J Distributors
236 Hanover St.
Boston, MA 02113
(617) 523-8490

Auricchio Cheese Inc.
5810 Highway N.N.
Denmark, WI 54208
(414) 863-2123

Balducci's
424 Sixth Ave.
New York, NY 10011

Bel Paese Cheese Sales Company
445 Brick Boulevard
Suite 203
Bricktown, NJ 08723

Crate and Barrel
Quincy Market
Boston, MA 02113

Dean & DeLuca
560 Broadway
New York, NY 10012
(212) 413-1691

G. B. Ratto
International Grocers
821 Washington St.
Oakland, CA 94607
(800) 228-3515

King Arthur Flour
Box 1010
Norwich, VT 05055
(802) 649-3881

Le Marchè
Seeds International
P.O. Box 566
Dixon, CA 95620

Manganaro's Foods
488 Ninth Ave.
New York, NY 10018
(212) 563-5331

Providence Cheese and
   Provisions Company
Atwells Ave.
Federal Hill
Providence, RI 02902

Shepherd's Garden Seeds
30 Irene St.
Torrington, CT 06790
(203) 482-3638

Williams-Sonoma
P.O. Box 7456
San Francisco, CA 94120
(415) 421-4242

INDEX